MODERNISM, IMPERIALISM, AND THE HISTORICAL SENSE

T0373853

Modernist art and literature sought to engage with the ideas of different cultures without eradicating the differences between them. In *Modernism, Imperialism, and the Historical Sense*, Paul Stasi explores the relationship between high modernist aesthetic forms and structures of empire in the twentieth century. Stasi's text offers new readings of James Joyce, Ezra Pound, T. S. Eliot, and Virginia Woolf by situating their work within an early moment of globalization. Combining the insights of Marxist historiography, aesthetic theory, and postcolonial criticism, Stasi's careful analysis reveals how these authors' aesthetic forms responded to, and helped shape, their unique historical moment. Of interest to readers in a range of disciplines, this book will appeal especially to scholars of British and American literature as well as students of literary criticism and postcolonial studies.

Paul Stasi received his Ph.D. from the University of California at Berkeley in 2006. He writes on twentieth-century Anglophone literature and has published articles on T. S. Eliot, Richard Flannagan, James Joyce, Ezra Pound, and Jean Toomer. He currently teaches at the University at Albany.

MODERNISM, IMPERIALISM, AND THE HISTORICAL SENSE

PAUL STASI

University at Albany, State University of New York

CAMBRIDGE
UNIVERSITY PRESS

Shaftesbury Road, Cambridge CB2 8EA, United Kingdom

One Liberty Plaza, 20th Floor, New York, NY 10006, USA

477 Williamstown Road, Port Melbourne, VIC 3207, Australia

314–321, 3rd Floor, Plot 3, Splendor Forum, Jasola District Centre, New Delhi – 110025, India

103 Penang Road, #05–06/07, Visioncrest Commercial, Singapore 238467

Cambridge University Press is part of Cambridge University Press & Assessment, a department of the University of Cambridge.

We share the University's mission to contribute to society through the pursuit of education, learning and research at the highest international levels of excellence.

www.cambridge.org
Information on this title: www.cambridge.org/9781009415286

First published 2012
First paperback edition 2023

A catalogue record for this publication is available from the British Library

Library of Congress Cataloging-in-Publication data
Stasi, Paul, 1972–
Modernism, imperialism, and the historical sense / Paul Stasi.
pages cm
Revision of the author's doctoral thesis, University
of California, Berkeley, 2006.
Includes bibliographical references and index.
ISBN 978-1-107-02144-0
1. Modernism (Literature) – United States. 2. Modernism (Literature) – Great
Britain. 3. Imperialism in literature   4. Eliot, T. S. (Thomas Stearns), 1888–1965 –
Criticism and interpretation. 5. Pound, Ezra, 1885–1972 – Criticism and interpretation.
6. Joyce, James, 1882–1941 – Criticism and interpretation. 7. Woolf, Virginia,
1882–1941 – Criticism and interpretation. I. Title.
PS228.M63S73   2012
810.9′112–dc23
2012006479

ISBN   978-1-107-02144-0   Hardback
ISBN   978-1-009-41528-6   Paperback

Contents

Acknowledgments

This book began as a dissertation at the University of California at Berkeley under the direction of Charles Altieri, who taught me how to think about art, and Colleen Lye, who taught me how to be a scholar. The groundwork for everything here, and indeed for all of my scholarship, comes from their guidance and formative conversations with Mark Allison, Mike Farry, Kevis Goodman, Omri Moses, and Douglas O'Hara.

I could not have found a more supportive and challenging intellectual environment than the English Department at the University at Albany. Kevin Bell, Bret Benjamin, Patricia E. Chu, Randy Craig, Hernan Diaz, Jennifer Greiman, Kir Kuiken, James Lilley, Barry Trachtenberg, and Laura Wilder have been exemplary colleagues and friends. James Lilley's astute reading of an early draft of Chapter 5 was invaluable. Patricia E. Chu helped me see the stakes of this project much more clearly than I could ever have on my own, reading through the palimpsest of my revisions to excise the ghosts of earlier drafts. Bret Benjamin has been a tremendous resource and friend, happily reading drafts, fielding panicked phone calls, and talking nonsense about Marx, basketball, and peak oil over exactly the right amount of scotch. Hernan Diaz's abdication is an indictment of our profession. Our sessions at 10 South Lake will be sorely missed and I promise to never set foot in Tulsa in their honor. Chris Iannini, scholar of pretty places without history, has been with me from the beginning, as has José Antonio Lucero, whose dream of building an opera house in the Amazon continues to inspire.

I would like to thank Mike Hill and the English department at SUNY Albany for granting me a writing leave to help complete this work, the anonymous readers at Cambridge whose comments made this a much better book, and Ray Ryan. A shorter version of Chapter 3 appeared as "'A sane balance of values': *The Cantos* as world literature." *Comparative Literature*, 62 no. 4 (Fall 2010): 361–75. I am grateful to Duke University Press and *Comparative Literature* for permission to reprint.

I thank my family for always encouraging me to pursue my interests, even when none of us knew where they might lead. And finally, there is Megan, my favorite person, who, along with the little girl, makes it all worthwhile.

Extracts from the following works of Ezra Pound are reprinted here by permission of Faber & Faber Ltd., London, and New Directions Publishing Corporation, New York, on behalf of the Ezra Pound Literary Property:

"Epilogue" & "Histrion" by Ezra Pound, from *Collected Early Poems*, copyright © 1976 by the Ezra Pound Literary Property Trust. Reprinted by permission of New Directions Publishing Corp., New York, and Faber & Faber Ltd., London.

"The Tree" by Ezra Pound, from *Personae*, copyright © 1926 by Ezra Pound. Reprinted by permission of New Directions Publishing Corp., New York, and Faber & Faber Ltd., London.

"Canto XLIX," by Ezra Pound, from *The Cantos*, copyright © 1975 by Ezra Pound. Reprinted by permission of Faber & Faber Ltd., London.

Abbreviations

Works of T. S. Eliot

CP   *Collected Poems, 1909–1962* (New York: Harcourt, Brace & World, 1963).

KE   *Knowledge and Experience in the Philosophy of F. H. Bradley* (New York: Columbia University Press, 1964).

SW   *The Sacred Wood* (New York: University Paperbacks, 1964).

Works of James Joyce

D   *Dubliners* (New York: Penguin, 1967).

P   *A Portrait of the Artist as a Young Man* (New York: Viking Press, 1964).

SH   *Stephen Hero* (New York: New Directions, 1963).

U   *Ulysses* (New York: Random House, 1961).

Works of Ezra Pound

CEP   *Collected Early Poems*, ed. Michael King (New York: New Directions, 1976).

LE   *Literary Essays of Ezra Pound*, ed. T. S. Eliot (New York: New Directions, 1968).

SP   *Selected Prose: 1909–1965*. ed. William Cookson (New York: New Directions, 1973).

Works of Virginia Woolf

E   *The Essays of Virginia Woolf*, eds. Andrew McNeillie and Stuart N. Clarke, 5 vols. (New York: HBJ, 1986), referred to as *E* followed by volume number: page number.

MD   *Mrs. Dalloway* (New York: Harcourt, 2005).

TTL   *To the Lighthouse* (New York: Harcourt, 1981).

VO   *The Voyage Out* (New York: Penguin Books, 1992).

Introduction: Imperial structures of feeling

HERE COMES EVERYBODY

Perhaps the least studied story in *Dubliners*, "After the Race" reads as an allegory of the relationship between a provincial Ireland and the Europe Joyce hoped it might someday join. Its protagonist, Jimmy Doyle, has invested in a race car owned by the Frenchman Charles Séguoin. The money comes from Jimmy's father, a "merchant prince" who "had begun life as an advanced Nationalist" but "modified his views" in time to earn a substantial living.[1] As the story begins, a car containing Jimmy, Ségouin, a young Canadian and a "huge Hungarian" races through Dublin to great applause.[2] Despite being pleased to be seen "in the company of these Continentals," Jimmy is "too excited to be genuinely happy" (*D* 44, 43). Nevertheless, after going home to dress, he meets his friends for dinner. "That night," Joyce tells us, Dublin "wore the mask of a capital" (*D* 46). After several glasses of wine, Jimmy feels the "buried zeal of his father wake to life within him" and he starts to quarrel with an Englishman who has joined their party (*D* 46). Fortunately, "the alert host ... lifted his glass to Humanity" and the men continue their revelry, eventually making their way to a yacht owned by a wealthy American (*D* 46). "This," Jimmy thinks to himself, "was seeing life" (*D* 47). Drinks continue to flow, cards are dealt and soon enough Jimmy has lost an indeterminately large amount of money: "Jimmy did not know exactly who was winning but he knew that he was losing. But it was his own fault for he frequently mistook his cards and the other men had to calculate his I.O.U.'s for him" (*D* 48). "He knew," Joyce continues, "that he would regret in the morning but at present he was glad of the rest, glad of the dark stupor that would cover up his folly" (*D* 48). This relief, however, is short lived; two lines later, the story ends with the Hungarian, "standing in a shaft of grey light: – Daybreak, gentlemen" (*D* 48).

If we are unsure of the lesson, the opening paragraph, as is so often the case in *Dubliners*, provides all the clues we need:

At the crest of the hill at Inchicore sightseers had gathered in clumps to watch the cars careering homeward and through this channel of poverty and inaction the Continent sped its wealth and industry. Now and again the clumps of people raised the cheer of the gratefully oppressed. Their sympathy, however, was for the blue cars – the cars of their friends, the French. (*D* 42)

The enemy of my enemy is my friend: so think the gratefully oppressed Irish, but Jimmy's experience demonstrates how historical opposition to England is not enough to secure friendship. Having given up nationalism for the prospect of financial gain, the Doyles find their financial lives still determined by the relations of center and periphery, as Jimmy becomes an allegorical figure for a provincial Ireland taken for a ride by the international community it would like to join. The daybreak at story's end reveals, then, the falseness of toasts to humanity in the face of capitalist modernity's uneven development. However, the story does not so much replace a false internationalism – let's call it cosmopolitanism – with nationalism, but rather suggests that this nationalism is itself only legible through the larger international structures that condition it. Abstract cosmopolitanism is replaced, here, by the pressures of existing international relations.

So it has gone in modernist criticism, as a movement once characterized by its ahistorical internationalism – whether in a celebratory or denunciatory fashion – has been replaced by a transnational set of texts deeply intertwined with the various discourses of their multiple locations. Modernism, in the familiar usage, has become modernisms. This work has proceeded in two relatively clear directions. On the one hand, there has been the effort by scholars such as Melba Cuddy-Keane, Paul Peppis, Lawrence Rainey, and Vincent Sherry (and many others) to return canonical modernism to its national scene.[3] Here we find a modernism no longer in opposition to mass culture, market society, or the publishing industry, but rather, defining itself through an appropriation of and, at times, direct participation in those discourses from which it most sought to distance itself. On the other hand, there has been what Douglas Mao and Rebecca Walkowitz identify in their 2008 state of the field essay "The New Modernist Studies" as "expansion," perhaps best exemplified by the collection *Geomodernisms*, which, in the words of its editors Laura Doyle and Laura Winkiel, "unveils both unsuspected 'modernist' experiments in 'marginal' texts and unsuspected correlations between those texts and others that appear either more conventional or more postmodern."[4] The old modernists have been put in their place, while the term *modernism* has been extended across time and space, becoming, in Susan Stanford Friedman's account, "the expressive dimension of" a modernity defined as "the velocity, acceleration, and dynamism of shattering change across a wide spectrum of social institutions" wherever it might find itself.[5]

Each of these critical trends is, of course, deeply influenced by postcolonial studies, which has not only revealed the imperial structures through which Europe managed to universalize its own particular set of cultural ideals and attitudes, but has also happily shifted scholarly attention to work from peripheral spaces. Modernism has emerged from its encounter with postcolonial studies productively chastened. Although this transformation of modernist studies can easily be attributed to a larger shift in literary criticism, and indeed society as a whole – even as the formalism of an earlier generation had less to do with the modernists themselves, who had always articulated a range of social and political concerns, than with the larger cultural climate – it is nevertheless instructive to observe the way in which this shift has been narrated. For when we do, we find that what Doyle and Winkiel call the "globalization of criticism" most often emerges in response to a larger shift in the *value* attributed to canonical modernism: its difficulty de-fanged by institutionalization, its aestheticism revealed to be complicit with even those oppressive social structures it sought to escape.[6]

This transformation emerges as the central conceit in Mao and Walkowitz's collection *Bad Modernisms,* in which the authors describe how the "permanent … opposition" of Irving Howe's modernism became the domestication found in Andreas Huyssen's influential *After the Great Divide*, where "conformism has all but obliterated the iconoclastic and subversive thrust of the historical avantgarde."[7] Modernism was no longer seen to be "at war against but rather continuous with tradition."[8] Friedman, as Mao and Walkowitz note, has her own version of this story. As a "young graduate student in 1965," Friedman writes, "Modernism was rebellion … resistance, rupture … the antidote to the poison of tradition."[9] For her graduate students thirty years later, "modernism was elitism. Modernism was the Establishment."[10] In each case, the key term is tradition. Bad modernism critiques it, conformist modernism is complicit with it, and so the retention of modernism's transgressive potential seems to require the search for a modernism that occurs elsewhere, away from those who are complicit with the establishment and to those who emerge from peripheral situations, other spaces, alternative traditions.

The irony of this story, however, is that this expansionary impulse – motivated by the critique of modernism's complicity with empire – threatens to replicate the very primitivist gesture it would disavow. In other words, we risk effacing the specificity of modernist cultural production if we use the term modernism as a placeholder either for period or form, each considered in isolation from one another. If we believe modernism to be related to empire, then expanding the definition of modernism to include peripheral formations, rather than achieving the seemingly anti-imperial goal of inclusion, might, in fact, efface the relationship between imperial center and aesthetic practice. The only way to confront the critique of modernism is not to redefine the term, to retreat, as it were, from history, but rather to examine more closely the relationship between aesthetic form and historical ground.

To this end, I argue that the characteristic devices of aesthetic modernism *depend* on the accumulation that only occurs in the centers of capitalist production. Indeed, when we look at modernist literature for figures of accumulation, we find them almost everywhere. Often these are formal in nature; modernist style forced into innovation by its awareness of the achievements of the past, by the fact that we know more than the writers who precede us and "they are that which we know."[11] No text captures this particular sense of modernism's place in literary history better than "Oxen of the Sun," in which Joyce recapitulates all the styles of English prose that have led to his own moment. Modernist form, that is to say, betrays a particular kind of self-consciousness about what Virginia Woolf called the "accumulated … deposit of tradition and inheritance" that makes even the "most ordinary young man or woman" at a tea-party "so thoroughly steeped in associations of all kinds" as to become "something venerable and subtle."[12] Woolf is summarizing Henry James's view of the English – a view with which she expresses a slightly bemused sense of agreement – but she repeats it nearly ten years later, complaining of her difficulty expressing unique perceptions in a language so well trodden. "There are the old cadences humming in one's head," Woolf writes, "the old phrases covering nothing so decently that it seems to be something after all" (*E* 2:249). Modernism's restless search for the new is here intimately tied to its awareness of the accumulated weight of the past.

Accumulation shades into overaccumulation, however, when it fails to find any viable way to realize its value and modernist literature is filled with characters who represent this particular problem. Stephen Dedalus's bored meditation on Aristotle, Blake, and historical potentiality conjured up while his students mechanically repeat lines from *Lycidas*; J. Alfred

Prufrock's declaration that he has known everything and yet finds it impossible to describe the butt-ends of his days and ways; Hugh Selwyn Mauberley's attachment to works of the past mocked as the "few thousand battered books" for which so many died, in a densely allusive poem that name-drops cultural works with abandon; Mr. Ramsay's plodding march through an alphabet of knowledge that remains entirely separate from the daily life that sustains him. Each of these characters contains a wealth of accumulated knowledge that cannot be realized in the historical moment in which he/she exists.

To make this claim is not, however, to assert that modernist art is some-how *coterminous* with capitalist accumulation. The analogy between the accumulation of culture and the accumulation of capital remains only an analogy and I will spend some time throughout this book distinguishing between the work of art and the commodity and, therefore, between these two forms of accumulation. Rather, my assertion is that we can only properly understand modernist aesthetics if we note their determination by the culture through which they are formed. For it is one of the most consistent lessons of modernist literature that there is no secure place outside of the structures that condition us. Indeed, it is this desire itself that is most often behind the modernist alienation that runs the gambit from Prufrock (for whom sociability feels like "sprawling on a pin") to Stephen Dedalus (who, Joyce demonstrates, is inexorably a product of the very nets of nationality and religion he would seek to escape) to Woolf's Rachel Vinrace (whose death is, in part, a metaphor for her inability to secure a place within the bourgeois social relations she so despises) to Mauberley (to whom Pound must bid good-bye before embarking on his *Cantos*). Each of these figures has a false idea of a heroic opposition that must evade any taint of complicity with the world in order to critique it. And it is precisely this understanding of historical determination as the evacuation of agency that leads to the view that heroes stand outside of their social order, while villains are those in whom we can detect the presence of its various ideologies.

Instead, we must understand how historical circumstances are riddled with contradictions, and so the aesthetic forms that arise from them are themselves contradictory, laced with critical potential even as they embody the self-same ideologies they would seek to resist. Recent work by scholars such as Simon Gikandi and Jahan Ramazani has begun to take on this challenge, suggesting the ways various postcolonial writers have refashioned modernist aesthetic devices for political ends. *Modernism, Imperialism and the Historical Sense* contributes to the emerging field of what we might call "postcolonial modernism," by demonstrating that it is precisely through their aesthetic forms, typically viewed as the mark of modernism's ahistoricism, that Eliot, Pound, Joyce, and Woolf engaged the structures of empire.[13] Only by understanding modernism's relationship to imperialism can we untangle what is a defining paradox of modernist writing: namely, its tendency to articulate a desire for novelty through references to work from the cultural past. Thus, Pound turns to Provençal poetry and eighteenth-century China, Joyce bases his modern epic on *The Odyssey* and both Eliot and Woolf, in distinct ways, develop their aesthetics out of readings of the English Renaissance. What historical pressures produced modernism's characteristic blend of stylistic innovation and canonical obeisance? This question is, perhaps, more familiar when framed as one about modernist politics as scholars have grappled with a literary movement that seems equal parts progressive and reactionary. To phrase the question as a purely political one, however, is to move our attention away from aesthetics while simultaneously reifying the distinction between aesthetics and politics. Instead, my aim is to trace the political implications of aesthetic form itself, attending to the ways art is both conditioned by its historical moment and yet, through its imaginative investments, capable of negating the world as it is, producing new phrases in excess of the historical content of its moment of production.

To achieve this goal, I situate modernism's aesthetic innovations alongside the structural transformations of what Eric Hobsbawm has called the Age of Empire, where imperial expansion was conditioned by a crisis of overaccumulation. No longer able to be absorbed profitably in its metropolitan centers, Western capital attempted to maintain its profits by acquiring new territories that could absorb the excess capital and commodities in which its value was locked. The result was an early moment of what we have come to call globalization: the increased unification of financial markets, the homogenization of culture, and the prevalence of informal means of control that supplement or, at times, replace military domination. Imperialist expansion occurs, then, alongside the emergence of that mass commodity culture that is one of the chief features of today's neo-imperialism and was also one of modernism's most consistent objects of attack. This attack on commodity culture needs, then, to be thought in relation to empire.

I begin this argument by identifying three main conceptual results of imperialist expansion. (1) Imperialism tended to increase cultural contact, but it did so under the relations of structural dependence characterized by the terms center and periphery. This relationship is represented by a conceptual structure I call Imperial Time – the contrast between an unending telic modernity and a world of reified unchanging traditions, which finds its clearest articulation in the atavistic primitivism characteristic of the period. Typically this primitivism sought to renew Western culture by an introjection of the exotic, ostensibly more "natural" forms of traditional culture. (2) Imperial culture is thus dominated by an interest in immediacy, either in the progressive forms of the modern world that erase traditional structures of feeling, or in the atavistic primitivism imagined to be that modern world's opposite number. These two forms of consciousness, however, are simply mirror images of each other, each lacking any sense of historical grounding. (3) This absence of historical grounding is further exacerbated by the structures of commodity culture, which in their perpetual need to manufacture desire construct an expressivist subject that tends toward the effacement of all forms of community. What results is a radically ahistorical individualism, constituted by a series of desires that are in service to a repressive social order but experienced subjectively as a form of liberation from that order.

Modernism's response to this situation is to emphasize the social ground of both subject and art object through what Eliot, in "Tradition and the Individual Talent," famously called "the historical sense" (*SW* 49). Eliot's essay describes a world in which tradition is no longer given, but must be acquired with "great labour" (*SW* 49). Its result is the "historical sense … [which] involves a perception, not only of the pastness of the past, but of its presence … [and] is what makes a writer traditional. And it is as the same time what makes a writer most acutely conscious of his place in time, of his contemporaneity" (*SW* 49). For "no poet, no artist of any art, has his complete meaning alone" (*SW* 49). The historical sense, then, is an understanding of the dialectical intertwining of the present and the past, the past only gaining meaning through its persistence into the present, the present only becoming meaningful in its relation to the past. In the realm of literature, tradition becomes the space within which history is registered.

This emphasis on the historical structures that condition the production of the work of art is seen most clearly in modernism's radical transformation of literary allusion. No longer simply the borrowing of a phrase or rhythm meant to jog the alert reader's memory, allusion becomes, within modernism, what Eliot called "stealing." And this stealing is one of the most striking formal features of modernist literature, as Eliot, Pound, Joyce, and, to a lesser but still significant extent, Woolf, construct their signature works out of materials from the cultural past. This formal device must be situated within the larger context of primitivism that dominates the early twentieth century from the atavistic vitalism of D. H. Lawrence to the commercial fads for African or Egyptian culture that have recently captured scholarly attention.[14] However, the turn to the past of Eliot, Pound, Joyce, and Woolf is never atavistic. Instead, the high cultural forms of modernist literary production are imagined to contain those values that consumer culture has tried to forget, but which persist nevertheless within its margins. In this way modernism resists what Dispesh Chakrabarty has called "History 1" – the "past posited by capital itself as its precondition" – in favor of "History 2," those aspects of the past that do not belong to capital's "life-process" but nevertheless "inhere in capital" even as they "interrupt and punctuate the run of capital's own logic."[15] The cultural materials that form the very fabric of modernist works of literature are thus inseparable from the capitalist history they are nevertheless mobilized to resist.

In reading modernist literary production in light of imperial culture, I bring two discrete discourses into conversation with one another. On the one hand, there is the relationship between Marxism and modernism, most famously embodied in the works of the Frankfurt School. Within this tradition, the mark of modernism's historical engagement is its autonomy, its absolute rejection of the structures of capitalist modernity. On the other hand, there is the oft-described rift between Marxism and postcolonial studies, Marxism seeing postcolonial studies as irredeemably culturalist, postcolonialism viewing Marxism as a Eurocentric discourse that fails to take into account peripheral experience.[16] Where these two discourses meet, I argue, is in the commodity form itself. For the commodity is, in Georg Lukács's famous account, "the central, structural problem of capitalism in all its aspects," its reification leading directly to the ahistorical consciousness of the self-legislating bourgeois subject, unmoored from his/her social ground.[17] At the same time, the commodity is, in the periphery, the very embodiment of the colony's dependence upon the neo-imperialist structures of the world market, its cheap price being "the heavy artillery with which [the bourgeoisie] batters down all Chinese walls, with which it forces the barbarians' intensely obstinate hatred of foreigners to capitulate."[18] The commodity, that is to say, structures the particular consciousness of center *and* periphery, embodying both the omnipresence and the erasure of colonial dependence.

This understanding of the commodity's dual function allows us to reread modernism's relationship to both Marxism and postcolonial studies. Grounding the modernist resistance to emergent cultural forms within a determinant political and economic structure suggests that its relationship to commodity culture is always, in part, a relationship to imperialism. Reading the commodity as the determining structure of peripheral consciousness allows for the introduction of power relations into postcolonial notions of hybridity that are all too-often overwhelmingly culturalist in their orientation. Neither modernism nor postcolonial studies, however, need be seen through the lens of romantic anticapitalism, for each can be understood to engage directly with one of capitalist modernity's determining forms.

The great virtue of Lukács's discussion of reification lies in its ability to see how forms of thought arise from particular moments. The same is true for aesthetic forms, which arise from particular places in response to particular social formations. Yet by virtue of being formal, they also have the ability to persist outside of the social orders from which they emerge, a fact that tends toward their reification. Fredric Jameson, for instance, argues that cultural forms should be seen as "attempts to resolve more fundamental contradictions – attempts which then outlive the situations for which they were devised, and survive, in reified forms, as 'cultural patterns.' Those patterns themselves then become part of the objective situation confronted by later generations."[19] Attaching modernism to its social ground is a way to understand both the contradictions that produced modernist aesthetics as well as how these formal resolutions might have continued relevance for a contemporary moment that remains in sway to some of the same structures of domination that conditioned modernist literary production. This, it seems to me, is the fundamental task of any Marxist aesthetics: how can we adequately do justice to both the shaping power of history and the efficacy of aesthetic form? How, that is to say, can we understand, without reifying either side, the relationship between aesthetics and history?

To answer this question, I would like to turn to Raymond Williams's important – and underutilized – concept of "structures of feeling," for with this concept Williams produces a nuanced sense of how the notion of determination never exhausts the ability of historical agents to articulate new possibilities latent within the contradictions of their historical moments. "Structures of feeling" are, for Williams, "social experiences in solution," emerging from "the endless comparison that must occur in the process of consciousness between the articulated and the lived."[20]

Structures of feeling, then, describe an area of experience that is all we might feel of "immediacy," that exists prior to conscious articulation – prior, that is, to the various ideological and social determinations that necessarily shape any communal discourse – and yet is always already social in character.

In this way, Williams preserves the possibility of emergent social for-mations, against the reifications of classical base/superstructure theory. In contrast, Williams offers a base that is itself consistently changing, a view that, in turn, allows for a less rigid conception of culture's relation to that base. To understand this argument more clearly, it is worth quoting Williams in full:

> *no mode of production and therefore no dominant social order and therefore no dom-inant culture ever in reality includes or exhausts all human practice, human energy and human intention* ... [thus] modes of domination ... select from and conse-quently exclude the full range of human practice. What they exclude may often be seen as the personal or the private, or as the natural or even the metaphys-ical. Indeed it is usually in one or other of these terms that the excluded area is expressed, since what the dominant has effectively seized is indeed the ruling definition of the social.[21]

However, for Williams, "all consciousness is social."[22] Paradoxically, then, the notion of "structures of feeling" emerges as a strong defense of the pol-itical efficacy of seemingly private experiences. For if these experiences are always already social they necessarily have a specific location in that social field of contestation we call culture. "Structures of feeling" name those kinds of "experiences to which the fixed forms do not speak at all, which indeed they do not recognize" but which might very well be tied to emer-gent social formations.[23] The articulation of these experiences in solution thus becomes one of the ways in which culture transforms itself, building something new out of inherited traditions.

The modernist literature of the European metropole is, as I will argue, virtually defined by this notion of an emergent structure of feeling, one entirely dependent upon inherited traditions and yet consistently striv-ing toward the realization of something else, whether in the attempts of Eliot's fragmented subjects to connect with one another, Pound's uto-pian desire to craft a world culture out of disparate cultural discourses, Joyce's recognition that a transformation of Ireland cannot simply reject the British culture within which it is submerged, or Woolf's realization that a reimagining of British nationalism cannot continue to voyage out, but must, instead, turn inward on itself. Similarly, the way out of the con-ceptual bind that I have outlined within modernist studies – the desire to rehabilitate the term "modernism" out of some residual allegiance to the rebellion of its earliest practitioners – is to return to the scene of modernist literary production and to confront its relationship to imperialism head-on.

In this way, I hope to continue the work of postcolonial studies, for in order to overcome the divide between a universal metropolitan center and a particularized periphery, we must also try to overcome the divide between aesthetics and politics that is the reflection of this more originary political divide. For literature from the periphery is still too often taken to be political, even if only in the tacit claim that writing about it is subversive, while the literature of metropolitan modernism remains primarily aesthetic, even when this aesthetic is seen as restrictive and totalizing. Clearly this is an unsatisfactory division, which, despite its good intentions – the desire to read political resistance in works of the economic periphery – only reinforces the hierarchies of global culture, relegating peripheral works to the unaesthetic realm of political struggle while retaining "aesthetic" merit, even in inverted form, for works from the center. We have, here, a kind of global division of cultural labor – the periphery is the body, the center the mind – that fails to do justice to the complex dynamics of politics and aesthetics at play in all parts of what Pascale Casanova has helpfully called "The World Republic of Letters."[24] Reshaping our understanding of works from the imperial center is one way we can produce a more nuanced account of how periphery and center shape each other.

THE VOYAGE IN

Modernism, Imperialism and the Historical Sense begins with an outline of the origins of both modernism and the ahistorical consciousness characteristic of commodity culture in the failed revolutions of 1848 as analyzed by Karl Marx. Turning its back on the working class and, therefore, its "world-historical mission," the bourgeoisie revealed itself, in 1848, to be pursuing its own naked class interests. The result was that the constitutive antagonisms of society were laid bare within the structures of an emergent democratic state. The point here is not that class conflict was invisible in the social order prior to this moment, but rather that class conflict emerged as the defining feature of the *political* stage. Onto this stage strode Louis Napoleon, that "gross mediocrity" who forced Marx to rethink his vision of both the bourgeoisie and the state itself. What Marx found in his analysis of 1848 was the tendency for capital to break free from social structures and posit itself as a super-ordinate social agency unmoored from any class interests, a vision perfectly matched by the supposedly neutral bourgeois state whose role is to mediate social conflict. These seemingly neutral structures, however, only represent the specific form of bourgeois class rule, which constitutes itself around an evacuated political center and an agentless vision of history. This agentless vision of history persists into the imperialist period, where expansion was imagined to be necessitated by the dictates of capital itself, as if no human intervention could prevent its iron laws from moving forward. At the same time, 1848 witnesses the first flowering of modernism in the works of Flaubert and Baudelaire, writers to whom each of my principal authors were deeply indebted and whose aesthetic forms they transformed in quite specific ways. I examine this relationship primarily through Eliot's engagement with the ahistorical consciousness of the Baudelairean *flâneur*, built upon the flows of imperial commodity culture.

Against this vision of an unmoored ahistorical subject, I turn to the *Eighteenth Brumaire*, to develop a Marxian notion of tradition as the space within which historical transformation is articulated. It is this idea of tradition that I see operative in the works of my principal authors. For T. S. Eliot, writing from within the center of the British Empire, tradition is primarily those works of the European cultural past that are effaced by the intertwined ideologies of primitivism and progress that Eliot's critical prose consistently attacks. In my second chapter's reading of Eliot's dissertation I demonstrate how the movement from subjective to communal structures of meaning is understood via an idea of mediation and a crucial distinction between what Eliot calls real and unreal objects. Rather than an inherent quality of the object itself, realness is, according to Eliot, a function of the relations an object contains, of the number of subjects for whom that object contains meaning. This distinction undergirds my reading of *The Waste Land*'s imperial structure of feeling. Within the space of the poem, Eliot attempts to make the unreal city real, presenting all those structural determinations that are effaced by imperial culture, which, in turn, produces the subjective alienation characteristic of the modern metropolis.

If *The Waste Land*'s final turn to India is meant as an acknowledgement of its role in creating metropolitan consciousness, Pound's turn to the East has much greater ambitions: nothing less than the construction of a universal culture that need not be irredeemably Eurocentric. In my third chapter, I discuss Pound's multicultural poetics in light of recent discussions of the limits and promises of both multicultural discourse and theories of the cosmopolitan. For unlike Eliot, Pound is not merely interested in revealing a layer of structural determinations that has been occluded, but in building a new culture for a future society that has yet to exist. Pound's interest in foreign cultures violates, then, that form of cultural relativism that equates culture with identity. In contrast, Pound argues for the public quality of culture, suggesting that it is contained not in identities but in art works themselves. Identities are thus malleable and are constantly altered by their encounter with works from other cultures. *The Cantos* seeks to envision a form of consciousness that would not simply assimilate the East into Western forms of understanding, but that might – within the realm of culture – overcome the conceptual forms of imperial domination.

In my fourth chapter I address the colony itself, situating Joyce's *Ulysses* within the competing ideologies of British imperialism and Irish nationalism. Presenting both the subject's construction by social discourses, and the ability of the laboring artist to alter those discourses, Joyce's mythic method emerges, in my account, as a way of reflecting upon Ireland's peripheral situation, its continual tracking of its own development against the standard Western narratives of development that Ireland only partly matches. This desire to force Ireland into already mapped out patterns of development is present both within early Marxist critiques of *Ulysses* – which read the novel as a reactionary evacuation of historical agency – and contemporary postcolonial reevaluations of the novel that valorize stasis as the specific condition of postcoloniality itself. In contrast, Joyce illustrates both through his characters and his endlessly inventive form, the construction of counter-hegemonic agency within the very structures that condition the colonial subject.

Writing from the opposite side of the colonial divide that frames Joyce's work, Virginia Woolf finds herself grappling with a remarkably similar issue: how is a British subject opposed to empire able to produce a creditable critique of the imperial structures that necessarily condition her? I answer this question by tracing a shift in Woolf's prose from the imperial setting of her first novel *The Voyage Out* to the domestic focus of works such as *Mrs. Dalloway*. With this shift, Woolf reveals the impossibility of standing outside one's social order, demonstrating the relentlessness with which patriarchal society conditions even such oppositional subjects as Rachel Vinrace. To this end, Woolf turns her focus to characters such as Mrs. Dalloway to discern what agencies might be latent within the British social system. *The Voyage Out* is transformed to a voyage in, as Woolf reins in the expansive imperialist British subject. She does so through a rereading of the English Renaissance that argues for the transformative powers of even the most complicit forms of cultural production.

In each of these readings, I see modernist literature as fully implicated in the imperial culture from which it emerges, irremediably tied to the commodity structure that is its asymptotic double. To say this is not, however, to reduce modernism to that culture, but rather to acknowledge its conditioning ground. Indeed, it is precisely the acknowledgment of this ground that is the mark of modernism's ability to resist it.

The persistence of the past: Modernism vs. imperial time

THE DISCOURSE OF EMPIRE

In *The Age of Empire*, Eric Hobsbawm describes the years 1875 through 1914 – the years in which the modernist generation was born and came of age – as "an era of profound identity crisis and transformation" for the newly ascendant bourgeoisie whose "very existence as a class of masters was undermined by the transformation of its own economic system."[1] The most important element of this transformation, according to Hobsbawm, was the rapid expanse of international capital. The world, in 1880, "was now genuinely global" as a "tightening web of transport drew even the backward and previously marginal into the world economy," which, in turn, "created a new interest among the old centres of wealth and development in these remote areas."[2] European civilization "now had need of the exotic." Importantly, this need was felt across all segments of society. In the realm of production "technological development now relied on raw materials which, for reasons of climate or the hazards of geology, were to be found exclusively or profusely in remote places."[3] At the same time, the growth of mass consumption produced an increased demand for products "long and characteristically known (at least in German) as 'colonial goods' and sold by the grocers of the developed worlds: sugar, tea, coffee, cocoa and its derivatives."[4] The result was that the daily lives of citizens in both the metropole and the colony were increasingly determined by the globalized financial relation that linked them. The impersonal structures of capital seemed to be rapidly undermining the individualistic values central to the bourgeoisie's hegemonic position, as well as the structure of the nation-state within which that hegemony operated, as everyday life in the metropole was increasingly conditioned by forces outside of its immediate control.

This situation seemed so new that it demanded a new word – imperialism – used across the political spectrum to describe a form of colonial conquest intimately linked to capitalist expansion.[5] Here we can turn to Lenin's 1917 *Imperialism: The Highest Stage of Capitalism* for a succinct summation of what were seen to be imperialism's five essential features:

1) The concentration of production and capital developed to such a high stage that it created monopolies which play a decisive role in economic life. 2) The merging of bank capital with industrial capital, and the creation, on the basis of this "finance capital," of a "financial oligarchy." 3) The export of capital, which has become extremely important, as distinguished from the export of commodities. 4) The formation of international capitalist monopolies which share the world among themselves. 5) The territorial division of the whole world among the greatest capitalist powers is completed.[6]

This last feature is, perhaps, the most important, as the inability of the great capitalist powers to capture more territory led to the fierce competition for markets generally considered one of the causes of the Great War. Thus imperialism, in the Marxist sense, tends to refer to inter-imperialist rivalry rather than any occurrence in the colonies themselves.

This narrowly schematic focus can seem to conceal what is, in fact, one of the most distinctive features of the Age of Empire, namely the way the nation was itself altered by its expansion. Indeed it was in defense of traditional nationalism that J. A. Hobson articulated his 1902 critique of imperialism. Imperialism, Hobson argued, tended toward a "perversion" of nationalism, whose "true nature and limits" were best articulated by J. S. Mill: "The strongest [cause of nationalist feeling] is identity of political antecedents, the possession of a national history and consequent community of recollections, collective pride and humiliation, pleasure and regret, connected with the same incidents in the past."[7] In its "attempts to overflow its natural banks and absorb the near or distant territory of reluctant and unassimilable peoples," imperialism represented, for Hobson, an untenable extension of the nation, ruining the nationalist construct of tradition through the forced assimilation of what was "unassimilable."[8] Hobson here seeks to defend the nation's boundaries, but he does so by at least recognizing the possibility of alternative social arrangements, arguing against the "notion that there exists one sound, just, rational system of government, suitable for all sorts and conditions of men, embodied in the elective representative institutions of Great Britain."[9]

Furthermore, imperialism, for Hobson, subverts not only the sovereignty of the colonies, but also that of the citizens of the metropole, for "the government of a great heterogeneous medley of lower races by department officials in London and their nominated emissaries lies outside the scope of popular knowledge and popular control."[10] The end result is that "the Imperial Government in our dependencies ... cannot be controlled directly or effectively by the will of the people."[11] When a great deal of the economic life of the nation is conducted elsewhere, as Fredric Jameson has argued, it becomes impossible for the metropolitan citizen to fully comprehend all the determinations that make up his/her social existence.[12] National sovereignty is thus, in Hobson's account, weakened universally; its very concept is threatened.

Integration into a world economy has, then, two paradoxical effects, which are developed by Nikolai Bukharin. On the one hand, integration works to "revolutionise the pre-capitalist methods of production in the most backward corners of the world, thus accelerating world commodity circulation in astounding proportions."[13] This revolution in the means of production leads to an increasing integration of economic life as national economic events are dictated by their insertion into a world market: "To a very large extent 'national' and local differences are leveled out in the general resultant world prices," in this way "substituting for the market conditions of an individual country, the world market conditions."[14] On the other hand, different countries are inserted into the world market in different ways, so that alongside this tendency toward homogenization is a tendency toward differentiation, toward the extension of the national-ist division between town and country on an international scale. "Entire countries," Bukharin writes, "appear to-day as 'towns,' namely the indus-trial countries, whereas entire agrarian territories appear to be 'country.'"[15] The periphery is thus included in the world economy in a structure of dependence, either as the rural source of raw materials and cheap labor, or as the designated market for the metropole's finance and commodities as described by Lenin. Capitalism's perpetually primitive accumulation rests as Rosa Luxemburg argued, on the need for an outside.[16] What Luxemburg missed, however, is the dialectical relationship by which capital both destroys and produces the outside on which it depends. The imperialist world emerges as a divided structure: "[A] smaller part in which 'progress' was indigenous and another much larger part in which it came as a foreign conqueror."[17] On the one hand a host of perpetually threatened traditions, on the other, an ever-expanding modernity. In each case a peculiarly ahis-torical consciousness results, one that is attached to either a reified sense of the traditional or a deterritorialized fetishization of the global.

When we turn to the origins of this world we will find that the devel-opment of these structures – the dispersal of the capitalist market – was created *precisely* by its concentration, by the crisis of *overproduction* that led to the expansion of market economies characteristic of the period. In what follows I will describe the origins of this expansionist impulse in the failed revolutions of 1848 that produced both the politics of spectacle associated with commodity culture and the aesthetic forms of literary modernism, prime among them the figure of the *flâneur*, who finds a home for himself in the generalized experience of dislocation this expansion creates, an experience James Clifford has named "ethnographic modernity."

THE FLÂNEUR, OR THE COMMODITY FORM
OF THE MAN OF LETTERS

Clifford begins his influential book *The Predicament of Culture* with poem XVIII of William Carlos Williams's *Spring and All*, whose first lines, "The pure products of America / go crazy--," Clifford finds emblematic of the cultural situation of the 1920s and, therefore, of literary modernism. To describe this situation, he coins the phrase *ethnographic modernity*: "ethnographic because Williams finds himself off center among scattered traditions; modernity since the condition of rootlessness and mobility he confronts is an increasingly common fate."[18] Rather than fight for "endangered authenticities," Clifford seeks to "make space for specific paths through modernity," an improvisatory approach to culture he aligns with the poet's famous dictum "Compose. (No ideas/but in things) Invent!"[19]

This same modernist injunction – "No ideas but in things" – appears in the introduction to Bill Brown's *A Sense of Things*, where it is used to suggest the world of a late-nineteenth- and early-twentieth-century America newly flooded with objects. Sacrificing "the clarity of thinking about things as objects of consumption," Brown hopes to answer the "fundamentally modernist" question about how meaning is encapsulated in and through the confrontation with objects.[20] Modernism, in his account, seeks an opaque object, but "what first reads like the effort to accept things in their physical quiddity becomes the effort to penetrate them, to see through them, and to find ... within an object ... the subject."[21]

Taken together, Brown and Clifford present a shift in the construction of the subject that is one way of articulating that ever-elusive concept of modernity. Formerly tied to place and organized around communal traditions, subjectivity seems, in the modern period, to be constituted by objects. This is as true of commodities as it is of cultural objects, particularly when we look to those cultural objects for reflections of our identity. Arguments about the politics of representation depend, then, on the condition of ethnographic modernity Clifford describes, for it is only in the presence of competing traditions that one can compare and evaluate the various forms of subjectivity these traditions project. The very desire for roots, we might say, is due to the omnipresence of routes, which detach both subject and object from the contextual structures within which they originally gained their significance.

This detachment has, of course, always been a feature of the commodity, which enters the market separated from the social labor that went into its production, but it has accelerated in the age of globalization in which the various international forces involved in the making of any particular product are nearly impossible for the consumer to track. Commodities, in our globalized world, have attained a form of mobility that has only brought them closer to the work of art, which in its post-Kantian capacity as a space of imaginative projection has always existed outside of any determining social ground. And yet this overstates the case, for it was precisely the artwork's entrance into the marketplace that guaranteed its autonomy from both church and state. Commodity and artwork have *always* been intertwined. They are, as Adorno argued, "torn halves of an integral freedom, to which, however, they do not add up."[22]

For the work of art, as understood by modernism, contains within its form sedimented history, both the history of its moment of production and the history of the critical engagements through which it has been continuously remade. Works of art, that is to say, are peculiar kinds of objects, whose value is not used up in consumption, whose stubborn materiality continually points to communal processes that transcend that materiality and create the object's value.[23] Modernism's characteristic, and seemingly contradictory, interest in both imagination and concretion seeks to do justice to this particular dialectic, suggesting simultaneously the transformative powers of imaginative work and the resistance of an object that cannot simply be subsumed to the present-tense needs of the perceiving subject. Eliot's "Tradition and the Individual Talent," Pound's interest in the sculptural and the revelatory, Joyce's continual comparison of naturalistic detail and Homeric myth, Woolf's investment in the continuities of local habitation and the immediacy of subjective experience – all of these formulations are versions of this dialectic, and they all serve to emphasize the work of art as an object that resists the expressivist logic by which the subject's relationship to the commodity is generally imagined.[24]

This expressivism suggests a simple proposition: I choose certain objects because they represent who I am. Immediately, though, this relation undergoes a dialectical reversal: Who I am, essentially, is constituted by the objects I consume. Commodities thus offer the promise of realizing one's core subjectivity through the consumption of objects, but attempting to locate this true self only leads to its endless deferral through the production of the various desires necessary to fuel a consumption-oriented social order. The quest for the self passes through its negation emerging as a capitulation to the most culturally validated narrative of subject construction: I am what I consume. We have, here, the peculiarly atomized and homogenized mass subject. Each subject follows the same social forces, which demand that it attempt to endlessly express its subjectivity through consumption: I am an individual because I own the same Nikes that everyone else does.

This consumptive subjectivity develops out of the structures of imperial capital, a fact that allows us to create a further link between Clifford's ethnographic modernity and Brown's flood of objects. Caused by a crisis of overproduction, imperialism worked toward the creation of a world economy, exporting finance and commodities to a periphery that was, as I have already suggested, moving – both conceptually and practically – ever closer to the center. Imperialism thus produces both those improvisatory paths through modernity and the flood of objects with which we navigate these paths.

Perhaps no figure has seemed more exemplary of these improvisatory paths than that of the *flâneur*, particularly as described by Walter Benjamin and elaborated on by a range of contemporary critics. Several features of this discourse are relevant here. The first is the connection, best articulated by Rob Shields, between the *flâneur* and the world of imperial capital that he – for the figure was almost always gendered male – surveys. For Shields the *flâneur* is a "displaced native," wandering a city "filled with foreigners and goods from distant lands."[25] His ability to successfully navigate the estranging streets of modernity represents a kind of wish fulfillment for the citizen of the European metropole. "The *flâneur*," Shields writes, "is a hero who excels under the stress of ... economic realities such as changing labour markets and commodity prices and social encounters with strangers and foreigners which *impinged* on the life world of Europeans."[26] His "gaze" is thus "part of a tactic to appropriate not only the local, physical spaces of the city as one's own 'turf' ... but also to participate in the popular sense of empire and even revel in the 'emporium.'"[27]

Hence the *flâneur*'s connection to the Arcades, which Benjamin called "forerunners of the department store" in which "art enters the service of the merchant."[28] The key to the *flâneur* is not so much the urban crowd, which Benjamin argued was "imprinted" on Baudelaire's work as "a hidden figure," but rather the objective conditions that create this crowd, namely "a pervasive structure formed by the mass production and dissemination of commodities."[29] Central to the experience of this "pervasive struc-ture" were the various expositions and fairs endemic to the period across Europe, which Benjamin described as "places of pilgrimage to the com-modity fetish" whose purpose was "to teach a 'lesson of things.'"[30] In England, the most famous of these expositions was the Crystal Palace Exhibition of 1851, identified by Thomas Richards as the origin of "the era of the spectacle."[31] At the Exhibition, "things now spoke for them-selves" and their message was "that all human life and cultural endeavor could be fully represented by exhibiting manufactured articles."[32] What the Great Exhibition showed, above all, was that "the capitalist system had not only created a dominant form of exchange but was also in the process of creating a dominant form of representation" that would, by the First World War, become "the centerpiece of everyday life."[33] This representational form was, of course, the fetishized commodity. The exhi-bitions thus constituted the randomly gathered urban crowd as a new polity under the rubric of consumption by "appealing to the[ir] fanta-sies," and directing these fantasies toward the commodities themselves.[34] The relations between individuals are here mediated through things, as consciousness itself is constituted by the belief that "merchandise can fill [the] needs of the imagination."[35]

Far from conflicting with national identity, this new identity was eas-ily grafted onto it, as "advertisers learned that the best way to sell people commodities was to sell them the ideology of England, from the national identity embodied in the monarchy to the imperial expansion taking place in Africa."[36] The commodity itself was the hero of this story, "appear[ing] as the prime mover of imperialist expansion." Thus imperial agency was effaced as it seemed that "the sheer plenitude of English material wealth" had itself "succeeded in creating an Empire the likes of which the world had never seen."[37] The expositions and arcades were essentially palaces both for displaying the imperial wealth congealed within the commodity form and for constructing a new social group – the urban crowd – through the mediation of that representational form.

And the *flâneur* who wandered within them was, according to Benjamin, the commodity form of the man of letters looking for a customer. "The *flâneur*," Benjamin writes, "is someone abandoned in the crowd. In this he shares the situation of the commodity."[38] Benjamin continues, juxtaposing Marx with a direct quotation from Baudelaire's prose poem "Crowds":

If the soul of the commodity which Marx occasionally mentions in jest existed, it would be the most empathetic ever encountered in the realm of souls, for it would have to see in everyone the buyer in whose hand and house it wants to nestle. Empathy is the nature of the intoxication to which the *flâneur* abandons himself in the crowd. "The poet enjoys the incomparable privilege of being himself and someone else as he sees fit. Like a roving soul in search of a body, he enters another person whenever he wishes. For him alone, all is open; if certain places seem closed to him, it is because in his view they are not worth inspecting." The commodity itself is the speaker here.[39]

Benjamin's discussion clearly picks up on the language of Marx's analysis of commodity fetishism, where the table made of "that common, everyday thing, wood ... steps forth as a commodity" and is thereby "changed into something transcendent."[40] Thus the mobility of the commodity, detached from social relations, is connected to the mobility of the *flâneur*, even as the quotation from the prose poem "Crowds" aptly captures the transcendent hopes of a poetic soul unimpeded by material restrictions. In his empathetic ability to enter the isolated members of the crowd, the *flâneur* posits himself as the subjective counterpart of the commodity form, helping to mediate a new form of experience created by an imperial metropole flooded with objects that connect its citizens, in ways barely perceptible, to the far-flung reaches of the globe.

We can differentiate this figure even further, for as Mary Gluck has shown there are, in fact, two distinct versions of the *flâneur*: "[T]he first is that of the popular *flâneur*. . . . The second is what I shall call the avant-garde *flâneur*" associated with Baudelaire.[41] The first figure was found in popular art, where he "raised uncertainty about the nature of modernity and its ability to generate cultural traditions of its own."[42] Often appearing in "the costumes of the ancients," the public *flâneur* seemed to ask whether "contemporary life was capable of producing heroic actions and epic art."[43] His ability to read the social types of the urban city gave a definitively positive answer to this question.

In contrast, the avant-garde *flâneur* "could no longer claim to embody the totality of the social and cultural values of an emerging modernity." Whereas the popular *flâneur* found "epic unity" in the "social spaces of the empirical city," the avant-garde *flâneur* could only reconstruct a fractured reality in the world of imagination.[44] "Modernity," Gluck concludes, "had ceased to be a social text ... it had become an aesthetic text, that needed to be freshly created through the artist's imaginative act."[45] Crucially for my argument, what separates these two figures is 1848. Though Gluck does not offer an analysis of this transition, she asserts that it is "undeniable ... that the phenomenally popular physiologies and panorama essays, which had dominated the cultural scene of the 1840s, lost their appeal almost overnight and became anachronistic by the time of the revolution of 1848."[46]

The year 1848, of course, has a privileged place in accounts of modernism. Not only is it directly thematized in what is typically considered one of the first modernist novels – Flaubert's *Sentimental Education* – but it also marks the moment when, according to Georg Lukács, the bourgeoisie turned against the proletariat, transforming itself from a class with a world-historical mission into a reactionary class seeking to preserve its own particular interests. For Lukács, this political development is the historical condition for the rejection of classical realism he found in the decadent works of literary modernism. At the same time, 1848 represents the entrance of the masses onto the political stage, and its result, the Second Empire of Louis Napoleon, which is the focus of Benjamin's study of the *flâneur*, "became a sort of laboratory of a more modern form of politics" dedicated to the management of the newly enfranchised crowd through manipulation and spectacle.[47] Furthermore, it is from within this new social formation that the expansionist drive of European capital emerges. In a variety of ways, then, 1848 gave birth to an emergent social formation whose conflicts and contradictions would become dominant during the modernist era.

That two of the most important forerunners of Anglo-American modernism – Flaubert and Baudelaire – began writing during this period is critical for my argument. For Eliot, Pound, Joyce, and Woolf take up the forms of an emergent French modernism, to which they all paid explicit and implicit homage, only to subject them to revision and critique in a relationship familiar to dialecticians through the untranslatable German term *aufhebung*.[48] My principal authors' desire to preserve and transform the aesthetic they inherit from their French predecessors suggests both the relevance *and* inadequacy of these aesthetic solutions for a form of imperial capital that was, in 1848, just taking shape.

The *flâneur* is, thus, the cultural form that best connects modernism's continental origins to the primarily London-based writers I discuss. However, as should already be clear, this is not a study of England or Englishness or the particular events of British imperialism. Rather, my interest is in the over-arching structures of international capital, which transcend and, indeed, threaten the independence of individual nation-states.[49] These transnational historical structures condition the aesthetic forms of literary modernism, forms that emerge not in response to a specific national situation – for what nation could unite a soon to be converted Brit, an Iowan living in Italy, an Irishman who spent the majority of his life on the Continent, and the daughter of the Victorian empire? – but to the scene of ethnographic modernity empire creates. Indeed, the careers of these writers depend, in various ways, on the dislocations of empire itself. In turning to 1848, then, I will be arguing for the specific ways modernism responds to a newly fragmented social world most readily understood by this particular historical moment, a moment that has produced a voluminous literature seeking to understand the relationship between notions of historical progress and aesthetic form. At the same time, I will develop, through a reading of Marx, a new understanding of tradition that results from this fundamental historical shift, and specify further the way modernism seeks to mobilize this tradition against the forms of ahistorical subjectivity constitutive of imperial commodity culture.

1848 AND THE IDEOLOGY OF MODERNISM

In *A Singular Modernity*, Fredric Jameson distinguishes between modernist aesthetic production proper and "modernism as ideology," which he calls an invention of the Cold War. Abandoning the utopian impulses of the early modernist period, this ideological investment in aesthetic autonomy seeks a "stabilization of the existing systems," reducing the transformative energies of modernism to "the more basic programme of modernization – which is simply a new word for that old thing, the bourgeois conception of progress."[50] In the following section I will turn to Marx's *Eighteenth Brumaire* to read the emergence of the historical situation that conditions the bourgeois conception of progress in its ideological form. Locating in the revolutions of 1848 the absent political center that has become fashionable in contemporary post-Marxist thinking, I will argue that modernism responds to this situation not with the idea of aesthetic autonomy – which has direct links to the romantic subject modernism consistently critiqued – but with an understanding of the situatedness of all discourse. The origins of modernism begin, then, from a situation of particularity that emerged out of the 1848 revolutions, when, as Roberto Schwarz argues, "the tide of popular revolutions forced the European bourgeoisie to recognize the particular nature of their own interests."[51] Here "the brute reality of class oppression laid bare the unreal side of the phraseology of liberty, equality and fraternity." The result, for Schwarz, is the revelation of the oppositions underlying the social order:

From the point of view of popular awareness, and of the self-awareness of the victors, the experience of the June massacres has the importance of a historic revelation. They reveal the true adversaries to each other and to themselves … Bourgeois normality, and with it the whole of contemporary language, began to live in a state of siege: words became soaked with incompatible meanings, produced by social antagonism; on one side, the official acceptations, on the other, those that the words held for the defeated, which were often semi-clandestine.[52]

Modernism, in Schwarz's account, emerges from precisely this heteroglossic discursive space.

Marx's *Eighteenth Brumaire* describes a similarly divided social world, leading to some of his most famous conclusions about the movement of history. In its opening we encounter the following distinction between the revolutions of the past and those of the present:

The social revolution of the nineteenth century cannot create its poetry from the past but only from the future. It cannot begin till it has stripped off all superstition from the past. Previous revolutions required recollections of world history in order to dull themselves to their own content. The revolution of the nineteenth century must let the dead bury the dead in order to realise its own content. There phrase transcended the content, here content transcends the phrase.[53]

Make it new, Marx proclaims; a new social order demands new articulations, for if the revolution seeks to bring a truly new social order into being, it cannot use phrases from a past it would seek to overcome. This rejection of the past must, however, be read alongside another equally famous passage, which suggests, instead, its persistence: "Men make their own history, but they do not make it just as they please in circumstances they choose for themselves; rather they make it in present circumstances, given and inherited. Tradition from all the dead generations weighs like a nightmare on the brain of the living."[54]

If before Marx sounded like Pound, here he becomes Stephen Dedalus, who similarly complained of the "nightmare of history" from which he was trying to awake. Marx, too, was hoping for an awakening and he here recognizes that any future revolution can only emerge out of the given circumstances. In making this claim, Marx is fighting against two competing ideologies. On the one hand, there is the form of historical determinism that would remove historical events from the realm of human agency. In a general way, we can associate this view with Hegel, for whom world history progressed via negation, sublating the agency of world-historical individuals through the cunning of reason. On the other hand, there is the complete separation of politics and economics which the self-contradictory alliance of the peasants and Bonaparte seemed to suggest.

In contrast to these two views, Marx offers the notion of tradition, a form of historical conditioning that is, itself, a product of human agency, and has, according to Neil Larsen, a "real, social power ... determining even the formal possibility of actuality."[55] "Tradition," Larsen continues, "or the 'given circumstances,' confers on events not merely the historical disguises in which to cloak their authentic content but also, and in a much more powerful maneuver, their meaning as 'events,' the sense that, in them, anything has happened at all."[56] The rejection of the forms of the past, then, does not represent a desire to stand outside of tradition, to imagine some entirely new space erupting into the social field. Instead, Marx is here making an argument about how history moves forward. Tradition represents something other than the mere repetition of the past; it is, rather, the space in and through which historical change is articulated. Moving from Pound to Joyce, we have arrived at Eliot.

Larsen, however, fails to notice this common ground, instead reading modernism as an ideological inversion of Marx. Where Marx describes "a historically objective 'crisis in representation,'" modernism sees representation as "a purely conceptual operation" containing "an intrinsic falsity."[57] Larsen thus locates modernism's roots in the historical crisis of 1848, a reading which fits in with the standard narrative of modernism's origins in nineteenth century France and the work of Flaubert and Baudelaire. As I have suggested, these events also become the basis for the development of imperial capital, for this crisis in representation is caused by the "tendency for capital in its real abstraction to break free from certain specific political – and in this sense, representational – relations and structures ... and, thereby, to take on the attributes of a superordinate social agency with no fixed political or cultural subjectivity."[58]

This social agency seems to exist only for its own sake, capital, in its self-reproduction, having the ability to make its presuppositions seem "not as conditions of its arising, but as results of its presence," an idea of autonomy that rhymes with the work of art that, in its auto-referentially, becomes the ground of its own determination.[59] In each case what is effaced is the social character of production, money begetting money as easily as genius channels beauty. In the case of capital, it is this endless self-reproduction that causes capital to separate from the social order, reducing quality to quantity in the service of expansion for expansion's sake. And it is precisely this ideology that undergirds imperialism, which was "born," according to Hannah Arendt, "when the ruling class in capitalist production came up against national limits to its economic expansion."[60] The political concept driving imperialism is, therefore, "not really political at all, but has its origin in the realm of business speculation, where expansion means the permanent broadening of industrial production and economic transactions characteristic of the nineteenth century."[61] Arendt elaborates: "Imperialist expansion had been touched off by a curious kind of economic crisis, the overproduction of capital and the emergence of 'superfluous' money, the result of oversaving, which could no longer find productive investment within the national borders … export of power followed meekly in the train of exported money."[62]

The concentration of capital leads to its dispersal, creating an "expansion of political power without the foundation of a body politic."[63] As in Hobson's argument, this expansion further disassociates the economic and political realms leading to a weakening of the affective bonds of the body politic. Into this void steps the ideology of race, "for there is under the conditions of an accumulating society, no other unifying bond available between individuals who … are losing all natural connections with their fellow man."[64] Moving first to the underdeveloped parts of the national territory, capital then expands to underdeveloped areas of the world, eradicating precapitalist economic modes and traditions in both metropole and colony. The ideology of race is here invented as a substitute for the traditions capital destroys *and* a justification for the very process performing that destruction.

The expansion Arendt describes is, of course, the increased export of capital characteristic of the Age of Empire, an export facilitated by two interrelated developments that increased the homogenization of economic structures: the continuing development of the joint stock company and the subsequent unity of financial and industrial capital Hilferding named "finance capital." Assembling capital from a range of small shareholders, the joint stock company "permits an enormous acceleration in the *centralisation* of capital, the amalgamation of many capitals into one."[65] This process allows the "owners of large blocks of capital … to gain control of the capital of many small shareholders."[66] The promise of increased participation – the justification of the joint stock company being that small capitalists could increase their earnings – comes here with a direct loss of control, generalized in the shift from free market to monopoly capital. As monopolies grow, Hilferding argues, there is a tendency for the various sectors of the economy to combine in "relations of mutual dependence and domination."[67] It is these relations of dependence that produce finance capital: "Finance capital signified the unification of capital. The previously separate spheres of industrial, commercial and bank capital are now brought under the common direction of high finance, in which the masters of industry and of the banks are united in a close personal association."[68] The rise of finance capital, thus leads to "the creation of a ruling class relatively unified in political affairs" whose relationship to the state becomes "much more close and direct."[69] What emerges is an increasingly totalized society, as the reach of the economic realm extends farther into the social world at the same time that economic control is taken out of the hands of the population at large.[70]

Reading Hilferding alongside Arendt, we can see that imperialism rests on a paradoxical separation and alliance of politics and economics. Hiding an economic policy within political clothing, the nation-state ends up extending political power over subjects who are not its members, who lack, that is, any properly political representation. Behind it all is the process of accumulation which, according to Arendt, creates "the 'progressive' ideology of the late nineteenth century ... ready to sacrifice everything and everybody to supposedly superhuman laws of history."[71] Imperial expansion becomes the extension of civilization to those tradition-bound, racially-other primitives still mired in precapitalist social formations. In this way imperialism attempts to create national unity out of a divided class society, giving "a new lease on life to political and social structures" – those same outworn phrases Marx argued needed to be overthrown – "which were quite obviously threatened by new social and political forces."[72] These new social forces, and the relative autonomy of the state within which they uneasily coexist, return us, at last, to the *Eighteenth Brumaire*.

The revolutionary wave that swept across Europe in 1848 had been much anticipated. The "unprecedented humiliation" of its failure required, then, a rethinking of the historical situation.[73] Marx's *Eighteenth Brumaire* represents a dramatic example of such a reconsideration and it has several important consequences for the historical moment of modernism's emergence. At issue, principally, is Marx's theory of the state. In *The Communist Manifesto* the state had appeared as "a committee for managing the common affairs of the whole bourgeoisie."[74] In *The Eighteenth Brumaire*, however, the bourgeoisie cedes its political rule to a "grotesque mediocrity," choosing to preserve its economic interests through the military stabilization of a volatile social structure.[75] An executive apparatus seems, here, to gain power over and against the dominant classes, granting the state autonomy with respect to class interests. It becomes, in effect, an absent center, a purely formal structure of rule that can be seized by any class that wins the political struggle. This purely formal state finds its match in a purely formal leader, who is himself a kind of floating signifier, occupying a hero's part despite being "the most simple-minded man in France."[76] Indeed it is his status as absent center that allows him to acquire "the most multifarious significance. Just because he was nothing, he could signify everything."[77]

Marx seems, then, to advance two different theories of the state: one instrumentalist – the state as a direct mechanism of the bourgeoisie's rule; the other formalist – the state as a structure that stands above class interest. This contradiction has led to much scholarly debate.[78] Rather than posit a theoretical discontinuity in Marx's thought, however, I would argue, following Bob Jessop, that *The Eighteenth Brumaire* describes "the transformation of the *institutional architecture of the state*."[79] For the state is not a neutral structure that remains unchanged by those whose interests it would serve. Instead, the autonomous state Marx here describes is one that perfectly matches the ideology of the bourgeoisie, who preserve their social and economic power *precisely* by separating it from the political sphere.[80] The relative autonomy of the state represents, in its formal structure, the interest of a particular class – the bourgeoisie – for whom the state exists precisely to guarantee its freedom to pursue economic interests without political interference.[81]

There are two key consequences of this separation of the economic and political realms for a Marxian analysis of history. The first is that there is no direct line from economic interest to ideology. Instead of "eternal and idealised interests that are attached to pregiven classes defined purely in terms of their position in the social relations of production," Marx analyzes the class struggle in its relation "to the present situation and its various strategic and tactical possibilities."[82] The second is that history lacks a smooth telic progression, proceeding instead through a series of contradictory starts and stops that are analyzed by Marx as the direct result of the various alliances that occur among classes with vastly different economic interests. Where a vulgar Marxism would insist on historical determination, Marx instead reads the struggle for hegemony.[83]

This reading of history is, simultaneously, a response to and critique of one of the most oft-noted consequences of the 1848 revolution: a change in the ideology of the bourgeoisie famously described, as we have seen, by Georg Lukács. Where previously the "bourgeoisie was ... the ideological leader of social development," it now, in its rejection of the demands of the proletariat, represented its "class ideologies in a much narrower sense."[84] This change is manifested, for Lukács as for Arendt, in the ideology of progress, which "undergoes a regression." "The fall of Hegelian philosophy," Lukács argues, "means the disappearance of the contradictory character of progress ... every element of contradiction is extinguished ... history is conceived as a smooth straightforward evolution."[85] No longer understood as the "prehistory of the present," history loses both its "living interest" and its direction, becoming a "collection and reproduction of interesting facts about the past."[86]

We can observe in Lukács's description the emergence of two forms of temporality. On the one hand, there is the endless temporal progression of the modern world. On the other, the reified world of the past, which is of antiquarian interest only. Counterposed to this is the characteristic Lukácsian notion of totality, the ability to place events within a history that is the unfolding of meaning, precisely the sense of history that the decisive events of 1848 tended to obscure. It is in the context of these two competing temporalities that we can read Marx's historical intervention. Read in this light, Marx's analysis both describes the ideological struggle that results from the bourgeoisie's abdication of its historical role and contradicts the ideology of progress which emerges, paradoxically, at the very moment of its betrayal. The subject's relationship to the "given historical circumstances" of tradition in *The Eighteenth Brumaire* overcomes the temporal duality Lukács outlines, rejecting both the smooth character of historical progress and the reified notion of a merely decorative past.

In contrast, modernism (for Lukács), represents a full capitulation to the bourgeoisie's regressive notion of progress and is, therefore, a betrayal of the values of critical realism. The world of the past, no longer "organically connected with the objective character of the present," becomes ornamental, a space where "a freely roaming subjectivity can fasten where and how it likes."[87] The archetype of this freely roaming artist is Flaubert – although we could also nominate Baudelaire – whose "deep hatred for modern society" led him to seek refuge in the Ancient Carthage depicted in *Salammbo*.[88]

It is in the context of this claim that I would like to return to Neil Larsen, who offers one of the most theoretically sophisticated critiques of modernism's supposed inversion of the historical crisis occasioned by 1848. Writing from an Adornian viewpoint – which represents, in his view, "modernism in full conceptual regalia" – Larsen presents a modernism for whom "representation no longer 'works,' no longer appears to offer the subject any cognitive access to the object."[89] In response, modernist writing works "through a medium that by its very nature disclaims all representational truth."[90] In this way, "modernism feeds on what is really, after all, the most conventional, and ideological, of historical representations: that of a historical past that does not trouble the subjective immediacy and self-identity of the present from which it is serenely – or tragically – contemplated."[91] The breakdown of traditional representation that Bonaparte represents does not, however, destroy the "premise of a representational identity per se ... but rather the *specific representational forms in which power is given.*"⁹² Modernism's refusal of history is, then, a refusal to understand the grounds of this particular crisis of representation, a claim that allows Larsen to distance modernism from the Marxian text within which he discloses the dialectical understanding of tradition I have already outlined. Modernism, in effect, reifies the evacuated center of power characteristic of capital in its imperial phase.

I will spend the rest of this book establishing the various ways the modernism of Eliot, Pound, Joyce, and Woolf specifically responded to this historical situation, but here I would like to mention two points that I will develop further. The first is that in making this claim, Larsen ignores the most standard narrative of modernism that we have: its rejection of the outdated forms of Victorian representation, a rejection that was motivated by a desire to reflect the changing modern world. Even those vague dismissals of "rhetoric" in which the modernists often engaged tended to have specific abuses in mind, leading less to a universal critique of representation as such, than to a technical distinction between effective forms of poetic invention. The second fact, which is often overlooked, is that even though modernism rejected its immediate predecessors, it characteristically articulated its aesthetic interests by and through examples from the works of the past. Thus we have Pound's investment in troubadour poetry, Joyce's virtuosic rewritings of Homer and Shakespeare, and Eliot's and Woolf's reimaginings of Renaissance literature. In each case we observe a modernism that understands its "subjective immediacy" largely in terms of its inherited traditions.

To understand why Larsen fails to address these elements of modernism's self-presentation, we can turn to a more recent essay entitled "Marxism, Postcolonialism and *The Eighteenth Brumaire.*" In this essay, Larsen largely reproduces the analysis previously outlined with one crucial difference. The misreading of Marx is no longer attributed to modernism, but to a postcolonialism that shares the post-structuralist belief that "Marxism can be purged of its 'Hegelian' birthmarks and incorporated successfully within the same critical spirit that animates the post-structuralist critique of the sign."⁹³ The object of Larsen's attack is Gayatri Spivak's "Can the Subaltern Speak." Larsen begins by noting the occasion of Spivak's remarks, the essay "Intellectuals and Power" in which Foucault and Deleuze reject "all pretensions of radical intellectuals to 'represent' the workers' struggle," proclaiming instead "a 'diffuse,' de-centered strategy, clearly *sans* party or 'revolutionary vanguard.'"⁹⁴ Spivak's response is to rebuke "such a neo-spontaneism for failing … to problematize its own metropolitan outlook." Drawing two opposed senses of the verb "to represent" out of Marx's text, Spivak argues that Foucault and Deleuze – and Western intellectuals generally – adhere to a problematic sense of representation as transparency, free of the international division of labor that is the condition of their own utterances. This view of representation continues to stage the subaltern as "Other:" "[T]he 'Subject's power to 'represent' (*vertreten*), resting on the powerlessness of the 'Other' to self-represent in this sense, is cloaked in a philosopheme of representation (*Darstellung*) that is, in principle, free."[95] For Larsen, Spivak's argument rests on reading a "crisis of subjective/collective agency as something intrinsic to *all* class difference" rather than something specific to a certain class "under given historical conditions."[96] Spivak thus remains, for Larsen, fundamentally within the orbit of the post-structural microphysics of power she seeks to critique.

I will not pretend to give a full account of the various twists and turns of Spivak's argument, but Larsen's critique, although fundamentally correct, misses a key element of her attack. For although Spivak does place her faith in a Derridian notion of "texuality" – going so far as to assert that "the narrow epistemic violence of imperialism gives us an imperfect allegory of the general violence that is the possibility of an episteme" – and, furthermore, tends toward a seemingly untheorized reification of an ahistorical "Western subject," she presents several interrelated concepts useful for a critique of empire.[97] Her essay works to divulge the ways the most seemingly radical critique of the subject tends, through its reliance on desire and libidinal economies, to reinstate the notion of an authentic privileged subject of knowledge. What this subject seems to know is precisely the Other as the place of concretion: "Reality," as Deleuze amazingly asserts, "is what actually happens in a factory."[98] Spivak's critique takes aim, then, at both the epistemic violence of "appropriating the other by assimilation," and the "self-contained version of the West" that "ignore[s] its production by the imperialist project."[99]

What Foucault and Deleuze's seemingly innocent gestures toward the Other suggest, for Spivak, is their commitment to a form of primitivism integral to their inability to theorize their position in the structures of globalization. Their reading of the Other as concretion, or as "a pure form of consciousness" is, in Spivak's estimation, a more or less direct reflection of a "contemporary international division of labor" that is itself "a displacement of the divided field of nineteenth-century territorial imperialism."[100] In response to the supposed transparency of the subject of knowledge,

Spivak argues for a form of self-reflexivity that can understand its position within this divided social field. "To confront" the Other, she writes, "is not to represent (*vertreten*) them but to learn to represent (*darstellen*) ourselves."[101]

Here we can return to the essay by Roberto Schwarz with which I began, for, in his reading, modernism – exemplified, as always, by Flaubert and Baudelaire – responds to the social antagonisms 1848 unleashed with precisely this type of self-reflexivity. "[S]ince the status of opinions, including authorial ones, does not allow open assent," modernism turns to a writing of technical rigor, which emphasizes the "primacy of narrative procedure over opinions."[102] Schwarz continues:

Authority and relative meaning are conferred through mediation of the literary method, above all by means of its effects of dislocation, which function as instances and allegories of the precedence that the social formation has over subjective intentions....

... *[A]mong the basic axioms of this new literary dispensation is the bankruptcy of ideas or intentions considered in the abstract....* Thoughts and emotions are qualified at every step, and in crushing fashion, by the place they occupy in the intrigue, and they exist only within that specific circumstance. The occasion, the immediate context ... becomes decisive.[103]

Modernist form, in Schwarz's Adornian reading, represents the determining power of social conditions, as individual desires are subordinated to the context in which they occur.[104] The subject is, here, relativized, not by its reduction to an endless chain of desire, but through the recognition of its position among competing traditions within the space of ethnographic modernity.

"No ideas but in things," can be rewritten, then, as the need to situate ideas within the objective structures in which they gain their significance. Williams's aphoristic slogan demands a form of historical thinking that resists the reification of conceptual thought, whether in the proclamation of an always already evacuated political center, a belief in a constitutive aporia in all forms of representation, or the Lukácsian faith "that a recognized and universally shared practice of representation exists and that it 'gives us the world' as it really is;" a faith Larsen seems, in part, to share.[105] All of these reifications serve to reinstate the subject of knowledge, for whom the social arrangement that constitutes him/her is accessible in its transparency. Modernism sets itself against this form of subjectivity, most clearly in its critique of romanticism, but also in its continual emphasis on construction and production, on the social labor of tradition within which subjects – and, crucially, art objects – gain their meaning.

REVOLVING WORLDS

Schwarz's modernism can seem, at first blush, to be simply another form of aestheticism as meaning is "conferred through [the] mediation of the literary method." The point, however, is not that aesthetics replace history – in any case an impossibility despite the frequency with which this charge is made – but rather that aesthetic form is *analogous* to historical form. Of course, history does not stand still. Social arrangements change and yet, in lines I have already quoted but which bear repeating here, the cultural forms that arise in response to them "outlive the situations for which they were devised, and survive, in reified forms, as 'cultural patterns.'"[106] For the modernists of my study, the aesthetic forms of Baudelaire and Flaubert were just such reified cultural patterns. The objective situation they confronted had shifted; no longer was the "immediate context" with which Flaubert, in Schwarz's account, qualified subjective intentions directly accessible to the artistic subject. This shift emerges, in a classic example of quantity turning into quality, due to the expansion of imperial relations. The national space within which Flaubert was still able to locate his contextual meanings was no longer, in the modernist period, the most important horizon for thinking about the relations among competing social forces; the antagonisms Schwarz describes were more and more international ones. And as I have already suggested, this expansion of social horizons is a key aspect of the "identity crisis" threatening the bourgeoisie's "very existence as a class of masters."

It is from this expanded international space that the aesthetic solutions of 1848 seem hermetically sealed, seem, that is to say, to be forms that require their own contextualization. From this perspective, the aesthetic mastery that Flaubert and Baudelaire proposed as solutions to their own historical moment reads as a mirror image of the bourgeoisie's self-confidence in the period of its ascendancy. *Flaubert and Baudelaire, that is to say, are constituted by the very bourgeoisie they loathed and whom they wished to shock.* In contrast, modernism, in its Anglo-American incarnation, tends to oscillate between artistic mastery and ostentatious displays of its own inability to totalize. *The Waste Land*'s famous lament that "I can connect nothing with nothing," the unresolved identity of M'Intosh that runs through *Ulysses*, Pound's habit of highlighting inaccuracies in his critical prose instead of searching out the correct reference, Woolf's refusal to specify the talk of Jacob's Cambridge friends, because she, as a woman, could not possibly have been present at the scene: each of these moments demonstrate the way in which the authors of my study are as interested in emphasizing their ability to capture the "unseizable forces" that drive us as they are in demonstrating their unseizability.[107]

Thus, the Flaubertian desire to remain invisible and all-powerful behind his work becomes, when paraphrased by Stephen Dedalus, simply another form of abstraction, mocked not only by Stephen's interlocutor, but by Joyce himself. As I will argue in greater detail, Joyce consistently undermines Stephen's most elevated aesthetic claims, demonstrating that the artistic desire to stand outside the work of art is simply the mirror image of the subject's desire to stand outside of its conditioning ground. In this way, Flaubertian narrative principles are used to contextualize the desires of the Flaubertian artist himself. With this gesture, Joyce manages to continue Flaubert's relentless emphasis on social formation over subjective intention while also pointing the way out of his hermetically sealed aesthetic text. Meaning, for Joyce, cannot be granted simply through aesthetic mediation, particularly for a colonial subject whose social order is determined by meanings that take place elsewhere.

Eliot, too, in his transformation of the *flâneur*, performs a similar act of sublation. Recall that for Gluck, the avant-garde *flâneur* operated as a kind of symbolic resolution to the problems of imperial capital, mediating the situation of ethnographic modernity in a world made newly illegible in the wake of the political transformations of 1848. Yet, this resolution remains, in large part, subjective for, as Charles Altieri has argued, "in Baudelairean lyricism all the ironies ultimately lead back to the exemplary sublimity of the speaker, both victim and hero of his corrosive intelligence and exquisite sensitivity."[108] Baudelaire, according to Altieri, could only register historical circumstances as the mark of this sensitivity. He had, as Eliot claimed, "great strength, but strength merely to *suffer* ... What he could do, with that immense passive strength ... was to study his suffering."[109]

It is precisely this valorization of artistic subjectivity that Eliot subjects to critique. Consider, in this light, the poem "Preludes," one of many early Eliot poems that rejects the aesthetic consolations of Baudelairean lyric, presenting us instead with a poetic subject unable to situate his exquisite perceptions within any larger structure that would grant them meaning. And yet, at the same time, Eliot demonstrates how this poetic subject is himself conditioned by the very social world for which he hopes to provide meaning. This contradiction is made most apparent in the poem's third stanza, as Eliot turns to an almost confrontational "you,"

encompassing, in the manner of Baudelaire's famous "Preface," both
reader and artistic subject:

> You dozed, and watched the night revealing
> The thousand sordid images
> Of which your soul was constituted;[110]

These lines present us with a version of the scandalous Kantian subject,
reduced to the presumed unity of its cognition of appearances, but Eliot
refuses to allow his artistic persona to reconstitute the world in his imagination.[111] Instead, poetic subjectivity remains entirely in excess of the object
world upon which it depends; its "vision of the street" is such "as the
street hardly understands" (*CP* 14).

Nowhere is this clearer than in the poem's final section, where the poetic
subject is described as "Impatient to assume the world." Subtly critiqued
via the word "assume," this idea is then immediately and directly mocked
by the poem's startling conclusion:

> I am moved by fancies that are curled
> Around these images, and cling:
> The notion of some infinitely gentle
> Infinitely suffering thing.
>
> Wipe your hand across your mouth, and laugh;
> The worlds revolve like ancient women
> Gathering fuel in vacant lots. (*CP* 14–5)

The notion of "some infinitely gentle / Infinitely suffering thing" seems to
suggest a union of Baudelaire's exquisite subjectivity and the object world
that stands outside of it. However, no sooner is this image raised than it
is dismissed. "The worlds revolve," Eliot suggests, despite the fancies of
poetic imagination.

"Preludes" thus rejects a purely aesthetic solution to the problems of
modernity, mocking the idealist assumptions of a poetic consciousness
that finds satisfaction in an image of suffering through which it can grant
significance to the depravations of modern life. In doing so, the poem
refuses the position of the Baudelairean *flâneur*. Far from the privileged
spectator of all he surveys, the narrator is simply one isolated subject
among many. Part of the squalid modern world, the poet can find no
internal resources for resisting it, his transcendentally pure consciousness
as unable to transform the world as the mechanically shuffling feet of the
returning workers referred to earlier in the poem in lines that hearken
back both to Baudelaire's crowd of consumers and the newly enfranchised
democratic masses.[112] Here, in the poem's final lines, we catch a glimpse

of the aesthetic of *The Waste Land* as the ancient and the modern are both present in a social order indifferent to the powers of poetic making. Crucially, this social order is plural: there are worlds beyond the space of the poem, worlds constitutive of the poetic subject in ways that subject can hardly imagine.

In what follows, I will attempt to demonstrate modernism's relationship to these other worlds in a reading of canonical modernism that does not ignore its constitution by the imperialist project. This reading is also an untangling of Spivak's reified "Western Subject," an investigation, then, of the conflicting strains and tensions within this particular form of subject-ivity as it was beginning to call into question the very structure of "appro-priation as assimilation" that is the object of Spivak's critique. The turn to other cultures in Eliot, Pound, and Joyce – and Woolf's related refusal to project herself into these cultures – differs from this appropriation in that it refuses to read the Other as some "pure form of consciousness." To do so would be to accede to the form of expressivism that was modern-ism's most consistent object of critique. Rather, these writers consistently seek to alter the appropriative subject of Western imperialism, either by reimagining its relation to its own locale or confronting it with values that are genuinely outside of its parameters, even as they reveal the subjective and situated interest of such efforts. In doing so, they suggest that history is of our own making, but the objects out of which we make it are the given circumstances, in this case: imperialist expansion, the intertwined notions of endless progress and static tradition, and the seeming loss of historical agency that can only be recuperated through the creation of various forms of community. Modernism attempts to disclose community through a dialectical understanding of tradition that rescues values from Europe's precapitalist past, suggesting both the recovery and persistence of the values capitalism imagines itself to have eliminated from view.

Modernist writing thus retains the redemptive stance associated with Benjamin's dialectical images, those constellations of then and now that "mirror the structure of history as a whole, viewed from the standpoint of its end."[113] Once again we encounter the methodological imperative to totalize. Modernism, though, achieves totality only in the momentary flashes Benjamin associates with redemptive temporality, and that Jameson has defended as utopian. For "radical alternatives, systemic transform-ations, cannot be theorized or even imagined within the conceptual field governed by the word 'modern.'"[114] We must, instead, think about the ways in which we are not modern, so that we might, someday, be something else. It remains now to ground these ideas in the things of modernism itself.

2

The Waste Land *and the unreal center of capitalist modernity*

The Waste Land is a poem defined by absence. The "dead tree gives no shelter, the cricket no relief, / And the dry stone no sound of water;" "The nymphs have departed;" "The river bears no empty bottles, sandwich papers, / Silk handkerchiefs, cardboard boxes, cigarette ends / Or other testimony of summer nights" (*CP* 53, 60). It is striking, then, to encounter in the poem's final section – which describes a place of "no water but only rock" – a ghostly presence:

> Who is the third who walks always beside you?
> When I count, there are only you and I together
> But when I look ahead up the white road
> There is always another one walking beside you
> Gliding wrapt in a brown mantle, hooded
> I do not know whether a man or a woman
> –But who is that on the other side of you? (*CP* 67)

Eliot's note provides an answer of sorts:

The following lines were stimulated by the account of one of the Antarctic expeditions (I forget which, but I think one of Shackleton's): it was related that the party of explorers, at the extremity of their strength, had the constant delusion that there was *one more member* than could actually be counted. (*CP* 74–5)

Despite the gesture towards inaccuracy, Eliot's memory is correct. The passage to which he is referring comes from *South: The Story of Shackleton's Last Expedition 1914–1917*. These dates should look familiar since they overlap with those of the Great War, one of several links between the two events. Shackleton's journey was advertised in January of 1914, receiving 5,000 applications for 56 slots. A "similarly overwhelming response" met Lord Kitchener's call to arms made seven months later: "[B]y September 15th, more than half a million volunteers had signed up for the hundred thousand new military slots."[1] "Englishmen," as Allyson Booth notes, "were apparently harboring a remarkable appetite for what was perceived, in 1914 at least, as adventure."[2]

Booth writes here in Philip Larkin's mode – "never such innocence again" – and it is this implied sea change in the perception of overseas "adventures" that is of interest. For the overlap of Shackleton's expedition with WWI marks a transitional moment in the experience of imperialism. No longer the heroic adventure memorialized by writers such as H. Rider Haggard, imperialism in the early twentieth century was already transitioning into the financialized forms of today's neo-imperialist order, a shift exemplified by Shackleton's journey.

For what precisely was to be gained by visiting the South Pole? The journey seems to exist simply to fill in the final blank space of Marlow's map of the world, representing not so much the desire for expansion as the end of expansion itself, the beginning of a new era in which "much of the world was mapped."[3] This absence of unconquered land is one of the pre-conditions for the intra-imperialist rivalry whose most dramatic expression was WWI, and for the particular form taken by imperial capital in the early part of the twentieth century. No longer able to rely on the discovery of new lands for profit, capital was forced, instead, to transform already conquered territories into markets for goods. The early twentieth century witnessed, then, the birth of a global system of capital built upon the inequalities of the imperialist period.[4] This global system, I will argue, hovers like a ghostly presence behind *The Waste Land*, determining the poem's play between absence and presence, its oscillation between subjective alienation and the wealth of cultural materials out of which it is composed. These two distinct modes of the poem emerge from this newly structured imperial system.

What we find in Eliot's work is a modernism that does not directly thematize empire – as has been the subject of so many recent studies of modernism and empire – but whose formal innovations must be read in relation to the new developments in imperial capital. Understanding this transition in imperialism's structure allows us to return that hallmark of modernist literature – aesthetic innovation – to its social grounding. More importantly, we observe here a shift from the narratives of an older imperial order – stories of Europeans gone astray in colonial spaces – to an attempt to represent something like the emerging global world. For although *The Waste Land* is situated largely within the metropole, the boundaries of that metropole are entirely porous. Indeed, to use the language of place for this poem seems singularly inappropriate. Despite

being, as I will elaborate in this chapter, organized around London's financial district, the poem radiates out across time and space in a way that
destabilizes the comfortable frame of the nation-state. The poem's form
mirrors, then, the overdetermined globalization of its historical moment.
Furthermore, in the same way that Eliot destabilizes space, he also destabilizes the subject, and so we return to that other chestnut of modernist criticism: impersonality. But this impersonality is here an attempt to
represent the historical conditions that have produced a particular form
of subjectivity. *The Waste Land* decenters both the bourgeois subject and
the boundaries of the nation-state, which mark the most secure frame for
understanding that subject. Even in the very heart of its own empire the
European subject no longer securely takes center stage. What takes its
place is a particular historical moment in the development of imperial
finance capital.[5]

The stakes of this argument can be further clarified, first by contrast-
ing Eliot to that elegist of imperialism's heroic phase, Joseph Conrad, and
then by distinguishing my own argument from Fredric Jameson's seminal
essay "Modernism and Imperialism." That Conrad is relevant to *The Waste
Land* is clear from the poem's cancelled epigraph, itself another ghostly
presence hovering behind Eliot's work:

Did he live his life again in every detail of desire, temptation, and surrender
during that supreme moment of complete knowledge? He cried in a whisper at
some image, at some vision, – he cried out twice, a cry that was no more than a
breath –
   "The horror! The horror!"[6]

Kurtz's surrender, of course, is to his primitive impulses, although the endless doubling of Conrad's narrative structure makes it difficult to untangle
the existential claim of human evil from the historically grounded sense
in which colonialism produces the very horrors it seems to be revealing, a
doubleness aptly captured by Marlow's maps, which turn blank spaces into
"place[s] of darkness."[7] England not only *has been* a place of darkness, but
its acts of conquest spread this darkness throughout the world, as imperialism insists on reading those places it colonizes as its own pre-history,
which it then retroactively articulates as one of darkness as well. The rhetoric of darkness serves, here, to create two fundamentally different ways
of inhabiting the world I have already associated with imperialism – the
civilized, and the intertwined realms of that civilization's past and Africa's
present – and this rhetoric is mobilized in an effort to keep these two temporalities distinct. The exact limit of Conrad's vision, as we have come

to understand it, is in his inability to see their collapse as anything other than horror.

Conrad's horror seems, furthermore, to be a perfect instance of what Fredric Jameson has described as "the pressure of something more transcendent, a kind of Kantian sublimity, against the here and now" that comes to stand in for "that other, vaster, unrepresentable space" that is, in some absolute sense, the colonized world.[8] Beginning with the claim that "the structure of imperialism also makes its mark on the inner forms and structures of" modernism, Jameson describes an imperial moment in which "a significant structural segment of the economic system as a whole is now located elsewhere."[9] The consequence of this fact is the subject's "inability to grasp the way the system functions as a whole ... [I]t can never be fully reconstructed; no enlargement of personal experience (in the knowledge of other social classes) no intensity of self-examination ... no scientific deductions on the basis of the internal evidence of First World data, can ever be enough to include this radical otherness of colonial life."[10] Eliot's poems, of course, present a striking example of this modern consciousness, unable to totalize the various determinations that constitute its social world. However, Eliot does not so much rest with the depiction of this consciousness as he situates it within the larger structures that condition it.

We can deepen, then, the contrast with Conrad. For Kurtz's "horror" – in all its sublime inscrutability – is precisely the collapse of that older heroic imperialist ideal which was all that redeemed the conquest of the earth. To understand this conquest as brutality is, necessarily, to understand the presence of an other for whom colonization has been brutal. The "horror" marks the irruption of this other experience into metropolitan consciousness, an irruption suppressed, at the story's end, by the name of the Intended. *Heart of Darkness* closes with imperialism's self-justification – its *intent* – in a manner that illustrates Conrad's attachment to that earlier imperialist mode. Sublimity here marks not only, or even primarily, an inability to totalize, but rather a refusal of the knowledge totality brings.

The sublime, however, is not an Eliotic mode and the teeming references of *The Waste Land* are neither vast, nor unrepresentable. What the poem insists upon, in direct contrast to Jameson's claim about modernism, is the necessity for totality, even as it presents the inability of individual subjects situated *within the poem* to totalize. The active reading the poem requires, then, is the active reading the new imperial order demands: one that does not fall into the sublime disappointments of Conrad nor resign itself to the inability to see. What we find in Eliot, *pace* Jameson, is not a modernism of sublimely unrepresentable space, but one that grapples with the particular form of empire that is its historical ground. Jameson's argument can only take us so far in understanding this particular aesthetic form, for it fails to see the precise ways in which Eliot does not simply disrupt "common-sense space perception," but instead produces a new aesthetic form for understanding the imbrications of various cultural and historical moments within the seemingly unified space of the imperial city.[11]

Crucially these moments come from both England's imperial present and the cultural past, which brings us to a final point of contrast with Conrad. For, despite one of its speaker's famous protest, "I can connect nothing with nothing," Eliot's poem continually connects moments of the past with moments of the present. Thus, the reference to Shackleton is also a reference to Christ, on the way to Emmaus, disappearing at the moment he is recognized. Similarly the Thames of "The Fire Sermon" is both the river of Edmund Spenser's *Prothalamion* and that of contemporary London, littered with the debris of contemporary culture. In each case, Eliot keeps these objects present by attesting to their absence. Consider again the lines from "The Fire Sermon": "The river bears no empty bottles, sandwich papers, / Silk handkerchiefs, cardboard boxes, cigarette ends / Or other testimony of summer nights." Quite clearly these lines describe an empty river, yet surely the most common experience of reading them is to imagine the presence of all these objects specifically named.

Two ideas are important to underline here. (1) Eliot consistently presents an experience of absence alongside the manifest presence of cultural objects. In doing so he anticipates the psychological insight of Jameson's description of modern subjectivity, while simultaneously emphasizing the objective presence of those cultural materials of which the contemporary world seems ignorant. (2) Rejecting the conflict between the primitive and the civilized – a conflict animating the horror Conrad expresses at their collapse – Eliot understands that the culture of the past depends as much on collective agreement as the culture of the present.[12] *The Waste Land*'s investment in this past, then, is neither nostalgic (it was better) nor progressive (it was barbaric), the two modes characteristic of an imperialism built upon the confrontation of a "modern" West with its various "premodern" Others. Instead, Eliot presents London as a kind of historical palimpsest, its contemporary existence encompassing experiences distant in both time and space. Eliot insists that these "unreal" experiences are central to an understanding of imperial London, as his poem works to produce the "historical sense" – that "perception, not only of the pastness of the past, but of its presence" – he felt was lacking in the modern world (*SW* 49). In doing so, he makes a strong argument for the power of culture as a resource for resisting imperial capital's desire to remake the world in its own image.

In what follows I will discuss *The Waste Land* alongside the terminology Eliot develops within his 1916 Harvard doctoral dissertation.[13] Writing against the ahistorical doctrine of Bergsonian immediate experience, Eliot constructs a theory of inter-subjectivity, which emphasizes the role of culture in the creation of subjects, objects, and the historical ground on which subjects meet. It is the revelation of these inter-subjective mediations that determines, for Eliot, the reality or unreality of objects. These terms then carry over into Eliot's depiction of imperial London. *The Waste Land*'s oscillation between subjective alienation and objective overdetermination – the wide range of cultural materials manifestly present, if in ghostly form, within the space of the desolate imperial city – is an attempt to make the "unreal city" real, to reveal the various structural determinations that constitute the imperial center.

THE BACKGROUND OF SOCIAL REALITY

In a contemporary moment newly overwhelmed with real objects – commodities of all sorts – Eliot's dissertation presents a strong defense of the importance of seemingly unreal ones – namely art, culture, and the past – all of which are as "woven into our reality" as language itself (*KE* 133). Ideas "may exist," Eliot writes, "previous to the articulation of language," but language must not be seen, simply, as "a development of our ideas; it is a development of reality as well" (*KE* 44). For "language shows a richness of content and intricacy of connections which it assumes to have really been there, but which are as well an enrichment of the reality grasped" (*KE* 44). Eliot here advances a notion of mediation, as reality is "enriched" through an understanding of connections that are, in part, produced through language. In his dissertation, Eliot describes both the conditions that seem to alienate subjects from one another and the way these subjects can reconnect through the construction of a common world built, in part, out of the "unreal" objects of language and culture. Anticipating our return to *The Waste Land*, we will see that the unreal aspects of London are precisely those experiences both temporally and spatially distant – Spenser, Shackleton – that haunt the city in the ghostly fashion I have been describing. The poem works to construct a real city out of the unreal experiences of its alienated subjects.

In the dissertation, Eliot begins his argument with a critique of Kantian dualism, situating both subjects and objects in a larger totality he calls, following F. H. Bradley, "immediate experience" (*KE* 15). In describing this experience, Eliot warns us against two related errors. First we must avoid "identifying experience with consciousness, or … considering experience as the adjective of a subject," and second "we must not confuse immediate experience with sensation, we must not think of it as a sort of panorama passing before a subject" (*KE* 15). Neither subjective nor object-ive, experience stands before this distinction as the ground from which the two emerge. Subject and object are thus two distinct points of view: "[E]verything, from one point of view, is subjective; and everything from another point of view is objective; and there is no *absolute* point of view from which a decision may be pronounced" (*KE* 21–2). "There are two sides," Eliot writes, "subject and object, neither of which is really stable, independent, the measure of the other" (*KE* 22). Furthermore, "consciousness, we shall find, is reducible to relations between objects, and objects we shall find to be reducible to relations between different states of consciousness" (*KE* 30). Subjectivity is here returned to its ground – it emerges and is altered by its contact with the world of objects – even as that object world is altered by its relation to the subject. Eliot clearly rejects both the idea of a self-legislating subject and of a subject wholly determined by its social world.

Instead he adopts the Bradleyean "finite centre," a term meant to sug-gest the individual as the site of various interactions with the object world. Within the world of the finite centre, we find that there is no fact/value split, for its values are fundamentally one with the facts it encounters. The finite centre is, then, a kind of Bergsonian vitalist subject, unbounded by any form of historical continuity.

Eliot, however, does not rest with this conception, eventually arriv-ing at a vision of subjectivity that emphasizes its historical conditioning. Consider, first, the following description of an encounter with the work of art:

We stand before a beautiful painting, and if we are sufficiently carried away, our feeling is a whole which is not, in a sense, *our* feeling, since the painting, which is an object independent of us, is quite as truly a constituent as our consciousness or our soul. The feeling is neither here nor anywhere: the painting is in the room, and my 'feelings' about the picture are in my 'mind.' (*KE* 20)

Subject and object are here co-extensive, there is a feeling that contains both, occurring only when the two interact. Similarly, Eliot writes that the world of "finite experience" always "involves selection and emphasis;" thus the realm of factual description is always supported by "interest and valuation" (*KE* 89). This interest varies "from moment to moment. So does the real, according to that fragment of it which happens to be the focus of our attention" (*KE* 89). Eliot is here operating within a Nietzschean mode, unseating conceptual reason by recognizing its fundamentally interested, that is to say subjective, nature. However, we cannot be misled into thinking Eliot does not believe in the real, for there is a "background of practical reality" in which we live "together in a coherence that cannot be formulated" (*KE* 89). This reality is "the felt background against which we project our theories, and with reference to which our speculations have their use. We all recognize the world as the same 'that'; it is when we attempt to describe it that our worlds fall apart" (*KE* 163).[14]

Eliot here describes something like an Althusserian absent cause – that background of action that remains unknowable, but, in a formative way, determines the ground of our action. This common structure of belief is what the later Eliot will call culture, and it is linked to his notion of tradition, which can only be obtained by "great labor" (*SW* 49). In the context of his dissertation this labor is social, or to be more precise, this labor is the *process of socialization itself*, the "real" world only coming into existence through the interactions between subjects.

At first, however, the interaction between subjects is what *produces* the very idea of subjectivity. Subjectivity is, in its very origin, fundamentally inter-subjective, created by the presence of an other before whom the limits of my perspective emerge. Returning to the example of the painting, we find Eliot asking, "For whom will my feeling be subjective? For the dispassionate observer, who seeing the same object without the same feeling, subtracts my feeling from the object, to make of it a separate and independent entity existing in my mind" (*KE* 24). The constitutive modern split between facts/values emerges here as the intrusion of the social world upon a previously whole finite centre. The introduction of other subjects crushes the individual's unified world. How, then, are these subjects able to interact with one another when each brings with it an entire world of holistic experience? What is the common ground upon which they meet?

The answer is that it is fundamentally the work of socialization to construct this common ground: "[T]he real world ... consists in the common meaning and 'identical reference' of various finite centres" (*KE* 140). Thus *socialization first removes the subject from its holistic experience and then forces it to reconstruct that experience with other subjectivities.* Socialization itself constructs our shared world of objects, "for the reality of the object does not lie in the object itself, but in the extent of the relations which the object possesses without significant falsification with itself" (*KE* 91). Eliot's understanding of the real world is, then, an understanding of mediation. The more relations an object has the more concrete it becomes. It is only "through the mediation of objects" that "we know other finite centres" (*KE* 151). The common human world emerges through mediation; concretion is a function of commonality, of the extension of relations throughout a range of finite centres. This extension is precisely the overcoming of subjective alienation.[15]

Eliot then turns his attention to a different class of "objects" – the past and characters from novels – which do not exist in the same way as those he has been discussing. Eliot begins his discussion of the past with the problem of memory. What, he asks, are we attempting to recover when we remember a past event? Taking as his example a speech that we once heard, Eliot suggests a crucial split between the event as it happened, and the event as we experienced it. The words that we remember, he argues, "were never an actual object of perception … the past which we aim at is the experience of an ideal individual, who should have been both internal and external to ourselves, who should have both known and experienced the past to which *in a very loose sense* our memory may be said to 'refer'" (*KE* 50).

To reconstruct this past requires the ability to differentiate between two points of view – internal and external – requires, that is to say, the introduction of a second party that we have seen to be necessary for the creation of the subjective element of experience. Crucially, though, this introduction also produces the objective element of experience; it is only through the confrontation of two points of view that we can build "the social consilience" that "goes toward the construction of *our* world" (*KE* 44, italics mine). This consilience *aims* towards the construction of that ideal individual who would be able to apprehend the past in its subjective and objective facets. Of course, the ideal individual never arrives.

We see, again, the importance of the idea of relations – and it is these relations, not some criteria of "objectivity" that determines the reality of our world. Thus, "we discover that it was just this continuity with experience, this fullness of relation, which gave us what we call our real objects, and just the discontinuity, the mere intention, which gave us our unreal objects" (*KE* 131). Real and unreal are the product of mediation, not intrinsic qualities of the objects themselves, and this idea extends to the characters of literature. *Vanity Fair*'s Becky Sharp, for instance, has a reality. She "exists as an event in the life of Thackeray, and as an event in the life of every reader in the same way that every real person exists as an event in the life of every other real person with whom he comes in contact" (*KE* 126). Thus, she is just as real as any "real" person, "but the object denoted by the word Becky does not exist, for it is simply the identical reference of several points of view" (*KE* 126).

We return here to the inter-subjective creation of a coherent world of meaning, and what is important to understand is not that the real world has been made equivalent to a fictional one, but rather the strong claims for the reality of seemingly fictional entities:

> The process of development of a real world, as we are apt to forget in our theor-ies, works in two directions; we have not first a real world to which we add our imaginings, nor have we a real world out of which we select *our* 'real' world, but the real and the unreal develop side by side. If we think of the world not as ready made – the world, that is, of meaning for us – but as constructed, or constructing itself, (for I am careful not to talk of the creative activity of mind, a phrase mean-ingless in metaphysics) at every moment, and never more than an approximate construction, a construction essentially practical in its nature: then the difficulties of real and unreal disappear. (*KE* 136)

Note the careful distinction Eliot makes concerning the world "of meaning *for us*" (*KE* 136, italics mine). Time and again he preempts the charge of idealism by insisting that there is a real world. It just cannot be separated from the structures of meaning within which we apprehend it. It is these same structures – the various relations and mediations by which we constitute the object world – that create the difference between real and unreal. The more relations an object has, the more subjects for whom it is meaningful, the more real it becomes. Eliot thus articulates a defense of the reality of cultural objects, a reality grounded in their histor-icity, in their relationship to the communal structures that constitute our social world.

Several aspects of this discussion are crucial for our reading of *The Waste Land*. The first is Eliot's vision of subjectivity. Eliot's subjects are actively engaged in the construction of a social totality, even as they are that total-ity's product. Similarly, the alienated subjects of the poem are the product of a specific moment in imperial capital, even as the poem itself presents the various materials one must totalize to (re)construct this moment. The second is the specificity of the idea of the unreal. Imperial London is "unreal" because of the discontinuities built into imperial experience; the work of the poem is to create continuity, to produce connections and relations among the various materials out of which it is composed. *The Waste Land* moves from discontinuity to continuity, constructing the real world of imperial capital out of the mediations of a series of finite centres interacting with all manner of unreal objects.

MAKING THE "UNREAL CITY" REAL

The Waste Land begins with a seemingly agentless speaking: "April is the cruelest month, breeding / Lilacs out of the dead land, mixing / memory and desire." By the end of the first verse paragraph, however, we have arrived at the banal musings of an unidentified individual: "I read, much of the night, and go south in the winter" (*CP* 53). Contained within the opening verse paragraph is a deliberate oscillation between the poem as the "expression of a generation" that it has often been taken to be and the "personal and wholly insignificant ... rhythmic grumbling" of Eliot's famous dismissal.[16] Not simply a contradiction, nor resolvable as equally plausible critical perspectives, these two views are produced by the poem itself; its great success, in the words of Charles Altieri, being its "capacity to correlate the psyche's most intimate fears with its most abstract cultural dependencies."[17] *The Waste Land* eschews the drama of individual suffering present in Eliot's early poems, a drama associated, as we have already seen, with a Baudelairean lyricism that can only register history as an index of subjective intensity. In contrast, *The Waste Land* seeks, in Altieri's words, to analyze "the conditions of feeling history imposes upon us."[18]

Altieri's "conditions of feeling" recalls Raymond Williams's "structures of feeling," a phrase meant to capture the historical dimension of subjective experience. The structure of feeling of this opening verse paragraph is the cruel mix of memory and desire, their presence within the impersonal first section of the stanza suggesting that they be read as historical conditions rather than subjective emotional states. And this history is quite specific, for the poem depicts the alienated, barren landscape at the "heart of the global capitalist economy," with its constant flow of objects, information, and people.[19] Thus, we have the claim of authentic German ancestry from a character born in Lithuania, and the demotic French of the Smyrna merchant, alongside a depiction of the upper and lower classes of the city. The poem similarly emphasizes trade, not only with the currants in Mr. Eugenides pockets, but in the journey down river, "Past the Isle of Dogs" – one of the great ports of late Victorian London – and the repeated references to the drowned Phoenician sailor, himself a representative of an earlier maritime empire.[20] Eliot's London is virtually teeming with the results of its position at the center of world trade.

This imperial structure is further highlighted by what, at first, seems a simple analogy between London and Rome, comprising two of three maps Eleanor Cook has argued are crucial to the poem. Cook's first map is of London itself. The second "coincides roughly with the Roman Empire at its most expansive and therefore also coincides roughly with the theater of war during World War I," and the third, which extends to India, is "Dante's map of the inhabited world."[21] The overlay of London with Rome leads Cook to read the poem as a "vision of imperial apocalypse," suggesting, in its repeated references to Carthage, both the decline of Rome that St. Augustine claimed could be traced to the decisive defeat of Carthage at Mylae, and John Maynard Keynes's association of the Versailles Treaty with the ruinous Carthaginian peace.[22] More recently, Michael Levenson has developed this argument, situating the poem in a post-WWI city in the grips of an "anarchic capitalist economy" built on "scandalous profiteering."[23]

These arguments are built, in part, on the specific geography of the poem, as the majority of its place names – London Bridge, King William Street, Saint Mary Woolnoth, Lower Thames Street, Queen Victoria Street, the Cannon Street Hotel, Magnus Martyr – are in the heart of London's financial district. Furthermore, both the church at Saint Mary Woolnoth and London Bridge were built on Roman ruins. What seems a modernist imposition of order is, in fact, a historically accurate palimpsest, as the poem records the presence of Ancient Rome under the streets of London's financial district, underlining finance's centrality to the new imperial formation.

Memory and desire need to be read, then, as structures of feeling created by this particular imperial environment, operating at both the personal and impersonal registers, which meet in the intertwining of these two emotional states. The subject caught between memory and desire *is* fundamentally the subject in the flow of history – our present moment poised between the past and a future seen as a question of the realization of desire or will. "What," Eliot asks, "are the roots that clutch?" (*CP* 53). What pieces of the past are adequate for the desiring subject, or phrased differently, how can a subject given over to its immediate desires retain a sense of history? What is the importance of the cultural tradition for a contemporary imperial subject no longer situated in a clearly bounded nation-state? For the poem is, as I have argued, teeming with references both to London's imperial present and its cultural past, and yet is, at the same time, dominated by the feeling of absence, isolation, and despair. *Subjectively*, we might say, London is empty, despite what the poem presents as its *objective* continuity with events distant in both time and space. Ever more connected to the world, London creates a subjective experience of increasing isolation. The form of *The Waste Land* seeks to do justice to this contradictory modern experience, presenting both the alienated modern consciousness *and* the mediating structures that condition that consciousness. Furthermore, the poem suggests that cognizing these structures – recognizing the cultural substratum that connects contemporary London both to its own past and its imperial periphery – might be the first step toward overcoming this alienation.

To concretize this argument, we can turn to the modern crowd. In *The Waste Land*, we encounter this crowd on London Bridge, in a scene that provides some insight into the conditions of feeling imposed by this particular historical juncture:

> Unreal City,
> Under the brown fog of a winter dawn,
> A crowd flowed over London Bridge, so many,
> I had not thought death had undone so many.
> Sighs, short and infrequent, were exhaled,
> And each man fixed his eyes before his feet. (*CP* 55)

Simultaneously the dead from WWI, present in the city through their absence, and the souls of Dante's *Inferno*, the crowd moves in a routine mechanical fashion, expanded on in one of the many cancelled sections of the original poem:

> London, the swarming life you kill and breed,
> Huddled between the concrete and the sky,
> Responsive to the momentary need,
> Vibrates unconscious to its formal density,
>
> Knowing neither how to think, nor how to feel,
> But lives in the awareness of the observing eye.
> London, your people is bound upon the wheel![24]

Even though this passage did not make it into the final draft, the wheel did, preserved in the last lines of "Death by Water," after the depiction of the drowned Phoenician, who has forgotten "the profit and the loss": "Gentile or Jew / O you who turn the wheel and look to windward, / Consider Phlebas, who was once handsome and tall as you" (*CP* 65). These lines describe the inevitable decay of empire – the Phoenicians having been, in their day, as dominant (and handsome) as the British in the early twentieth century. Death is presented as a great leveler, revealing the impotence of financial gain. The fact that the death is "by water" suggests that this outcome is contained within the very means of imperial domination itself: the control of trade through the control of the seas that was the hallmark of both the British and Phoenician Empires. The drowned Phoenician is, then, a warning to those who control the wheels upon which the people of London are bound, a connection that helps establish England's imperial status as the structural condition for the alienated crowd of the poem. This alienation is expressed through an intertwining of the organic and the mechanical, as subservience to the "momentary need" effaces human agency, leading to an "unconscious" submission to the wheels of fate.

Life in the modern city is largely given over to this combination of the immediate and the mechanical, a fact best illustrated in the scene between the typist and the young man carbuncular, who are described by their roles in the system of imperial capital. The young man is a "small house agent's clerk," a middleman within the inflationary system dominating the post-WWI city (*CP* 62). Eliot reinforces his status as a profiteer by comparing him to a Bradford millionaire, as it was said that the industrialists of Bradford profited mightily from the recent war. The typist, too, is part of the machinery of industrial capital, her very identity circumscribed by the machine she operates. The encounter between the two is, predictably, a routinized one:

> Flushed and decided, he assaults at once;
> Exploring hands encounter no defence;
> His vanity requires no response,
> And makes a welcome of indifference.
> . . .
> She turns and looks a moment in the glass,
> Hardly aware of her departed lover;
> Her brain allows one half-formed thought to pass:
> 'Well now that's done: and I'm glad it's over,' . . .
> She smoothes her hair with automatic hand,
> And puts a record on the gramophone. (*CP* 62)

This scene, as it has been typically understood, is an indictment of human relations under the regime of capital, the typist as mechanical as the machine she operates, the house agent's clerk exploiting her for personal gain as ruthlessly as he does his customers.

Crucially, though, this critique is elaborated through a blending of the organic and the mechanical, the "human engine" throbbing with automatic desire. With this linkage, *The Waste Land*'s critique of capital resists that hypostatization of the concrete that Moishe Postone has described as characteristic of romantic anti-capitalism. Beginning with the seemingly paradoxical valorization of both blood and the machine in the ideology of National Socialism, Postone reveals their common origin in a form of fetishized anti-capitalism "based on a one-sided attack on the abstract."[25] Within this ideology, "*both* blood and the machine are seen as concrete counterprinciples to the abstract."[26] Eliot's presentation of these two concepts *within* a critique of capital, suggests a similar awareness of their complicity. Neither the organic nor the mechanical is offered by Eliot as a solution to the problems of capitalist modernity. His critique of capital, then, is after something larger: not simply a critique of routinization, but an attempt to suggest the way this routinization goes hand in hand with a certain nostalgia for the body.

The poem similarly refuses that other great hope of romantic anti-capitalism: the soil. For the land of the poem is desolate and barren, ravaged by the deterritorialization of imperial finance that, in reorganizing the world in its image, tends towards the eradications of pre-existing boundaries. The poem presents, then, the simultaneous destruction the capitalist system works on the land and on the people who inhabit it, its impersonal speaking a formal analogue to the precedence of social formation over personal expression that, as we have seen, Roberto Schwarz reads as the hallmark of modernist literary form. Immediately, though, we can see the risks involved in this formal structure, for how does the poem avoid reproducing "on an aesthetic level the formal terrorism that had beaten the crowd into a featureless mass"?[27] Similarly, if the poem seeks to overcome the rootless perspective of the Baudelairean *flâneur*, its method seems to rest, as Maud Ellmann has argued, on an "uprooting of words from other authors, texts, and nations," performing "a textual diaspora in which the writings of the past deracinate themselves and recombine with words of other ages, languages and authors."[28] How, in other words, does the poem, in its desire to represent the conditions of modernity, avoid replicating the dialectical intertwining of fragmentation and homogenization characteristic of imperial capital?

The Waste Land takes on these questions directly in two related ways: through the character of Tiresias, and through the direct quotation of Baudelaire at the close of "The Burial of the Dead." Eliot famously referred to Tiresias as "the most important personage in the poem," despite his being a "mere spectator," and it is through his eyes that we observe the scene with the typist. Eliot's note elaborates his significance: "Just as the one-eyed merchant, seller of currants, melts into the Phoenician Sailor, and the latter is not wholly distinct from Ferdinand Prince of Naples, so all the women are one woman, and the two sexes meet in Tiresias. What Tiresias *sees*, in fact, is the substance of the poem" (*CP* 72). As I have already argued, the scene Tiresias observes represents a loss of human individuality, and yet his perception – via the "all women are one woman" formula – courts a similar type of reduction. Able to enter the characters of the poem at will, Tiresias is as mobile in spirit as the Baudelairean *flâneur*. Those he observes, how-ever, lack all individuality, interchangeably melting one into another.

Tiresias, however, is not only a spectator. He also exists within the space of the poem itself, as does the Baudelaire whose mobile spirit he recalls. The line from Baudelaire appears at the end of "The Burial of the Dead." Amidst the ghostly crowd on London Bridge, one figure stands out as the speaker spots his friend Stetson and presents us with the following monologue:

> 'You who were with me in the ships at Mylae!
> 'That corpse you planted last year in your garden,
> 'Has it begun to sprout? Will it bloom this year?
> 'Or has the sudden frost disturbed its bed?
> 'O keep the Dog far hence, that's friend to men,
> 'Or with his nails he'll dig it up again!
> 'You! hypocrite lecteur! – mon semblable, – mon frère!' (*CP* 55)

Again we must avoid reading the overlap of Mylae and WWI as an example of Eliot's "mythic method," for that would return us to the genius of the exquisitely suffering artist creating meaning where none is present. Here, though, the artist is not separate from the world he is decrying. Not simply a passive spectator, he is embedded within the narrative itself, a fact that creates a triangle of engagement – the reader, the speaker, and Stetson. Each perspective is situated here in a definable poetic space, thus evading the Baudelairean dyad, which would posit Stetson as the figure to be observed by an author and his hypocrite double. If we are to respond to the world as Eliot does, it will not be through our exquisite sensibility, or the "enlargement of personal experience… self-examination … [or] scien-tific deductions on the basis of the internal evidence of First World data" Jameson argues is impossible under imperial capital. The route to know-ledge is not through subjective experience, then, but rather through the historical structures that condition that experience, the pervasive structure of commodity capital that, as we have seen, Benjamin found to condition the *flâneur* and the modern crowd that was his symptomatic double, both present here on London Bridge.

And yet even though Eliot works to show us the meanings present within the world already – for the past's persistence is not a subjective imposition but rather the recognition of an obscured historico-cultural substrata that, nevertheless, exists – this world is not just there waiting for a subject to recognize it. There is not, as we have seen Eliot argue in his dissertation, a "real world to which we add our imaginings" nor is there a "real world out of which we select *our* 'real' world." Instead, the real world is constructed through mediation. Transforming the unreal city into a real one requires the activity of a constructing subject. To this end, *The Waste Land* – despite Eliot's note – does not offer us any stable, Tiresias-like perspective around which the poem's various fragments cohere. Instead it works, as Lawrence Rainey has recently argued, to produce local coherences, structures of meaning that are contingent and provisional.[29] Any reading of the poem must be an *active* reading, for the poem's indeterminacy requires us to produce local coherence in a process that emphasizes the labor of culture, the creation of meaning out of the unreal structures of past and present. The structure of the poem thus presents the capitalist dialectic of fragmentation and homogenization *through the figure of negation*, situating its fragments within a larger structure that grants them their meaning, while allowing them to persist in their difference. Yet even this is inexact, for the context does not grant meaning; rather the context is *precisely the juxtaposition of these diverse fragments themselves.* These fragments are not, then, "deracinated" – a term that suggests a nostalgia for some stable essential context that would determine their meaning and from which they have been shorn – but rather gain their meaning through their existence within the structure of the poem, even as Stetson emerges out of the urban crowd as a function of an experience he shares with the poem's speaker. Particularity is only recognizable within a larger communal structure, and this structure is not something that is pre-given, but rather something that emerges as the result of active construction.

This observation has important implications for a reading of the ending of the poem. I have been arguing that London – as the center of a global empire – seems to lack that "continuity with experience" that gives us "what we call our real objects" (*KE* 131). Separated from its own past, and from events that determine its present, the city creates the conditions of unreality in which its agentless citizens live. The poem's structure seeks to capture both this unreality and this agentless condition, and so we must read its various binary constructions – each a version of the dialectical relationship between the abstract and the concrete described by Postone – within the context of this unreality. The mechanical and the organic, land and water, facts and values: the terms of each of these defin-ing oppositions are shown to be constitutive of one another, as the space of the poem becomes an analogue of the historical spaces in which value is socially constituted, even as its various discourses are analogous to the flows of information and capital that move through the imperial center. Here, then, is the context for understanding the final section's turn to India, not as a representation of "Dante's map of the inhabited world," but rather as an explicit inclusion of the periphery into the world of the metropole itself. In this reading, setting one's lands in order can only occur with the recognition of India's ghostly presence in contemporary London.

Eliot's note locates three themes within the poem's final section: "[T]he journey to Emmaus, the approach to the Chapel Perilous … and the present decay of eastern Europe" (*CP* 74). This last comment has often been taken to refer to the Russian Revolution, but Levenson disagrees, detecting a further connection to Keynes, who saw the "structural collapse of nineteenth-century capitalism" wrecking havoc on Central and Eastern Europe.[30] Here, the "most dreadful material evils which men can suffer – famine, cold, disease, war" were parts of contemporary experience.[31] Thus, the landscape of section V – "Here is no water but only rock / Rock and no water and the sandy road" – suggests the actual circumstances of the ravaged lands to London's east (*CP* 66).

The poem, thus, moves past the "Falling towers" of empire – "Jerusalem Athens Alexandria / Vienna London" – before finally arriving in India:[32]

> Ganga was sunken, and the limp leaves
> Waited for rain, while the black clouds
> Gathered far distant, over Himavant. (*CP* 67, 68)

India, too, is parched and barren, and as Mike Davis's *Late Victorian Holocausts* demonstrates, this is a historically specific reference, for India under British rule was subject to famines that were the direct result of the imperial regime of finance and free trade. Due neither to a scarcity of resources, nor to what Britain imagined as India's eternal backwardness, the series of famines in the late Victorian period occurred precisely at the moment when colonial societies "were being dynamically conscripted into a London-centered world economy."[33] The devastation that accompanied this process was horrific. During the "the age of Kipling, that 'glorious imperial half century' from 1872 to 1921, the life expectancy of ordinary Indians fell by a staggering 20 percent."[34] The famines of 1907–8 alone took an estimated 2.1 to 3.2 million lives and cast a long mortality shadow over the first decades of the twentieth century. Their immune responses weakened by the long ordeal of hunger, the rural poor in western and northern India were mowed down in the millions by epidemic waves of malaria, tuberculosis and plague. The Black Death, spread by drought-induced rat migrations, entrenched itself in the former famine districts of the U.P. and the Punjab, where it had claimed 8 million further victims by 1914.[35]

Famines in India were, then, a relatively recent and common occurrence in the years just prior to *The Waste Land*'s composition, and they were the direct result of the seizure of what had been communally managed farms and water sources, which were now geared toward individual ownership and export to British markets, the result, that is to say, of the destruction of traditional ways of life in favor of the demands of imperial capital.[36] As in Ireland during the potato famine, the late nineteenth century witnessed the starvation of farmers who were producing grain to be exported to England.[37] England, however, refused to understand its complicity in the situation, believing instead in the benefits of its rule: "The British, of course, had a vested interest in claiming that they had liberated the populace from a dark age of Mogul despotism."[38] The famines were, they insisted, the result of "extreme weather, not imperialism."[39] They were, that is to say, inevitable and beyond human control.

Eliot, as I have argued, rejected this intertwining of primitivism, progress, and fatalistic determinism. His cultural past is not the realm of the noble savage, but rather a crucial, if occluded, element of contemporary life. Thus in "The Fire Sermon," the Thames is not, as in Conrad, the site of an originary darkness, but rather, in its allusion to Spenser, the site of a form of community through which the present understands its own alienation. The same process occurs in the poem's turn to India. India is not, for Eliot, a land without agency or a place of partially civilized barbarism that needs to be overcome by European modernity. Rather, in the poem's closing lines, Eliot turns to India's high culture – the Upanishads – and in doing so, seeks to confront the West with a set of values that are external to it. This moment in the poem is neither a nostalgic nor Orientalist exploitation of Asiatic culture. It is, instead, a structural cognate to the nostalgic and progressive fetishizations of the past of imperial culture, but one that is mobilized for quite different values.

These values are embodied in three words from the Upanishads: *datta, dayadhvam, damyata* (glossed by Eliot as give, sympathize, control). The movement of the poem's last lines, then, is a movement out of the prison of bourgeois subjectivity, a turn toward the Other through sympathy and generosity. Eliot presents here his own version of the critique of imperial consciousness – able to approach the Other only by assimilating it into its own cultural terms – launched by Gayatri Spivak.[40] Here the movement is not one of assimilation, but rather of "the awful daring of a moment's surrender," the complement, that is, to the virtue of control (*CP* 68).

It is difficult to understand exactly how to connect control to the virtues with which it is aligned. It would seem to refer to self-control, a limiting of desire that is another way out of pure expressivity.[41] Eliot's note, however, removes the word "self" and the image of control we encounter is inter-subjective:

> *Damyata*: The boat responded
> Gaily, to the hand expert with sail and oar
> The sea was calm, your heart would have responded
> Gaily, when invited, beating obedient
> To controlling hands (*CP* 69)

Control, here, is control over another, the "beating obedient" heart recalling the throbbing "human engine," even as the controlling hands suggest those that earlier made "a welcome of indifference." Yet the differences between the two passages are equally striking as indifference turns into a gaiety that occurs "when invited." The poem seems, in this passage, to accept the burdens of an agency before which Eliot's verse typically hesitates, presenting a vision of inter-subjectivity that, although still marked by the presence of power, seems at least to be consensual. Or, rather, "would have" been consensual, had it occurred.[42]

The poem's solutions remain, then, entirely provisional – resting on something that "would have" happened – as the momentary consolation of these lines collapses in a final "antic swirl of quotation"[43]:

> I sat upon the shore
> Fishing, with the arid plain behind me
> Shall I at least set my lands in order?
> London Bridge is falling down falling down falling down
> *Poi s' ascose nel foco che gli affina*
> *Quando fiam uti chelidon* – O swallow swallow
> *Le Prince d'Aquitaine à la tour abolie*
> These fragments I have shored against my ruins
> Why then Ile fit you. Hieronymo's mad againe.
> Datta. Dayadhvam. Damyata.
>   Shantih   shantih   shantih (*CP* 69)

An eleventh-century nursery rhyme, a quotation from Dante, a pre-Christian Latin poem, Gérard de Nerval and Thomas Kyd: all these references are strung together in a recapitulation and condensation of the poem's formal structure reinforced by the quotation from *The Spanish Tragedy*. This line – "Why then Ile fit you" – is spoken by Hieronymo as he agrees to write a play to be performed by his enemies, who will unwittingly carry real swords and thus enact his revenge. Hieronymo's play is, as he explains, to be composed in several different languages,

> That it may breed the more variety:
> As you, my Lord, in Latin, I in Greek,
> You in Italian, and for because I know
> That Bellimperia hath practised the French
> In courtly French shall all her phrases be.[44]

As Hugh Kenner notes, "each of these languages occurs in *The Waste Land*; all but Greek in the list of shored fragments" directly preceding the quotation from Kyd.[45] More importantly, each of these lines is concerned with poetic making, so that the end of the poem offers a reflection upon its own construction, even as its juxtaposition of Nerval and Kyd presents "the two poetic traditions that by [Eliot's] own testimony most influenced the development of his poetry: [French] symbolism and Elizabethan drama."[46] We thus return to the contrast between the individual expressivist subject – the swallow referring to the story of Philomela, so often, if problematically, mobilized as a symbol of pure poetic speaking – and the communal structures Eliot praised in Elizabethan drama.

In keeping with the turn to the East, this communal structure is itself international, and so once again the poem refuses the nostalgic nationalism that would seek to close the borders of the porous imperial city. For *The Spanish Tragedy* also refers to Philomela, a reference Eliot, in his 1927 essay "Seneca in Elizabethan Translation," argues comes from an outside source, that is, nevertheless, peculiarly "indigenous." Calling *The Spanish Tragedy* "the most significant popular play under Senecan influence," Eliot discovers within it "another element" that "allies it to something more indigenous."[47] This element is best exemplified by Hieronymo biting off his own tongue. Eliot elaborates: "There is nothing like this in Seneca. But if this is very unlike Seneca, it is very like the contemporary drama of Italy. Nothing could better illustrate the accidental character of literary 'influence.'"[48]

The Spanish Tragedy is, then, a hybrid form; its "indigenous element" comes from Italy and so the very distinction between indigenous and imported is collapsed. Furthermore, its particular type of hybridity is determined by accident. In its final moments, *The Waste Land* turns to contingency, its echo chamber of meaning described once again as an act of subjective construction: "These fragments *I* have shored against *my* ruin" (emphasis added). This turn to the subjective is emphatically not a return of individual expressivity, for even the pure singing of the nightingale is here shown to be eminently structural, an Italian influence on a Spanish Tragedy (and an English play) that is rooted in Latin, and present as an echo in the modern verse of Swinburne and Tennyson, to which the phrase "O swallow swallow" alludes.[49] The constructivist impulse of this stanza is further underlined by what Eliot calls its "formal ending": the repeated "shantih" translated by Eliot as "the Peace which passeth understanding" (*CP* 76).

The formal structures of the poem are recapitulated at its conclusion: fragments that stubbornly resist mythic coherence, a human agency that constructs its meaning through the "labour of tradition," a poetic form that accommodates hybridity and rejects the homogenizing force of capitalist modernity. And yet as much as Eliot's early poems, *The Waste Land* resists a purely aesthetic solution to the problems of modern life; as in "Preludes" the worlds revolve regardless of poetic intent. Instead of a solution, we have a process, the subjective attempt to give coherence to a history that is without telos, the need to construct a real world from the unreal one we are given. Rising from the abstract to the concrete, *The Waste Land* seeks to produce London's imperial reality within the space of poetry, not as that reality's replacement, but rather as a consideration of its structural determinations. The poem is not, ultimately, an escape from history, nor is it resigned before the sublime unrepresentability of imperial space as Jameson would have it. Rather, it is situated within history's continual production of difference, offering itself as part of the necessarily constant process of re-imagining the world in the face of historical change. For despite the momentary peace of the poem's conclusion, "Hieronymo's mad againe."

3

Cosmopolitan kulchur: The Cantos *as world literature*

COSMOPOLITAN KULCHUR

You might as well give courses in "American chemistry," neglecting all foreign discoveries.   – Ezra Pound, on "American literature"[1]

Despite claiming that "the most powerful cultural legacy of imperialism was ... an education in western ways for minorities of various kinds," Eric Hobsbawm nevertheless feels compelled to follow this assertion with a question: "What of the opposite effect of the dependent world on the dominant?"[2] His answer seems to be that it was negligible. Whereas "exoticism had been a by-product of European expansion since the sixteenth century ... the novelty of the nineteenth century was that non-Europeans and their societies were increasingly, and generally treated as inferior ... they were fit subjects for conquest, or at least for conversion to the values of the only *real* civilization."[3] Imperialism thus tended to increase culture contact under the rubric of Western superiority, creating a seemingly one-way street of influence that was, as we have already seen, aligned with a historical narrative of cultural development. In this way, the increased contact between cultures of the imperialist period was, in part, behind the transformations Hobsbawm identifies in late nineteenth-century nationalist thinking, among them the view that "national self-determination ... applied ... to any and all groups which claimed to be a 'nation'" and the "novel tendency to define a nation in terms of ethnicity and especially in terms of language."[4]

The Age of Empire, then, was also an age of nationalism, as these two intertwined developments encouraged a strong sense of cultural difference that could just as easily produce the theories of European superiority that justified imperial domination as it could those that critiqued colonial rule. J. A. Hobson, for instance, articulated his own critique of imperialism via the terms of cultural difference, calling it a "debasement of ... genuine nationalism" for England to "overflow its natural banks and absorb the near or distant territory of reluctant and unassimilable peoples."⁵ In an indirect way, Hobson provides an answer to Hobsbawm's question: The dependent world's potential impact on the dominant one is the prospect of dissolution – Europe's culture threatened by an influx of "unassimilable peoples." The same protectionism that Hobson rejects in the economic realm – described as the very basis of an imperialism that "repudiates Free Trade" – is here defended in the realm of culture.⁶ Hobson wants the spoils of free trade; what he doesn't want are the people who accompany these spoils, and certainly not their unassimilable cultures. His solution to this dilemma is to call for an internationalism that would preserve national differences and, in this way, protect the nation from those it has conquered.

Not all commentators on early twentieth–century life, however, feared the international mix of its urban environments. Georg Simmel, for instance, writing one year after Hobson's text, found much to admire in the city, even as he described the ways in which its cosmopolitan nature emerged from the flows of global capital. In his famous essay "The Metropolis and Mental Life," Simmel presents a portrait of the modern city that "has always been the seat of the money economy."⁷ Money, for Simmel, represents rational abstraction: "[C]oncerned only with what is common to all … it reduces all quality and individuality to the question: How much?"⁸ Money is thus at the very root of the "rational relations" in which "man is reckoned with like a number," a rationality reflected in the anonymity of the city's economic life, where production is conducted entirely for an impersonal market wherein citizens represent their interests with "an unmerciful matter-of-factness."⁹ This anonymity is not, however, without its positive side, for "it grants to the individual a kind and an amount of personal freedom which has no analogy whatsoever under other conditions."¹⁰ Furthermore, this positive freedom is a reflection of the city's "functional extension beyond its physical borders."¹¹ This expansion, however, is dialectical, simultaneously cultivating freedom and diminishing the power of the individual, who now finds him/herself subject to a range of impersonal forces outside of his/her immediate horizon, in an argument we have already encountered in Fredric Jameson's "Modernism and Imperialism." The city's expansion "into a far-flung national or international area" represents both a gain and a loss against the more rigid structures of an earlier way of life.¹²

I quote Simmel at length, because his argument provides a helpful framework for thinking about Ezra Pound's particular brand of cosmopolitanism. For Pound, like Simmel, was a critic of both money and the

rational abstractions he felt it promoted, even as he celebrated the virtues
of the modern metropolis, which could resist both "the yelp of 'nationality'" and the "desire to coerce others into uniformity" (*SP* 190, 189).[13] In
contrast to this assertion of national difference, and its paradoxical desire
for conformity, Pound advocated a form of international culture resting
not on the "elimination of differences" but rather on "the right of differences to exist" (*LE* 298). Pound's effort to construct a universal culture,
then, did not, in his estimation, require the effacement of particularity.

Consider, in this light, Canto II, which famously begins with Robert
Browning and then moves through Li Po and Picasso before ending with
Homer:

> Hang it all, Robert Browning,
> There can be but the one "Sordello."
> But Sordello, and my Sordello?
> Lo Sordels si fo di Mantovana.
> So-shu churned in the sea.
> Seal sports in the spray-whited circles of cliff-wash,
> Sleek head, daughter of Lir,
>   eyes of Picasso
> Under black fur-hood, lithe daughter of Ocean;
> And the wave runs in the beach-groove:
> "Eleanor, ἑλέναυς and ἑλέπτολις!"
>   And poor old Homer blind, blind, as a bat,
> Ear, ear for the sea-surge, murmur of old men's voices;[14]

The sources here are many. Pound refers both to Browning's epic poem
"Sordello" and also – as the untranslated line from an early life of Sordello
tells us – to the twelfth-century Mantuan poet. Sordello also appears
in Dante, who was famously guided by another Mantuan, Virgil, who
was for Dante as Browning is for Pound: a source of poetic inspiration,
whose work must be updated for contemporary concerns. We then move
from twelfth-century Europe to twelfth-century China and the poet
So-shu, criticized for producing foam rather than waves. And this interest in concretion is cross-cultural, as Homer is praised for his faithful
representations of sea and voice. Alongside concretion, however, there is
also metamorphosis – for the seal is associated with Proteus and shifts,
in Pound's lines, from the ancient Celtic sea-god Lir (appearing in the
twelfth-century Welsh prose collection *The Mabinogion*) to the contemporary art of Picasso.

Pound's interests here are international, but this internationalism is not
only a matter of Pound's form; it is also contained within the very works

he cites. For Sordello also appears in Dante's *De Vulgari Eloquentia*, where he is praised for his linguistic internationalism in a text that, according to Teodolinda Barolini, is "a polemic against linguistic provincialism."[15] Similarly, the reference to Eleanor that ends this quotation speaks both of Helen of Troy and Eleanor of Aquitaine, whom Pound admired for combining the music of Spain with the poetry of Southern France. Even the Welsh works to which Pound refers have an interesting cross-cultural provenance: their name is an English misappropriation of the original Welsh word.

Canto II is, then, an example of what its poetic fragments contain: an illustration of the various routes, mediations, and translations through which culture is transmitted. Indeed, for Pound, culture is always in motion. In contrast to a "static" culture, Pound "values the diachronic traces of thought and language, the historical directions of their...paths of dissemination."[16] If the poem as a whole aims, in Charles Altieri's words, to translate "what the past has established into realities for the present," these realities are decidedly international.[17] Furthermore, although the poem opens up the possibility of a cultural synthesis as Pound's concrete poetic objects are altered by the context in which they occur, these quotations also remain stubbornly particular. My explication, for example, does not change a reader's fundamental inability to integrate Provençal, English, and Ancient Greek into some new organic, untextured whole. The difference, as Gertrude Stein would say, is spreading.

Yet, despite what we might call Pound's "multicultural poetics," his work has not been embraced by contemporary scholars interested in expanding the canon or overturning the nationalist divisions of literary scholarship. Instead, the Pound most commonly in circulation is a fascist and an anti-Semite, Exhibit A in the intertwined rejections of what is dismissively called "the ideology of the aesthetic" and the concept of totality, both seen to be irredeemably totalitarian. Pound, of course, did not help his case, and it is not my intent to excuse his anti-Semitism, which was real and appalling even if, often, intended as an economic critique, or his fascism, which was less real and more naïve, if equally dismaying.[18] What I hope to do, instead, is to recover the positive value of Pound's interest in other cultures, situating it within both the world of imperial capital he consistently critiqued, and our own discourses of multiculturalism and cosmopolitanism, themselves intimately intertwined with globalization.[19]

In making this argument, I will be combining two strands of contemporary Pound scholarship: the one focused on Pound's economic critique – typically read in relation to fascism – the other interested in the cultural politics of Orientalism. Each of these aspects of Pound's work, I maintain, must be thought in terms of the other, for Pound's critique of the commodity is fundamentally a critique of the appropriations constitutive of the imperialist bourgeois subject. Pound counters this appropriation with the presentation of foreign materials that challenge the hegemony of a Eurocentric consciousness. Only when situated clearly within this imperial framework does the political critique latent within Pound's multicultural interests come into view.[20]

MULTICULTURAL FORMALISM

Any more developed phase [of culture] must of necessity include criteria which are, as criteria, capable of comparison with the best alien criteria. In one sense it can almost be said: there are no alien criteria.

– Ezra Pound, "National Culture" (*SP* 163)

There has been, in recent years, a widespread dissatisfaction with what I will call multicultural formalism, the abstract demand to respect different cultures and systems of belief alongside the prohibition against filling in those differences with content, attempting in this way to avoid any tinge of cultural essentialism.[21] It is clear that Pound's effort to combine East and West, to advance an international standard of value based upon a comparison of different cultures is an affront to this regime of difference, and it may be this fact, as much as his admiration for Mussolini, that has marginalized his multicultural efforts within contemporary scholarship. For the scholarship of difference is invested in the maintenance of the borders of culture and the preservation of those authenticities endangered by ethnographic modernity.[22] Multiculturalism thus tends toward a vision of culture as a "closed, self-sufficient and sacrosanct unity," valuing "difference in and for itself."[23] Pound, in contrast, understands culture as a hybrid phenomenon, a continual process of travel and translation that can bring a version of the *Odyssey* written in Medieval Latin to a twentieth–century Parisian bookstall, only to be translated into an Anglo-Saxonized idiom by a man born in Idaho. The opening gesture of *The Cantos* is, then, a celebration of the circuitous routes that have produced some of the most venerated forms of Western culture. Even the culture of the past – where we might expect the projection of cultural wholeness and stability – is, for Pound, about wandering, whether that of Odysseus or the Provençal troubadours. Pound's epic similarly travels among various cultural traditions, seeking continually to expand the borders of English language poetry.

It is possible to see this effort as a form of cultural imperialism. Yet Pound betrays none of the superiority characteristic of Orientalist constructions of the East, nor does he find Asia to be an unchanging realm of picturesque values in the manner of the primitivism that is itself another face of imperial superiority. Rather, Pound builds a common world culture out of the discreet histories of East and West – the intrigues of Renaissance Italy, early America, or the Chinese Court – and the cultural objects produced by those histories, seeking to construct a universalism that need not be irredeemably Eurocentric. To be sure, this effort is utopian and contains many problems – among them the obvious impossibility of approaching the East without some fundamentally Western-tinged, and to that extent Orientalist, perspective – but it is not, for all that, an effort that we should abandon. Neither is it a problem we can just wish away, for the homogenization of culture proceeds apace, and it does so primarily through the advance of a global capitalism whose universality not only masks its own particular interests but also produces, as its symptom, a rhetoric of diversity with which it is intimately intertwined.[24]

This rhetoric presents culture as a synonym for identity, and in doing so tends to valorize cultural difference as an existential fact of human existence.[25] The end result, as E. San Juan Jr. has argued, is an occlusion of "the material conditions of racist practices and institutions" constitutive of many of these supposedly cultural distinctions, and the rearticulation of these distinctions as a series of "privatized sensibilities" that "become the chief organs of consumerist experience."[26] Culture becomes a form of private property, mobilized by capitalism as the basis for further consumption. Again we see the intertwining of expressivist subjectivity and the culture of consumption, which here takes on a communal register: I consume these things because that's what my people do.

Pound, of course, argued strenuously against both poetic expressivism and the capitalist culture in which he lived. Among what Cary Wolfe calls his "palpable attractions" are his "early defense of individual difference in the face of economic Taylorization and imperialism, his recognition that the aesthetic is at once fully social and even economic" and his claim that you cannot "be a good artist and a good capitalist subject at the same time."[27] What is most radical about Pound's critique of imperial culture, however, is his decoupling of culture and identity, his belief that culture is public, lodged within works of art rather than in subjects. Pound thus develops a fundamentally modern sense of the subject's constitution through its encounter with the object world, but he does so by strongly differentiating the concretion of the art object from

the fungibility associated with the commodity under the exchange relations characteristic of a market society.[28]

Indeed, one of the key aspects of Pound's literary production is a
defense of the "ontology of objects" that, according to John Guillory, has
separated the commodity from the art object since the birth of the discourses of aesthetics and political economy out of moral philosophy in
the eighteenth century.[29] In Pound's account, art objects are objectifications of subjective states of emotion, which in turn shape the subjectivities
of those who encounter them. Works of art are not consumed in their
use, nor are they to be appropriated by the viewing subject, but rather
they are the agents of appropriation themselves, and they bring with
them, in Pound's estimation, the social conditions present at their making. Poetry is, for Pound, part of the public sphere, and the entirety of his
literary effort is dedicated to critiquing various forms of the proprietary –
whether that of lyric subjectivity, aestheticism, or the hoarding of money
and goods.[30] Pound's conception of the poetic object, like Eliot's notion
of tradition, represents, then, a critique of both the temporality I have
associated with imperialism – a temporality constituted by the opposed
reifications of a frozen tradition and empty, homogenous time – and of
a consumer culture dedicated to immediacy and intimately intertwined
with this new form of imperialism. Against the hoarding of goods, Pound
advocates the circulation of cultural artifacts, which contain the values he
felt were absent from contemporary discourse: "The struggle still was, and
still might be, to preserve some of the values that make life worth living."[31]
These values are what Pound hopes to produce and preserve through *The
Cantos*'s juxtaposition of often untranslated fragments from disparate
cultural locations. Pound thus differentiates the chaotic influx of ideas –
which he welcomes – from that of wealth – which he rejects, and he does
so by arguing against the equation of culture and identity characteristic of
the cultural nationalism of both his time and our own, producing instead
a form best described as world literature.

POETIC ROUTES

What is wanted is not to restore a vanished, or revive a vanishing culture under
modern conditions which make it impossible, but to grow a contemporary culture from the old roots.   – T. S. Eliot[32]

Over the past decade, Franco Moretti's 2000 essay "Conjectures on
World Literature" has provoked – sometimes directly, sometimes not – a

series of responses dealing with the concept of world literature.[33] In that piece, after noting the vast number of literary works produced in the contemporary moment, Moretti suggests that in order to accommodate this influx of material we must alter our basic reading habits, turning from close textual analysis to what he calls "distant reading."[34] This form of reading reveals a "law of literary evolution," which Moretti defines as the compromise between an imposed form and a local content, a literary version of the center/periphery relations disclosed by world systems theory.[35] Only by focusing on these larger patterns can the study of world literature achieve what Moretti sees as its core goal: "[T]o be a thorn in the side, a permanent intellectual challenge to national literatures."[36] This last sentence could just as easily have been written by Ezra Pound, who similarly argued that "we should read less, far less than we do" (*SP* 23). Although Pound's interest in world literature proceeds by the close examination of key passages rather than the distant reading Moretti advocates and, as such, is closer to the "comparatism that sustains at once global reach and textual closeness" – a comparatism Emily Apter associates with the work of Leo Spitzer and recommends in reply to Moretti's model[37] – Pound retains what I think is Moretti's core insight: namely, that relations among nations and cultures make themselves felt within literary texts as a question of form. Indeed, one of the central aims of *The Cantos* is, as Pound states in an unpublished letter, "to indicate the stream wherethru and whereby" cultural artifacts are transmitted.[38]

The Cantos thus emerges as a challenge to the artificial divide that the nationalization of literary traditions creates between texts, which habitually cross national borders. For Pound wrote what can only be called World Literature. Drawing on Greek, Latin, Provençal, French, Egyptian, Japanese, and Chinese materials – to name just a few – he produced a body of work that is remarkable both in its range and in its ability to push against the national boundaries within which we continue to investigate literary production. Even his translations, which have been the subject of a great deal of critical controversy, are not so much domestications of the foreign as they are "self-foreignizing operations."[39] Pound, as Hugh Kenner has argued, "never translates 'into' something already existing in English," but instead seeks to make "something correspondingly new" happen in his native tongue.[40] For Pound, translation is never simply a neutral transfer of meaning from one language to another, but rather an effort to "expand and deepen his language by means of the foreign language,"[41] since "different languages ... have worked out certain mechanisms of communication and registration. No one language is complete" (*LE* 36). Furthermore, Pound believed it was impossible for "any man in our time [to] think with only one language" (*LE* 36). The polyglot world of *The Cantos*, then, is a direct response to the globalizing world in which Pound lived, an attempt to provide the contact between cultures he saw as necessary for a renaissance in twentieth-century literature.

Of his explicit translations – for it is possible to view much of his work under this rubric – *Cathay* has recently drawn the most scholarly attention, as critics have considered how best to understand Pound's lifelong fascination with China.[42] Did Pound simply appropriate Chinese materials in support of his already stated preference for precision and order? Or were his poetics substantially altered by his encounter with Chinese thought?

For Christine Froula, the answer is the latter. In her view, Pound's discovery of the work of Ernest Fenollosa and his subsequent writing of the poems of *Cathay* produced the basic poetic principle guiding the composition of *The Cantos*: "Pound was about to embark on *The Cantos*, his internationalist-modernist English epic, when he came upon Fenollosa's prophecy of the dawning century's new and startling 'chapter' in the 'book of the world' from which would issue 'strange futures,' 'world-embracing cultures half-weaned from Europe,' 'hitherto undreamed responsibilities for nations and races.'"[43] As "Fenollosa's first audience," Pound "wrote toward such a future," basing his epic on an ideogrammic method that "assimilates his encounter with Chinese to *The Cantos*' very structure."[44] Pound's simultaneous incorporation of both foreign materials and "foreignizing translation[s]" into his poem disrupts, according to Froula, "the dominance and transparency of the poem's English ground," making it "a microcosmic register of modernity's shrinking globe."[45] "Cosmopolitan and time-traveling from its first page," *The Cantos* emerges as an epic of globalization, an attempt to represent – or, more accurately, bring into being – a world culture comprised of both Eastern and Western values.[46]

Froula's characterization of the poem seems to me fundamentally accurate, but her metaphor of a "shrinking globe" is inexact; its agency is misplaced. For it is not so much that the globe is shrinking, but rather that Pound is traversing it, actively seeking materials he hopes will produce a revolution in English language poetry. "Our literature," Pound writes (speaking of literature written in English), "is always in full bloom after contact with France…the disease of both England and America during the last century is due precisely to a stoppage of circulation" (*SP* 200). The antidote to this stoppage of circulation is "the importation of models ... for writing," a task to which Pound tirelessly dedicated himself, since he was, in T. S. Eliot's words, "first and foremost, a teacher and campaigner" (*LE* xii). Pound is a poetic wanderer, a modern version of the troubadour poets who dominate his early verse. Thus, *The Cantos* begins "on the godly sea" and ends – or at last stops – with a nautical encounter in its last line: "You in the dinghy (piccioletta) astern there!" (CIX.788).[47] The renewal of culture Pound sought was not, then, a matter of "roots" but "routes": the contact between cultures and the circulation of cultural objects Pound insisted was the key to any true civilization.

Of course, Pound's age was not, in his estimation, a great one. Its civilization was "botched," ruined by commerce, war, and what a 1917 essay called "The Enemy": provincialism.[48] Provincialism, according to Pound, consists of two related errors: "[A]n ignorance of the manners, customs and nature of people living outside one's own village, parish, or nation" and "a desire to coerce others into uniformity" (*SP* 189). These errors are in turn inseparable from the "evil" of "the 'university system' of Germany." Murdering to dissect, the German system trains individuals to explore "some minute particular problem *unconnected* with life, *unconnected* with main principles" (*SP* 191). Burying "himself in 'problems'," the German-trained student thus turns "away from any sense of proportion between the 'problems' and vital values" (*SP* 192). Because the scholarship of his era placed culture in an isolated realm, it threatened the very basis of civilization, for civilization, Pound quotes approvingly from Rudyard Kipling, is transportation.

Pound's critique of provincialism blends here with praise for the modern metropolis, where we find "the only things that matter," namely "peace, our ideas of justice, of liberty, of as much of these as are feasible, the immaterial as well as material things" (*SP* 200). This list of advantages is striking, for alongside peace, justice, and liberty – restricted to what is "feasible" – it contains a crucial admission of the necessity of material goods. "At present," the essay continues, "the centre of the world is somewhere on an imaginary line between London and Paris, the sooner that line is shortened, the better for all of us, the richer the life of the world" (*SP* 200). Obviously enough, Pound is here describing the process of globalization. Although his primary interest remains culture, his references to "material things," Kipling, and transportation suggest an awareness of the economic transactions that facilitate the contact between cultures.

This doubling of culture and commerce is linked explicitly to the spoils of imperial adventure in the early poem "Epilogue," dedicated "to my five books containing mediaeval studies, experiments and translations":

> I bring you the spoils, my nation,
> I, who went out in exile,
>   Am returned to thee with gifts.
>
> I, who have laboured long in the tombs,
>   Am come back therefrom with riches.
>
> Behold my spices and robes, my nation,
> My gifts of Tyre.
>
> Here are my rimes of the south;
> Here are strange fashions of music;
> Here is my knowledge.
>
> Behold, I am come with patterns;
> Behold, I return with devices,
> Cunning the craft, cunning the work, the fashion.[49]

The imperial analogy is clear enough – Provençal poetry as Pound's Elgin marbles – and it forces us to consider the relationship between his cosmopolitan sensibilities and the imperial culture in which he lived. For the alternative to the "yelp of 'nationality'" seems to be the spoils of imperialism, although in a distinction that will become crucial, Pound wishes these spoils to be public. It is to the idea of circulation, then, that I will next turn.

UNCONSUMABLE ARTIFACTS

> I believe in some lasting sap
>   at work in the trunk of things.
>   – Ezra Pound, "Redondillas" (*CEP* 217)

Pound's Hell Cantos are filled with those he blamed for causing World War I, among them the "Profiteers drinking blood sweetened with sh-t," the "financiers / lashing them with steel wires" and "the perverters of language, / the perverts, who have set money-lust / Before the pleasures of the senses;" (XIV.61). Rotting in their own filth, "sh-tting flies," and "rumbling with imperialism," these villains are presented in a variety of scatological metaphors representing a bastardized form of production that fails to fulfill any social function (XV.64). Thus, Canto XIV closes with the following verse paragraph:

> The slough of unamiable liars,
>> bog of stupidities,
> malevolent stupidities, and stupidities,
> the soil living pus, full of vermin,
> dead maggots begetting live maggots,
>> slum owners,
> usurers squeezing crab-lice, pandars to authority,
> pets-de-loup, sitting on the piles of stone books,
> obscuring the texts with philology,
>> hiding them under their persons,
>
>> ...
>
> monopolists, obstructors of knowledge,
>> obstructors of distribution. (XIV.63)

That Pound blamed WWI on the destructive combination of military, financial, and journalistic profiteering is not unusual, but his linking of usury, philology, and monopoly surely is. What unites these seemingly disparate realms, for Pound, is obstruction, the hoarding of money and knowledge, the burying of what should be of public utility under a mound of philological filth.

In contrast, Pound argued that "the ultimate goal of scholarship" is "popularization ... [putting] the greatest amount of the best literature ... within the easiest reach of the public" (*SP* 198). The best "a critic can do for the reader or audience or spectator is to focus his gaze or audition" directly on the works themselves (*LE* 13). For artworks are part of the cultural heritage, providing "a great percentage of the lasting and unassailable data regarding the nature of man" (*LE* 42). As such they "exceed the boundaries of private ownership," (*SP* 63) becoming part of the "permanent property ... given to the race at large" (*LE* 47). The cultural heritage – also defined as "the whole aggregate of human inventions" – represents a transcendence of the individual, proving that "the overplus of what a group of men can do acting together, over and above the sum of what they can do each acting alone, is a reality" (*SP* 275).

Works of art are thus imagined by Pound in explicit contrast to commodities. They are in "a class by themselves, as they are always in use and never consumed; or they are, in jargon, 'consumed' but not destroyed by consumption" (*SP* 215). Although *The Cantos* confronts us as an exhibition of poetic objects that rivals those of imperial and cultural conquest so ubiquitous in the late nineteenth and early twentieth century, the logic they teach is fundamentally different from the fungibility associated with the commodity. For Pound's objects do not construct a consuming subject, nor are they marshaled in support of a national or imperial project. What they represent, instead, are utility and value, two qualities obscured by the reifications of both aestheticism *and* commodity culture.[50]

Indeed, for Pound, the work of art's utility *is* its value: "The *mot juste* is of public utility. I can't help it. I am not offering this fact as a sop to aesthetes who want all authors to be fundamentally useless. We are governed by words, the laws are graven in words, and literature is the sole means of keeping these words living and accurate" (*LE* 409). Literature, in Pound's estimation, serves the community by keeping the language accurate, hence the lifelong importance he placed on "precision of statement" and "particularization," values that form the core of the "spirit of romance" Pound attempted to bring to contemporary society (*LE* 215).[51] For works of art emerge out of particular situations: "[T]hat which the philosopher presents as truth, the poet presents as that which appears as truth to a certain mind under certain conditions" (*SP* 361). By being true to his/her perception, the artist presents a specific truth, and the externalization of this truth creates a kind of permanent testimony that can be activated by a method of scholarship that does not bury the past under a mound of philological filth, but rather understands that the "forces, elements or qualities which were potent in the mediaeval literature of the Latin tongues," for instance, might be "still potent in our own."[52]

It is this residual potency that differentiates Pound's poetic objects from the inert things of commodity culture, *and* his sense of history from the unending progress of a telic modernity. This idea can best be illustrated by Canto VII in which Pound quotes a phrase from Flaubert's "Un Coeur Simple" that has become a kind of critical touchstone, finding a prominent place in essays by Roland Barthes, Fredric Jameson, and Bill Brown.[53] Pound quotes the lines as follows: "Un peu moisi, plancher plus bas que le jardin. / 'Contre le lambris, fauteuil de paille, / 'Un vieux piano, et sous le baromètre ...' [A little musty, the floor being below garden level. Against the wainscot, a wicker armchair, and old piano, and under the barometer]" (VII.24).[54]

For Jameson, this description is emblematic of Deleuze and Guattari's notion of decoding, defined as "the secularization of the older sacred codes," although we will have to quote Flaubert's original passage in full to follow his argument:

Eight mahogany chairs were lined up against the white-painted wainscoting, and under the barometer stood an old piano loaded with a pyramid of boxes and cartons. On either side of the chimney piece, which was carved out of yellow marble in the Louis Quinze style, there was a tapestry-covered armchair, and in the middle was a clock designed to look like a temple of Vesta. The whole room smelt a little musty, as the floor was on a lower level than the garden.[55]

What Flaubert's description allows us to see, Jameson argues, is that the move from one social formation to another does not proceed without resistance. Thus, the merely additive space of modernity – eight interchangeable chairs, arrayed along a blank white wall – is countered by the piano, with its pyramid of boxes, trying desperately to "recentre space" and "pull back the contents of the room into a genuine centred hierarchy" characteristic of an earlier, sacred form of society.[56] Importantly, it is culture itself – the piano, the temple-shaped clock – that embodies this resistance, even though its futility is aptly illustrated by the conscription of the temple in the service of modernity's empty, homogenous time.

Jameson then turns to Pound's Canto VII, which he calls "the great transitional moment, in which for the first time the epic swings away from that archaic immediacy in which the gods existed in the early *Cantos* towards the junk-filled contemporary space of a *belle époque* on its way to the First World War."[57] Thus, we find the "Beer-bottle on the statue's pediment" (VII.25). "That Fritz," Pound continues, "is the era, to-day against the past" (VII.25). Pound's point, however, is not simply that the artist can observe the contrast between then and now – and thus produce what Jameson calls the "modernist" reading, which seeks to recuperate the sacred through the symbolic structures of a hermetically sealed text in an act of artistic will – but rather that the contemporary moment itself contains such juxtapositions.[58] Jameson is, then, correct when he argues that "the Poundian drawing room is haunted by the surcharged energy of older dwellings" but wrong to assert that this makes "historical commemoration possible."[59] For Pound's poem is not about commemoration at all – to believe in commemoration is to accede to the linear narrative of a modernity that has overturned all prior values. Instead, Pound contrasts the stale objects of a bourgeois interior – through which one discerns the subjectivity of their owners – to the moments of the past that have lasting value, suggesting in the process the persistence of those very values capitalism imagines it has eliminated.

This contrast between two forms of objects is articulated within an abbreviated history of poetry, which moves from Homer to Ovid to Bertran de Bons, whose poems, like certain paintings of the period are "not mere succession of strokes, sightless narration," but rather sharply observed perceptions (VII.24). The passage then turns to Dante, Flaubert, and finally Henry James in a "ghostly visit" that produces the comparison with the past from which I have already quoted:

> The Elysée carries a name on
> And the bus behind me gives me a date for peg;
> Low ceiling and the Erard and the silver,
> These are in "time." Four chairs, the bow-front dresser,
> The panier of the desk, cloth top sunk in.
>   "Beer-bottle on the statue's pediment!
> "That, Fritz, is the era, to-day against the past,
> "Contemporary." And the passion endures.
> Against their action, aromas. Rooms, against chronicles. (VII.25)

We would seem to be in the world of Flaubertian description – empty objects existing in their empty seriality. And the comparison is with the world of the past: statues, passion, action, and chronicles arrayed against beer-bottles, rooms, and aromas. Clearly the works of the past are the seat of value, but equally clear is the fact that they remain a part of the contemporary world.

More importantly, though, they are still alive, as the concluding section of the Canto reveals. Pound recalls a dancer he once knew and one of his own poems – "Ione dead the long year" – now seven years older, the woman seven years "deader." It would seem the entire process of remembrance is rejected: "And all that day, another day: / Thin husks I had known as men, / Dry casques of departed locusts / speaking a shell of speech ..." (VII.26). Here Pound finds "only the husk of talk" rather than the living speech that inspired Homer in lines I have already quoted from Canto II and which Pound repeats at the opening of the Canto with which we are concerned (VII.26).[60] Yet as the Canto proceeds, something happens:

> Life to make mock of motion:
> For the husks, before me, move,
>   The words rattle: shells given out by shells.
> The live man, out of lands and prisons,
>   shakes the dry pods,
> Probes for old wills and friendships, and the big locust-casques
> Bend to the tawdry table,

> Lift up their spoons to mouths, put forks in cutlets,
> And make sound like the sound of voices. (VII.27)

Pace Jameson, Pound is not commemorating anything. He is, instead, insisting on the vital presence of what seem to the contemporary world to be dry husks, and, furthermore, asserting their difference from the meaningless objects that fill the bourgeois interior. For Pound's interest is not in material things per se, but in the objectifications of subjective experiences – voices contained in husks.

His effort to "find out what sort of things endure, and what sort of things are transient" (*SP* 125) is realized, then, in *The Cantos*, which presents his "ideograph of the good": all those works of the past whose husks still move (*LE* 37). *The Cantos,* therefore, works on at least two registers at once. On the one hand, it represents what Pound called "a tale of the tribe," although as Altieri has pointed out this is not a "tribe familiar to us," but rather a new tribe that "might be created out of our history."[61] On the other hand, it can be seen as a "record of struggle," or what Froula has called the "track of a human being in time," an emphasis that, similarly, suggests the poem's openness to historical transformation, its interest in what the works from the past it collects have to say to the present and future of humanity.[62] The individual and the communal meet, as Pound attempts faithfully to represent all those works of lasting value that he has seen with precision and particularity – the very values obscured by the rational exchange of contemporary capitalism – including them in both their original languages and in the myriad forms through which they have been transmitted. This presentation is meant to have public utility, for Pound is, to repeat Eliot's precise characterization, "first and foremost, a teacher and a campaigner."

Against the world of imperialist appropriation – the obsessive hoarding Pound saw as characteristic of usury, philology, and monopoly – Pound offers a public poetry that puts into circulation the various artifacts out of which it is constructed. Furthermore, the immanent value of these objects forces the reader to confront them in their stubborn particularity, forces, that is to say, a confrontation with the object that disables the easy assimilation of the poetry's contents into some prior subjective context. Once again, as in Eliot, value is not to be found in the sensitivity of the artistic subject who can grant meaning to a world from which it is absent. Instead, poetic works themselves refashion the reading subject in a process Pound outlines in his early poems. Analyzing these poems will help us to understand what Pound imagined would occur when a reader encountered the multicultural structure of *The Cantos*.

TREES AND GODS

> I sing of the special case,
>   The truth is the individual.
>   – Ezra Pound, "Redondillas" (*CEP* 219)

Pound's 1908 poem "Histrion" tells what "no man hath dared to write": namely, that "the souls of all men great / At times pass through us, / And we are melted into them, and are not / Save reflexions of their souls" (*CEP* 71). At times, we are Dante, François Villon, and many others. The last stanza explains this phenomenon:

> 'Tis as in midmost us there glows a sphere
> Translucent, molten gold, that is the "I"
> And into this some form projects itself:
> Christus, or John, or eke the Florentine;
> And as the clear space is not if a form's
> Imposed thereon,
> So we cease from all being for the time,
> And these, the Masters of the Soul, live on. (*CEP* 71)

Far from the expressivist logic that dominates consumer culture – the choice of objects to represent one's interiority – Pound here presents us with something like the inverse: I am constituted by what I consume. The poetic object is permanent; it is the subject itself that is fungible.

This vision of the subject is developed in "The Tree," a poem Pound placed at the beginning of *Personae*. The title seems to suggest a form of rootedness that stands in contrast to the wandering Pound of troubadour lyric. The poem itself, though, presents a different story:

> I stood still and was a tree amid the wood,
> Knowing the truth of things unseen before;
> Of Daphne and the laurel bow
> And that god-feasting couple old
> That grew elm-oak amid the wold.
> 'Twas not until the gods had been
> Kindly entreated, and been brought within
> Unto the heart of their heart's home
> That they might do this wonder thing;
> Nathless I have been a tree amid the wood
> And many a new thing understood
> That was rank folly to my head before.[63]

"The Tree" begins with a stillness that opens its speaker, via observation, to knowledge of his/her environment, to the awareness of "unseen things" and an understanding of others – Daphne, the "god-feasting" couple – who have themselves become trees. This sort of sympathetic understanding requires a process of internalization, as the gods' entrance into "the heart of their heart's home" is what makes one a tree in the first place.

What, however, does Pound mean by the gods? He asked himself this question in "Religio, or The Child's Guide to Knowledge." The answer: "A god is an eternal state of mind … When is a god manifest? When the state of mind takes form…. By what characteristic may we know the divine forms? By beauty" (*SP* 47). The gods are objectified states of mind that possess beauty, that is to say, works of art, defined in the essay "Arnold Dolmetsch" as "impersonal or objective stor[ies] woven out of … emotion" (*LE* 432). We can add these works to the list of Poundian texts that teach one how to read. Reading, as presented here, requires a stillness, an openness that allows the work of art to project itself into one's interiority. Pound's lifelong interest in the poetic object – his tireless campaign to make the best poetry popular – must also, then, be seen as a critique of the subject. In direct contrast to Spivak's definition of the imperialist subject appropriating the other by assimilation, Pound's poetic subject is itself appropriated by an other *to which* it is assimilated. The diverse cultural material of *The Cantos* is meant to construct a subject that is in direct opposition to the self-contained Western subject, who, within the space of Pound's epic, is literally transformed by the works he or she encounters.

As we have already seen, Pound's defense of poetry consistently articulated itself as a critique of imperialism, a claim for poetry's importance to an ideal civilization he distinguished sharply from a "mere bloated empire" (*LE* 21). When poets fail in their task of keeping words living and accurate – producing instead "an inaccurate art … that makes false reports" – then "the whole machinery of social and of individual thought and order goes to pot," leading directly to "imperial and sentimental exploitations" (*LE* 43, 21). In contrast, the "serious artist" works through precision: "[He] is scientific in that he presents the image of his desire, of his hate, of his indifference as precisely that, as precisely the image of his own desire, hate or indifference. The more precise his record the more lasting and unassailable his work of art" (*LE* 46). Thus, while Pound maintains a theory of individual agency that rests on a version of sincerity – one that culminates in his refusal to see the structural problems of capital, blaming all wrongs on deliberate conspiracies and manipulation – he also refuses to accord any one perspective the status of objective or universal truth.[64] For Pound insisted that "our only measure of truth is … our own perception of truth" (*LE* 431). The problem is when someone tries to pass off his partial truth as *the* truth, when the myths or stories that represent individual testimony become "only lies and propaganda" used "to preserve the empire" (*LE* 432). Instead, truth emerges from the combination of a series of particular situations, seen with intensity and clarity by subjects willing to take responsibility for their own seeing. In emphasizing the situatedness of discourse, Pound avoids the transparency Spivak associates with the imperial Western subject. To say, then, that *Cathay* is an event in English, as Hugh Kenner insisted, is not only or even primarily to say that its Chinese sources are irrelevant. It is, rather, to insist that the poetry be understood as issuing *from the Western perspective from which it originates.*

Yet as I have said, time and again, *The Cantos* works to disrupt this perspective, turning without warning from Malatesta to the earthly Paradise of Kung's garden in Canto XIII, itself clearly meant as a contrast to the War Cantos that directly precede it. The poem's structure, that is to say, destabilizes the traditional text/context relationship by which the "other" text is appropriated into a Western context, asking instead that we critique contemporary Europe from the perspective of Ancient China. As the poem moves on, and the various contexts multiply – ranging from Ancient Greece, to Revolutionary America, to Dynastic China – it becomes as impossible to situate oneself squarely within a hegemonic Western subject position as it does to rest comfortably in the English language that is, ostensibly, the poem's dominant idiom. Perspectives in the poem may emerge from discrete locations – often marked by the poet himself, if in obscure ways – but in their circulation with other perspectives they fail to attain anything like universality. They remain, instead, partial records of specific moments and specific ways of seeing. Pound's poetry thus does not disclose a universal human condition; rather, it seeks to construct one out of diverse cultural histories in a process akin to what Judith Butler calls "cultural translation."

Butler's argument begins with the familiar claim that universality is only a cloak for some particular interest surreptitiously elevated to universal status, but goes on to suggest that this might not be such a bad thing after all. Critiquing the hierarchical "ordering of ... identifications ... produced by a discourse on multiculturalism," she argues that the universal "begins to become articulated precisely through challenges to its existing formulations."[65] Thus, we can rest neither with "the enumeration of radical particularisms between which no communication is possible" – Butler's version of multiculturalism – nor with the assimilation of particularity to "a presupposed universalism."[66] Instead "the futural articulation of the universal ... can happen only if we find ways to effect cultural translations between … various cultural examples."[67] In a similar spirit, Pound argues that "the whole of great art is a struggle for communication," which makes it "possible for individuals to meet across national borders" (*LE* 298, 296). *The Cantos* represents this struggle to communicate across the great border between East and West. By way of conclusion, then, I would like to examine two moments when Pound turns to China to suggest how Western values might be productively transformed by an encounter with the East.

Against the Hell Cantos's image of chaotic obstruction, we have the Confucian Canto (Canto XIII) that directly precedes it. Set in a "dynastic temple" by the "cedar grove," the Canto begins with Kung (Confucius) asking his followers how he should conduct his life. Their answers vary, and Tian asks Kung who is correct: "They have all answered correctly," Kung responds, "That is to say, each in his nature" (XIII.58). The canto begins, then, in particularity with the various perspectives expressed by Kung's disciples. It continues through imagism – "The old swimming hole, / and the boys flopping off the planks," – before arriving at its theme: "If a man have not order within him," Kung says, "He can not spread order about him … and [he] said nothing of the life after death" (XIII.58, 59). Despite its seemingly ancient pastoral setting – a setting reinforced by its imagistic moments – Canto XIII offers the West a reminder of the intertwining of moral and civic virtue Pound felt it had abandoned. A picturesque Asia becomes, here, the source of practical knowledge. Unlike the appropriating bourgeoisie subject, Kung's ideal subject understands both the partiality of its own perspective and its grounding within a specific social order.

The famous Seven Lakes Canto also begins as picturesque pastoral: "For the seven lakes, and by no man these verses: / Rain; empty river; a voyage, / Fire from frozen cloud, heavy rain in the twilight / Under the cabin roof was one lantern" (XLIX.244). As is well known, the canto is modeled on a "screen book" Pound received in 1928, which contained "eight ink paintings, eight poems in Chinese, and eight poems in Japanese," all depicting the same traditional landscape.[68] This subject, according to Zhiamong Qian, "is a monument of Chinese culture, an example of how poets and artists in China (and in Japan) have continuously made an old theme new."[69] To support this point, Qian quotes Laurence Binyon – one of many scholars Pound relied on for his information about Chinese art and culture – who argued that the repetition of familiar landscapes in generation after generation of Chinese painting forces us to overcome "our foolish and petty misconceptions of originality."[70] The landscape, then, offers an example of a cultural object that is not the property of one individual subject, but rather illustrates a theme that circulates across time, made newly relevant by each generation of artists who take it up. The Canto itself reinforces the public nature of this particular theme, as Pound transforms something private – a screen book given to him as a gift – into a publicly circulating artifact.

He does this most dramatically at the Canto's end, where the opening imagistic scenes take on a strong moral valence.[71] "State by creating riches shd. thereby get into debt?" Pound writes, "This is infamy; this is Geryon. / This canal goes still to TenShi / though the old king built it for pleasure" (XLIX.245). These lines – quoting Thomas Jefferson, Dante, and a Japanese history of China – are followed first by a transliteration of a Chinese poem and then by one of Pound's own translations: "Sun up; work / sundown; to rest / dig well and drink of the water / dig field; eat of the grain / Imperial power is? and to us what is it?" (XLIX.245). Concrete images turn into the concretion of labor, with utility emphasized against both finance capital and imperialist appropriation in a vision that reads back onto the poem's imagistic moments. For Pound believed the artist to be on the side of the farmer: "The artist is one of the few producers. He, the farmer and the artisan create wealth; the rest shift and consume it" (*LE* 222). What *The Cantos* tries to produce is a language adequate to the globalized world in which Pound lived, a language that would both represent and respond to the increased contact across cultures he observed. Thus, in this Canto, Pound illustrates how Chinese paintings can be connected to a Japanese historian, an American politician, and a medieval Italian author – all to make a point about early twentieth-century political culture within the boundaries of one poetic space.

Which returns us once again to the question of world literature. Earlier, I referred to the "law of literary evolution" that Moretti's investigation into world literature disclosed. This law suggests that literature always involves a "structural compromise" between the "foreign and the local."[72] The development of the novel becomes the history of the relationship between a form brought from elsewhere and a local content it can only partially represent. World literature is not, then, simply what Moretti studies or what his essay aims to produce as a concept. Instead, world literature is what all literatures always already are, despite our tendency to analyze them in isolation. The "world" part of "world literature" resides in its form. "World literature," Moretti contends, "is not an object, it's a *problem*, and a problem that asks for a new critical method."[73] Writing nearly a hundred years earlier, Pound articulated a similar position. A globalized world asks for a new poetic method, one that can both acknowledge the history embedded within cultural objects and work toward the production of a universal world culture built out of the particularity of non-consumable works of art.

Seven Lakes ends with what Pound called a "glimpse of Paradiso."[74] "The fourth; the dimension of stillness. / And the power over wild beasts" (XLIX.245). Although the exact meaning of these lines is somewhat obscure – why, for instance, is the Dionysian power over wild beasts important in Paradise? – they convey a sense of futurity that recaptures some of the pastoral longing of the Canto's opening. This longing has, by the end of the Canto, been refigured as something to be achieved – something to be produced. For despite his paradisal longings, Pound, like Kung, says nothing of life after death. The only true paradise in *The Cantos* is the earthly one to which it points. Living in a world in which it was impossible to think with only one language, Pound attempted to work with what he was given, creating a world literature that would resist both abstract exchangeability and the nationalist rhetoric of cultural purity. Our own regime of multicultural formalism shows that he was not victorious, but his efforts are examples from which we can learn – and that is exactly how he would have wanted it.

4

Turning consumption into production: Ulysses and the construction of postcolonial agency

What we really need is a wholesale displacement of the thematics of modernity by the desire called Utopia. We need to combine a Poundian mission to identify Utopian tendencies with a Benjaminian geography of their sources and a gauging of their pressure at what are now multiples sea levels. Ontologies of the present demand archeologies of the future, not forecasts of the past.

– Fredric Jameson, (*A Singular Modernity* 215)

The situation of Stephen Dedalus, that self-proclaimed savior of the Irish whose flight to Paris has crash-landed into the British-owned Martello Tower, is perhaps best exemplified as he sits down to his morning meal. With him is the usurper Mulligan, "the oxy chap" Haines, and an old Irish milk woman "serving her conqueror and her gay betrayer."[1] Clearly enough, this woman represents a non-idealized image of Ireland, a "wandering crone" trapped in a position of structural dependence, so alienated from her own culture that she mistakes Haines's Gaelic for French (*U* 14). Stephen is not sure how to behave towards this woman; not knowing whether "to serve or to upbraid," he remains aloof (*U* 14). Mulligan, though, has no such compunction, as he is happy to display his superiority, play the fool, and serve the old woman up for Haines's amusement. In a similar fashion, Mulligan had earlier told Stephen that Haines found his remark about Irish art – "the cracked lookingglass of a servant" – clever and that perhaps he might touch him for a guinea (*U* 7). When Stephen asks for money, however, he has none of Mulligan's fawning charm, and his abruptness clearly embarrasses the Englishman who laughs and ends the conversation. Haines's desire to "make a collection of [Stephen's] sayings" must be read alongside the fact that he is the only one at breakfast who has Gaelic (*U* 16). Having already taken its language, the conqueror seeks also to commodify Ireland's culture – without monetary compensation – and he does so alongside a famous denial of agency: "[W]e feel in England that we have treated you rather unfairly. It seems

history is to blame" (*U* 20). With these words, Haines distances himself
from the primitive accumulation of his ancestors, failing to realize its continuities with his own neo-colonial form of cultural accumulation.

In such a situation where is Stephen to turn? His every action seems
circumscribed by the masters he seeks to escape. Rejecting both the
Wildean pose of Mulligan's compromises *and* the image of Irish authenticity – an old milk woman whose poverty is itself the mark of colonial
dependence – Stephen seems to have nowhere to stand. Thus, according
to Declan Kiberd, Joyce shifts "his investigation from the mind of Stephen
Dedalus," which cannot "be further elaborated in that society," to "the setting which thwarts its articulation."[2] Stephen's impasse is, for Kiberd, due
to the social order in which he lives. Once again, it seems that history is
to blame.

Kiberd is not alone, however, among postcolonial critics of Joyce in
their unwitting echo of Haines's agentless vision of history. Indeed, recent
accounts of *Ulysses* have tended to agree with the novel's earliest Marxist
readers, who found what Eliot called the book's "mythical method" to
be ahistorical, representing, in Lukács's famous account, "a belief in the
basically static character of events."[3] What for Lukács was critique has, in
contemporary accounts, turned into praise, as the static character of the
novel is attributed not to Joyce's form, but rather to the structural inequalities of Ireland's colonial condition, which Joyce's form reflects.[4] Lacking
any historical agent capable of transcending this situation, Dublin must
remain paralyzed.

It is difficult, however, to imagine Joyce acceding to this agentless vision
of history, for although he was quite clear about the effects of English tyranny on the Irish soul, he placed almost equal blame upon an Ireland that
he felt had not been faithful to itself.[5] Joyce, that is to say, emphasized the
agency of both colonizer and colonized in creating Irish reality, rejecting
the common ground between Stephen's paralysis and Haines's denial of
responsibility. Furthermore, if, as Nicholas Brown has argued, "any consequent historicization of *Ulysses* must begin from the question of form,"
surely such a historicization must proceed from what is the most salient
feature of that form: not pessimism, or the representation of historical
blockage, but rather an endless sense of possibility, of the ability of the
individual to take up and remake the "materials put at his disposal by
literary tradition."[6] Tradition is not, for Joyce, a straitjacket that prevents
Irish agency; history is not only a nightmare. Indeed, to view one's social
order in these terms is to hold to a naïve view of the authentic space from
which change must emerge, a view Joyce explicitly critiques through his

depiction of Stephen. For tradition is not what *prevents* historical change, but rather, as I have argued throughout this work, the very space through which historical change emerges. And that tradition is present in *Ulysses* in those literary materials upon which Joyce works, in, that is to say, the novel's formal transformations of a host of inherited styles.

Postcolonial critiques of Joyce have conceded too much, then, by imagining an imperial structure so totalizing in its determinations that it can fix Irish interiors with as much success as it controls their external lives. Furthermore, in its emphasis on historical blockage, this form of criticism ends up replicating the grand European narratives upon which those earlier Marxist dismissals were built, narratives that tended to read Ireland's divergence from the standard path of European development as pathology. Instead, Joyce develops Ireland's simultaneous difference from and participation in the larger community called Europe, by disclosing those agencies present within a situation of colonial dependence.

In what follows, I will demonstrate the common ground between these two critical tendencies and locate them within the binary of authenticity/ collaboration constitutive of Stephen's consciousness. I will then discuss the mythic method in light of Ireland's peripheral condition before demonstrating Joyce's careful construction of agency from within those discourses of religion and imperial commodity culture that seem most to deny it. Ultimately, I see Joyce presenting utopian hope and political discouragement in equal measure, achieving something like the archeology of the future Jameson calls for in my opening epigraph: the revelation of the utopian tendencies latent in present conditions.

POTATO SOAP

It might be argued, following [Roberto] Schwarz, that an obsessive "experience of incongruity" – occasioned by the fact that dependent cultures are always interpreting their own realities with intellectual methodologies created somewhere else and whose basis lies in other social processes – is indeed a typical character of postcolonial societies.   – Joseph Cleary, ("Misplaced Ideas?" 107)

When Leopold Bloom enters Nighttown – "as much the world of an imperialized experience as it is of the unconscious" – he is nearly knocked down by young Jacky Caffrey, chased by his brother Tommy.[7] Reeling from the encounter, Bloom checks to make sure he has not been pickpocketed: "(*Shocked, on weak hams, he halts. Tommy and Jacky vanish there, there. Bloom pats with parcelled hands watch, fobpocket, bookpocket, pursepocket, sweets of sin, potato soap*)" (*U* 428). A watch, a penny dreadful, a potato, and a bar of soap: the items in Bloom's pockets are chosen with typical Joycean care, for each embodies some aspect of Ireland's colonial situation. The watch, that ubiquitous symbol of modernity, coexists with the fetishistic potato – "poor Mama's panacea" (*U* 427) – that Bloom carries for good luck, an "emblem and relic" both of his mother and "of that natural economy which, with the Irish potato famine in Ireland in 1845–47, had been laid open for dismantling with one excruciating jolt."[8] Then there is the novel, *Sweets of Sin*, purchased for Bloom's wife Molly and reminiscent of the style of "Nausicaa," the chapter in which we met both the feuding Caffrey brothers and that almost entirely commodified "specimen of winsome Irish girlhood," Gerty MacDowell (*U* 340). Finally, there is, one more time, that soap, which will take center stage later on in the chapter:

([Bloom] points to the south, then to the east. A cake of new clean lemon soap arises, diffusing light and perfume.)

THE SOAP

We're a capital couple are Bloom and I;
He brightens the earth, I polish the sky. (*U* 431)

The soap has, here, as Stephen Dedalus might say, achieved its epiphany. Revealing itself to be a thing "abounding in metaphysical subtleties and theological niceties," the soap rises above the surrounding world via Bloom's religious conjuration.[9] When it does, announcing, according to Garry Leonard, "the dawn of commodity culture," it delivers a message in the form of an advertising jingle uniting subject and object under the sign of capital.[10] Occurring within a chapter devoted to Bloom's subjective fantasies, the soap's song suggests the way private desire is constructed by the world of commodities, just as Molly's desire is instigated by the commodified narrative of a mass-market paperback.

The commodity relation in Nighttown, however, has a specificity that transcends the simple advent of modernity implied by Leonard's phrase, for in its paring with the potato, it represents a British imperial counterpart to the pre-modern Irish talisman. This relationship seems, at first, to be a historical one: Pianola replaces barbitos; soap replaces potato. Yet, as with Pound, Joyce is not suggesting that the pre-modern world has vanished. Rather, he is showing its persistence in a way that is specific to what David Lloyd has called Ireland's "anomalous state": its simultaneous existence in the so-called first and third worlds of economic development.[11] From this perspective, the "backwardness" of Ireland is a "deliberately engineered subaltern economic status," and as such, is the very condition of Irish modernity.[12]

Marxist criticism, particularly of the early twentieth century, has often been unable to address this particular form of modernity, a blindness we can see operative in Georg Lukács's famous dismissal of modernist literature.[13] Lukács's description of modernism's two main tendencies – the reduction of "detail to the level of mere particularity," and the "gradual revelation of the human condition" – seems, obviously enough, derived from Joyce's method.[14] "Technique," Lukács continues, becomes "something absolute," a formal choice reflected in the presentation of a heroic subject who stands outside of the social order: "[The hero] does not develop through contact with the world; he neither forms nor is formed by it."[15] As with Kafka, the counterpoint to Joyce is Thomas Mann. "The world of Thomas Mann," Lukács writes approvingly, "is free from transcendental reference: place, time and detail are rooted firmly in a particular social and historical situation."[16] Now, these conclusions are surely remarkable. *Ulysses,* for instance, is so rooted in place that Joyce once famously boasted one could reconstruct Dublin from its pages.[17] And *A Portrait of the Artist as a Young Man* quite clearly presents the arrogance of a young artist hoping to form the world, even as it displays, in intimate detail, the way that artist is, in fact, formed by the world in which he lives.[18]

More to the point, however, is that Joyce's world is not one that could be said to be "free from transcendental reference" and the world of consumers and petty-bourgeoisie he presents is "rooted firmly in a particular social and historical situation": that of Ireland under colonialism. The failure of a certain form of Marxist criticism to do justice to Joyce's writing represents, then, the general problem with applying "cultural histories" derived with "a metropolitan European or Euro-American capitalist history in mind" to the Irish situation.[19] For, as Joe Cleary has argued, "Irish history ... evolved in ways that did not conform in some decisive respects to developments in the metropolitan cultures" that inform the work of such major Marxist critics as Lukács and Fredric Jameson.[20] Rather, Ireland evolved in a condition of peripheral dependence, and to "be peripheral is precisely to be compelled to develop within constraints, sets of forces, and agendas – economic, political, cultural, intellectual – that have largely been prescribed or conditioned by developments in the metropolis."[21] In the Irish colonial context, then, the developments of the imperial center function as a kind of "transcendental reference" against which Irish difference is continually measured, a dilemma replayed in those Marxist critiques of *Ulysses* that are only able to notice Joyce's deviation from the standard narratives of capitalist development. It is in light of Ireland's peripheral condition that I wish to read Joyce's mythic method, not simply as a formal device or a "scientific discovery," but as part of the novel's presentation of both "Ireland under British domination" and "the whole occident under the domination of capital" (*LE* 407).[22]

As we have already seen, one of the forms of this domination is consumer culture, whose characteristics, according to Rosalind Williams, are "a radical division between the activities of production and of consumption, the prevalence of standardized merchandise sold in large volume, the ceaseless introduction of new products, widespread reliance on money and credit, and ubiquitous publicity."[23] It is easy enough to locate these items in *Ulysses*, a text that virtually teems with commodities and advertisements as a range of critics have shown.[24] *Ulysses* also quite clearly displays a social world with a wide gap between production and consumption, reflected in the novel's characters, whose days are organized less by labor than by food and drink. Consumption, however, as Enda Duffy has noted, takes on a different valence in the periphery where "the pleasure of consumption is always overshadowed by . . . explicit evidence of exploitation."[25] For the commodity itself "is likely to have been imported from the imperial center." Thus, "the relationship that the fetishized commodity comes to mediate . . . is that between the native consumer and the alien producer," a fact that explains, for Duffy, the violence of "Circe," which demonstrates that the native consumer must be "coerced into being a consumer."[26]

The native consumer's response is to devise a range of strategies for resisting this interpellation, and while Duffy's account of these responses is compelling, his overall framework remains trapped within a binary of resistance and collaboration Joyce's novel refuses. This claim can be substantiated by a return to "Circe's" potato soap, which represents not merely the existence of the pre-modern alongside the modern, but rather the persistence of the pre-modern *into the very structure of the modern itself.* For the soap in Joyce's chapter is as much fetish as Bloom's talisman, and it was precisely in its role as fetish that the soap, as recent criticism has demonstrated, was mobilized by imperial narratives of progress.[27] Indeed the Unilever Corporation's motto – "Soap is civilization" – suggested the commodity as the agent of civilizational progress, as if consumption could lead directly to culture.[28] This tremendous hyperbole arose, according to Anne McClintock, from a culture of fear, which saw the presence of "racial deviants" in "the heart of the modern, imperial metropolis" as the sign of racial degeneration – itself the unavoidable inverse of Victorian narratives of progress.[29] One of the curious side effects of this fear was the prevalence

of advertisements showing how "Victorian cleaning rituals were ped-
dled globally as the God-given sign of Britain's evolutionary superiority."
Invariably depicting a native entranced by a magical bar of soap, these ads
invested the soap with "fetish powers," ultimately making the commodity
itself the hero of imperial expansion.[30]

Thomas Richards analyzes one such ad – a Pears' Soap advertisement
from 1887 – in detail:

> It depicts a group of "dervishes" looking at a legend, "PEARS SOAP IS THE BEST,"
> chalked on a rock ... This advertisement presents the "dervishes" as illiterate sav-
> ages who cannot appreciate the value of things, so much so that the British do
> not even bother to make the inscription intelligible to them ... What separates
> [this ad] from earlier advertisements of its kind is its claim, writ large above the
> scene, that the commodity offers "THE FORMULA OF BRITISH CONQUEST."[31]

"The real significance of this claim," Richards continues, lies "in the fact
that it was used by English imperialists of the 1890's to represent commodities as a magic medium through which English power and influence
could be enforced and enlarged in the colonial world."[32]

With these ads, we are back to the contrast between the temporality
of imperial progress and what McClintock calls the "anachronistic space"
of the primitive native, who will become civilized by becoming British,
or at least by purchasing British commodities.[33] Among these anachronistic natives, as Vincent Cheng and others have discussed in detail, were
the Irish, typically caricatured as Neanderthals, a kind of missing link
between the ape and the civilized Brit.[34] Despite the persistent vision of
cartoonists such as John Tenniel and Thomas Nast, however, the Irish
were not actually a different race from the British. The difference between
the two groups was, therefore, most often articulated as a distinction
of culture, between what Matthew Arnold saw as the sentimental Celt
and the practical Saxon, a distinction which was then replicated by the
Irish Revival.[35] Joyce's linkage of the soap and the potato – fetishes of the
British and the Irish respectively – suggests, then, the similarities between
the imperial narrative of progress, embedded in the commodity, and the
Irish nationalist response that idealized a lost world of Celtic purity, and
in doing so critiques the binary of resistance or coercion upon which
critics such as Duffy rely. Resistance can only come from within the
structures of domination that constitute Irish life, not from the outside.
Purity turns, in Joyce, into hybridity, but this hybridity is not, simply,
a happy fact of the postcolonial condition. Rather, it is the direct result
of the forms of domination under which the Irish live. The nationalist

vision of a pure race – whether British or Irish – effaces this domination and the resultant hybrid subjects it creates. Nationalism, that is to say, threatens to become as ahistorical as the cosmopolitanism it was meant to replace.[36]

What we must attempt to do, when we read Joyce, is to avoid the choice between potato and soap – between, let us say, authenticity and collaboration – *as well as* that between a detached cosmopolitanism, on the one hand, and the shared ground of Irish and British nationalisms on the other. Instead, we find Joyce attempting to answer Patrick McGee's great question: "How does one formulate a counter-hegemonic vision within the framework of hegemonic culture?"[37] The answer, for Joyce, is to work with the tools of hegemony themselves, in his case, the commodity, Catholicism, and the mythic structures of imperial and Irish nationalism, this last reflected in Joyce's mythic method.

As I will show, this method is not, as Eliot would have it, a "way of controlling, ordering, of giving a shape and a significance to the immense panorama of futility and anarchy which is contemporary history."[38] Nor is it, as Pound believed, "part of Joyce's mediaevalism and ... chiefly his own affair" (*LE* 406). Instead, *Ulysses's* formal comparison of the minutiae of Dublin in 1904 with *The Odyssey* tracks the similarities and discontinuities between the national and the cosmopolitan, between Irish particularity and what Horkheimer and Adorno called "the basic text of European civilization."[39] As in *Dialectic of Enlightenment*, Joyce's use of *The Odyssey* suggests a critique of those intertwined concepts of nostalgia and progress, seen in Joyce to be the provenance of Irish and British nationalisms, respectively. In contrast, Joyce suggests that any truly free Irish future must work within the given conditions of Irish daily life, and yet, at the same time, cannot abandon the utopian hopes represented by what Timothy Brennan has called the "national longing for form."[40]

Like Pound, then, Joyce sets out with Odysseus, but unlike the American poet, he grounds his cosmopolitan journey within a specific cityscape: that of Dublin under British rule. And like Eliot, Joyce is interested in showing the multiple determinations that constitute the lived space of the modern metropolis, but he betrays none of Eliot's fear of degeneration and his city is not the site of an alienated subjective consciousness. Rather there is, in Joyce, an overwhelming sense of the subject's social constitution, a deep awareness of the condition of living as the "servant of two masters," which emerges from the specific experience of the periphery (*U* 20). For the metropole can remain blithely unaware of what is, for the periphery, an omnipresent fact: namely, the colonial relationship itself. Unlike Eliot, then, Joyce does not need to present those determining structures that are invisible in the metropolitan space. Rather, the task in the periphery is to locate some form of agency within an omnipresent relationship of dependence. This relationship is addressed both by Stephen's construction of an aesthetic out of the religious and imperial discourses to which he is subject, and by Joyce's mythic method, to which I shall now turn.

NOSTALGIA, PROGRESS AND THE MYTHIC METHOD

The central thesis of *Dialectic of Enlightenment* is summed up by its authors quite succinctly: "Myth is already enlightenment, and enlightenment reverts to mythology."[41] Expanding upon this premise, they present the book's animating paradox: "Enlightenment, understood in the widest sense as the advance of thought, has always aimed at liberating human beings from fear and installing them as masters. Yet the wholly enlightened earth is radiant with triumphant calamity."[42] Virtually the opening gesture of the book is a critique of progress, for, as Adorno remarks in *Negative Dialectics*, "no universal history leads from savagery to humanitarianism, but there is one leading from the slingshot to the megaton bomb."[43] What is not entirely clear at first, though, is *Dialectic of Enlightenment*'s equally strong critique of nostalgia. For the claim that Odysseus is "the prototype of the bourgeois individual," is not meant to relocate the origins of capitalism in ancient Greece.[44] Rather, the rereading of *The Odyssey* in terms of capital must be seen as a polemical move, a response to the idealizations of Greek culture that, in the early twentieth century, ran the intellectual gamut from fascism, through Heidegger's shepherds of Being, to Lukács's organic pre-modern past. *Dialectic of Enlightenment* offers, then, a critique of both progress and nostalgia – enlightenment and myth – and, in doing so, suggests that the two concepts are intertwined, the nostalgic ideal born out of a modern "consciousness suffering from the fissured state of the world and conjuring up a past unity out of its own depravations."[45] The relationship between the archaic and the modern – which Benjamin saw as central to commodity production and he and Adorno imagined as at the heart of their "shared work" – is here mobilized to critique what I have been calling imperial temporality.[46]

In *Ulysses*, this temporality is most obviously present in the shared ideology of British and Irish nationalism, each of which views history through the lens of an external determining structure, as in the famous comment of Mr. Deasy, Stephen's boss and an Orangeman loyal to the crown: "All history moves towards one great goal, the manifestation of God" (*U* 34). Stephen's response is telling:

Stephen jerked his thumb towards the window, saying:
– That is God.
Hooray! Ay Whrrwhee!
– What? Mr Deasy asked.
– A shout in the street, Stephen answered, shrugging his shoulders. (*U* 34)

Stephen is, of course, making a joke – a goal has just been scored in the hockey game outside – and his recent meditations on sport as a kind of warfare suggest a sinister interpretation of history's perpetual production of "force, hatred" and "the very opposite of that that is really life" (*U* 325). At the same time, however, Stephen has here transformed Deasy's religious telos into the banality of random occurrence, countering progress with chaos.

The unwitting accomplice of Mr. Deasy's narrative of progress is the nostalgia evinced by Irish nationalism, which also reads history through the imposition of a religiously derived narrative: that of the Jews in Egypt. The best example of this in *Ulysses* is the speech of John F. Taylor, recited from memory by Professor McHugh in "Aelous." Having just heard Gerald Fitzgibbon – who plays the part of the high priest admonishing Moses in McHugh's oration – speak against the Irish language, Taylor rose and addressed the crowd:

Great was my admiration in listening to the remarks … by my learned friend. It seemed to me that I had been transported into a country far away from this country, into an age remote from this age, that I stood in ancient Egypt and that I was listening to the speech of some highpriest of that land addressed to the youthful Moses.

. . . .

Why will you jews not accept our culture, our religion, and our language? …

But, ladies and gentlemen, had the youthful Moses listened to and accepted that view of life, had he bowed his head and bowed his will and bowed his spirit before that arrogant admonition he would never have brought the chosen people out of their house of bondage. (*U* 138, 139)

When the speech begins Stephen thinks "Noble words coming. Look out. Could you try your hand at it yourself?" (*U* 138). A mere two pages later he does, producing a kind of mini-*Dubliners* tale that deflates Taylor's rhetoric in much the same fashion as he had earlier countered Mr. Deasy's neo-Hegelian historical certainty.

Stephen's effort is called "*A Pisgah Sight of Palestine or the Parable of the Plums*" and it concerns "two Dublin vestals … elderly and pious" who "want to see the views of Dublin from the top of Nelson's pillar" (*U* 145, 141). Climbing up the 120 foot pillar, the ladies "settle down on their striped petticoats, peering up at the statue of the onehandled adulterer" which sits atop the column (*U* 144). Here they remain, spitting plums and gazing at the city. As might be expected, Stephen's story confuses his audience. Placed alongside his response to Mr. Deasy *and* the speech of John F. Taylor, however, we can see that Stephen is deflating both of these competing religious views of history, suggesting instead an interest in the formlessness of the everyday with its lack of immanent meaning. The similarity of Stephen's responses helps underline the similarity of the discourses to which he responds, demonstrating how the transcendent was marshaled for both Mr. Deasy's ideology of progress and the nostalgic nationalism that proceeds, as the title that accompanies Taylor's speech suggests, "**FROM THE FATHERS**" (*U* 139).

In his attempt to remain with the here and now, however, Stephen misses the way the turn to the transcendent was itself part of that here and now, and it is this fact that Joyce reflects in his mythic method, not just as a deflation of the various pieties of British and Irish nationalisms, but as a way of representing Ireland's peripheral situation, continually tracking its here and now against the seemingly transcendent structures of an imposed imperial culture. At one and the same time elevating the everyday and deflating the mythic, Joyce's turn to the archetypal marks a rejection of both the notion of progress – a choice for cyclical recurrence over historical evolution – and the nationalist dream of an unspoiled Irish past – in its deflation of that mythic past's supposed nobility. In doing so, Joyce has connected himself to Europe, not only in the choice of a Greek myth – rather than, say, a Celtic one – but also in the book's title, which is not, after all, *The Odyssey* or even *Odysseus*, but rather *Ulysses*. Embedded within this link between myth and history, then, is a third term: that of the cultural tradition. For *The Odyssey* does not come to Joyce directly, but rather through Dante and Tennyson, as indeed Greek culture itself comes through Rome and the Renaissance, themselves mediated by Walter Pater and a Victorian world that so consistently imagined itself as a latter-day Roman Empire. Here we can glimpse what Seamus Deane has called the "fictive nature of politics" – that is the way the realm of culture is mobilized to produce those famously imagined communities constitutive of the modern nation.[47] The mythic method allows Joyce both to give credit to the way these universals inform our mode of being in the world *and* to

suggest that they only reach us through the concrete history of the contemporary world's cultural traditions.

The European cultural tradition, then, is what mediates between the
world of Greek myth and that of early twentieth-century Dublin, and this
tradition is most obvious in *Ulysses*'s endlessly shifting style, itself a marker
of the competing discourses that condition our perception of the world.
These styles, however, are not simply the neutral domain of cultural mediation, but rather the most dramatic sign of the novel's artistry, the clearest indication of the constructing hand of Joyce the artist. Individual
agency is thus disclosed within the heart of the subject's social constitution. Furthermore, the multiplicity of style refuses to accord any one discourse a position of universality. As with Eliot, Joyce's cultural tradition
is the space through which individual transformations of the social order
are made legible. And as with Pound, the truth is individual, but in Joyce
this truth does not emerge from clarity of perception, from the fidelity
to the real achieved via the technically sound work of art. Instead, truths
emerge from social situations – from the specific discourses that structure each chapter – as they are reflected through the consciousness of a
producing subject.

Through the multiplication of social discourses, Joyce presents the inadequacy of any one perspective's ability to describe the totality of his social
order, even as the content of the novel demonstrates the way these various
discourses shape the daily life of its characters. Joyce's form emerges from
what we might call an Irish difference, one that replaces the totalizing
aims of an imperial English culture with the multiple determinations of
an Irish reality that is constitutively hybrid. No doubt this hybridity is a
feature of any culture, but the specific form Irish hybridity takes, as Joyce
makes clear, is the result of a relationship of domination whose elements
include both commodities and the very historical and cultural narratives
through which the Irish perceive their social world. Hybridity is not, then,
simply the neutral ground upon which both colonized and colonizer meet
as in, say, the work of Homi Bhabha.[48] *Rather the hybridity of the colonized
subject contains the structure of domination within its very form.*

We have already seen that the answer to this imposition cannot simply be the formlessness of Stephen's parable. Instead, Joyce is interested
in the form-granting of individual construction, something I have argued
is emphasized by the novel's style. Reframing McGee's question, then,
we can see the novel seeking to turn a hegemonically constituted consumption – the Irish subject's construction by imperial and religious
discourses – into a counter-hegemonic production, into the creation of

counter-hegemonic meaning out of the given circumstances. For just as Ireland's current predicament did not come into being of its own volition, so a new potentially free Ireland will not emerge on its own. Rather, it will require an agency that can be grounded in the given conditions of the Irish situation, one that refuses the false binary of authenticity and collaboration and finds a way to turn a reliance on received traditions into the production of new ones.

To understand this further, we must examine the various subjectivities through which Joyce represents the Irish colonial situation and their relationship to the commodity culture that is such a dominant part of that situation. In doing so, we will see the production of meaning disclosed within the most seemingly hegemonically conditioned subjects, a subjective process that Joyce will mirror in the revelation of the communal values that structure Dublin life. Furthermore, it is within this very national community that the seeds of Ireland's participation in the larger European community can be found. In making this argument, I will show that Joyce does not, as is often tacitly assumed, agree with the aesthetic theories of Stephen Dedalus. Rather, through the revelation of the inadequacy of Stephen's theories, he outlines his own aesthetic vision, demonstrating the path by which Stephen can ultimately become the writer of *Ulysses* itself.

CONSUMING SUBJECTS I: STEPHEN DEDALUS

"The fetish character of the commodity is not a fact of consciousness; rather, it is dialectical, in the eminent sense that it produces consciousness."   – Adorno[49]

"An esthetic image," Stephen Dedalus remarks in the final chapter of *Portrait*, "is presented to us either in space or in time … [it] is first luminously apprehended as selfbounded and selfcontained upon the immeasurable background of space or time which is not it. You apprehend it as *one* thing. You see it as one whole. You apprehend its wholeness."[50] Yet, when Stephen sets about attempting to *create* aesthetic images, they do not seem quite so separate from the world as he had hoped. Indeed, time and again Stephen comes up against the fact that the tools of his chosen art – words – are unavoidably enmeshed in a chain of meanings from which they can never fully detach themselves. Stephen's response to this fact is two-fold. On the one hand, he chastises himself for failing to produce his own language. On the other hand, he faults himself for infidelity both to the world he seeks to describe and to the words of the literary tradition he prizes.

Stephen's artistic aims, that is to say, embody the contradictions of Flaubertian realism. Simultaneously driven by the desire to write a book about nothing and the need for an absolute fidelity to the real, Flaubert, as we have already seen, imagined the artist as a God hiding behind his work, and, in this way, saw the novel as a form that transcended the tawdry bourgeois world it described.[51] Stephen repeats Flaubert's famous lines soon after describing the aesthetic image, and is immediately mocked by his friend Lynch:

The artist, like the God of the creation, remains within or behind or beyond or above his handiwork, invisible, refined out of existence, indifferent, paring his fingernails.
– Trying to refine them also out of existence, said Lynch. (*P* 215)

Lynch's rejoinder undercuts the grandeur of Stephen's phrase, even as a few pages earlier "[a] crude grey light ... and a smell of wet branches ... seemed to war against the course of Stephen's thought" (*P* 207). What Joyce shows, in these moments and through Stephen's struggles with language more generally, is that his poetic creations will always, necessarily, be dependent on the world of wet branches and crude light they seek to escape and that, furthermore, they can attain efficacy *only through this dependence.* Artistic construction, in Joyce, takes shape against a background of structural dependence embodied, at its largest level, in the imperial commodity relation.

Stephen, however, seeks to separate the work of art from the commodity, declaring that in aesthetic matters one must be careful "to know whether words are being used according to the literary tradition or according to the tradition of the marketplace" (*P* 188). In *Stephen Hero*, this same observation is developed at greater length: "Words are simply receptacles for human thought: in the literary tradition they receive more valuable thoughts than they receive in the market-place."[52] Despite this distinction in value, Stephen's aim seems to be to remove words from tradition itself, and in this way make them his own: "Soon Stephen began to explore the language for himself and to choose, and thereby rescue once for all, the words and phrases most amenable to his theory" (*SH* 26).

This goal, however, is not as easy as it sounds, for the very interiority Stephen seeks to express is itself permeated with the world he wishes to escape. Sitting in a lecture Stephen finds himself irritated at "the voice, the accent, the mind" of a fellow student "and he allowed the offence to carry him towards wilful unkindness, bidding his mind think that the student's father would have done better had he sent his son to Belfast to study and have saved something on the train fare by so doing" (*P* 193). No sooner is this thought described than it is disavowed: "That thought is not mine, he said to himself quickly" (*P* 193). Stephen has here simply parroted the form of disapproval appropriate to his fellow student's social type.

More damningly, this same inability to separate word from world is present in Stephen's many aborted attempts at artistic creation. Consider the moment when he first guesses that his friend Cranly has some sort of relationship with the object of his admiration, the mysterious EC. First we are told, in a more or less neutral style, of her movements: "She passed out from the porch of the library and bowed across Stephen in reply to Cranly's greeting" (*P* 232). Stephen notices a "flush on Cranly's cheek" (*P* 232) and sinks into thought, which inevitably returns him to EC's apparition, her movements now rewritten in Stephen's idiom:

> She had passed through the dusk. And therefore the air was silent save for one soft hiss that fell. And therefore the tongues about him had ceased their babble. Darkness was falling.
> *Darkness falls from the air*
> A trembling joy, lambent as a faint light, played like a fairy host around him. But why? Her passage through the darkening air or the verse with its black vowels and its opening sound, rich and lutelike? (*P* 232–3)

Stephen finds himself here in a characteristic confusion, one summed up succinctly in *Ulysses* by Martha Clifford's inadvertent error: "I called you naughty boy because I do not like that other world" (*U* 75). From where does Stephen gain pleasure? The world before him or the remembered words of Thomas Nash?

There is a third term, though – the past that produced those words – and Stephen's mind drifts back to "the age of Dowland and Byrd and Nash" (*P* 233). No sooner does this occur than he falls into despair. "What was their shimmer," he asks, "but the shimmer of the scum that mantled the cesspool of the court of a slobbering Stuart?" (*P* 233). In this phrase we can observe an important movement, as the "shimmer" first hovers between EC's eyes and the words used to describe her, before crash-landing into the context in which the poetic lines first took shape, the "court of a slobbering Stuart." The inability of words to leave their contexts behind is here used as a tool to undermine their efficacy. Yet, at the same time, these words continue to structure Stephen's thoughts, so much so as to produce in him the sensation of a memory associated with the historical context embedded in Nash's line: "And he tasted in the language of memory ambered wines, dying fallings of sweet airs, the proud pavan: and saw with the eyes of memory kind gentlewomen in Covent Garden wooing from their balconies" (*P* 233). In what sense, though, can Stephen be said to remember these Elizabethan scenes? Stephen himself is not sure, and so he rejects these thoughts: "That was not the way to think of her. It was not even the way in which he thought of her" (*P* 233). "Could his mind" he asks "then not trust itself?" (*P* 233). Even his memories seem structured by old phrases and the contexts they produce, phrases which, in a further twist of the knife, he has not even remembered correctly. For Nash spoke of brightness not darkness: "All the images [the line] awakened were false. His mind bred vermin" (*P* 234).[53]

The problem, once again, is two-fold, for Stephen desires both to express his spirit in "unfettered freedom" and to give an adequate expression to the world as it is (*P* 246). Thus, an encounter with a woman selling flowers had earlier called forth this meditation: "The blue flowers which she lifted towards him and her young blue eyes seemed to him at that instant images of guilelessness; and he halted till the image had vanished and he saw only her ragged dress and damp coarse hair and hoydenish face" (*P* 183). Forcefully turning his mind from abstraction to concretion, Stephen tries to avoid turning the woman's ragged dress into a symbol. He wishes, that is, to hold to the here and now. Yet, as we have already seen, the real world context of words – their value in the marketplace, their origin in the courts of slobbering Stuarts – troubles this desire for purity, whether of perceiving subject or perceived world. The most realistic text, like the purest form of expression, necessarily depends on other contexts for its articulation.

Aesthetic images are thus determined, in their very structure, by their social context and, crucially, this context is both that of the moments out of which they emerge, as well as the present-day contexts in which they attain their meaning. This last idea can best be illustrated by examining Stephen's disagreement with the Dean of Studies over the word tundish. Stephen has used the word tundish for funnel, much to the Dean's confusion, and the moment calls from Stephen the following famous meditation:

The language in which we are speaking is his before it is mine. How different are the words *home, Christ, ale, master,* on his lips and on mine! I cannot speak or write these words without unrest of spirit. His language, so familiar and so foreign, will always be for me an acquired speech. I have not made or accepted its words. My voice holds them at bay. My soul frets in the shadow of his language. (*P* 189)

The choice of words here is telling – home, with its suggestion of home rule, and the related mastery of religion and drink – and they situate the discussion of language, obviously enough, within the orbit of colonial rule. Furthermore, as Stephen later discovers, tundish is not an Irish term, but "English and good old blunt English too" (*P* 251). Why, then, does the Dean of Studies get to be right? Turning to the *OED* we find Stephen's realization substantiated, but we also learn that tundish has a "local" usage and a more restricted meaning than the general term "funnel." Irish and English, then, are placeholders for a distinction between the local and the universal, even as that distinction is itself grounded in an actual context, the power differential of teacher/student, colonizer/colonized. The difference between tundish and funnel is, we might say, of less importance than the overall framework through which such differences are articulated; the language available for that articulation is itself marked by the grounds from which it arises. Power relations are here shown to be embedded within the very words through which Stephen understands his social order. The world seems inescapable.

It is in this context that we can return to his doctrine of the epiphany, which refashions the language of both religion and commodity for aesthetic purposes, demonstrating the very historical embededdness it seeks to overcome. In traditional religious doctrine an epiphany is "[a] manifestation or appearance of some divine or superhuman being" (*OED*, sense 1). For Stephen, however, the epiphany, is, in its two key articulations, the liberation of the objects of the world and the revelation of an aesthetic image. The first definition is given in *Stephen Hero*:

> By an epiphany he meant a sudden spiritual manifestation, whether in the vulgarity of speech or of gesture or in a memorable phase of the mind itself ... He told Cranly that the clock of the Ballast Office was capable of an epiphany ... I will pass it time after time, allude to it, refer to it, catch a glimpse of it. It is only an item in the catalogue of Dublin's street furniture. Then all at once I see it and I know at once what it is: epiphany. (*SH* 211)

Epiphanies here fluctuate between subject and object, both a function of the subject's gaze and something seemingly latent within the object itself. It is this latter idea that Stephen develops. Working with three Aquinian terms – *integritas, consonantia,* and *claritas* – he presents a three-stage theory of aesthetic apprehension. First, "your mind ... divides the entire universe into two parts, the object, and the void which is not the object" (*SH* 212). Here the object is seen to be "one integral thing, that is *a* thing" (*SH* 212). The next stage is the recognition that the object is "in the strict sense of the word, a *thing*, a definitely constituted entity" (*SH* 212). Finally, he reaches the third quality, defined as *quidditas* or "the moment which I call epiphany ... when ... we recognize that it is *that* thing which it is. Its soul, its whatness, leaps to us from the vestment of its appearance. The soul of the commonest object, the structure of which is so adjusted, seems to us radiant. The object achieves its epiphany" (*SH* 213).

In *Portrait*, Stephen presents a similar theory, but with a change of emphasis from the object, to the perceiving/creating subject. Referring to the obscure third term *claritas*, Stephen again defines it as "*quidditas, the whatness* of a thing," only now this seems less a property of objects than of aesthetic images themselves:

> This supreme quality [*quidditas*] is felt by the artist when the esthetic image is first conceived in his imagination … The instant wherein that supreme quality of beauty, the clear radiance of the esthetic image, is apprehended luminously by the mind which has been arrested by its wholeness and fascinated by its harmony is the luminous silent stasis of esthetic pleasure. (*P* 213)

Here the epiphany seems wholly contained by artistic creation – it is a function of the artist's work, and is, fundamentally, static, in line with a theory of art that favors contemplation over the action excited by "improper arts" (*P* 205).

Now we have seen objects with souls before – in Marx's and Benjamin's ironic descriptions of the commodity – and Garry Leonard has picked up on this connection, arguing that "the object with a soul in Stephen's aesthetic theory is … a commodity."[54] For Leonard, this realization is meant to deflate Stephen's artistic pretensions, but this reading remains within the same paradigm as Stephen, one that oscillates between authenticity and collaboration, one that imagines context in the form of an Elizabethan cesspool and then uses that cesspool to invalidate the image born there. To be part of a commodity culture, however, means that one needs to confront the fact of commodification *as it structures both internal and external experience.* Thus, we need to read the relationship of epiphany and commodity through the key terms of Stephen's disquisitions: object and image. This means, on the one hand, confronting the object in all its whatness, as an object with its own properties rescued from the capitalist regime of endless exchangeability. On the other hand, it means recognizing artistic creation as the *production* of an image born from the world that yet manages, at the same time, to be distinct from that world.

Image and object, we might say, stand at the conjunction of subjects and objects *as they are structured by the world of reified commodities.* In its oscillation between subject and object centered theories of art, Stephen's theory reflects not so much the confrontation between these two modes, as the ground upon which they interact, something like Eliot's "immediate experience" out of which subjects and objects emerge. But this experience is, in Joyce, conditioned by the discourses of religion and commodity constitutive of Ireland's dual subjection and it is not to be wished away through the construction of an aesthetic that divorces itself from the world as Stephen would like. To rescue the "words and phrases most amenable to [one's] theory," is not, finally, to remove them from their context, but rather to engage with that context *as it is present within the very concepts denoted by those words and phrases*. In this way, agency is disclosed within the boundaries of commodified experience itself, not as something that rests outside its determinations. Surprisingly enough, it is through the character of Gerty McDowell that Joyce most clearly presents this lesson.

CONSUMING SUBJECTS II: GERTY MCDOWELL

No character in *Ulysses* appears more thoroughly commodified than Gerty McDowell, whose interiority dominates the first half of "Nausicaa." The word interiority, however, is misplaced for trying to answer "Nausicaa's" dramatic question – "who was Gerty?" – is harder than it seems, as both Gerty's interior and exterior seem to be the product of the commodities she consumes (*U* 340). Her entire body, for instance, is constructed out of women's magazines. Thus, we learn that "her hands were of finely veined alabaster with tapering fingers and as white as lemon juice and queen of ointments could make them" (*U* 340), while her eyebrows are "silkilyseductive" thanks to "Madame Vera Verity, directress of the Woman Beautiful page of the Princess novelette" (*U* 341), and although her physique is fragile, "those iron jelloids she had been taking of late had done her a world of good" (*U* 340).

Gerty's interior, too, is as filled with commodified narratives as her body is prepared with advertised commodities. This is why she is able to view Bloom – a forty-year old man masturbating on the beach – as a "foreigner" with a "pale intellectual face," an exotic stranger "more sinned against than sinning," lacerated with "wounds that wanted healing with heartbalm" (*U* 349, 350). We are, of course, meant to note the obvious folly of Gerty's perception, and yet no sooner is this point stated than we must immediately deal with the equally obvious fact that, for all its commodified form, this description of Bloom is not, in fact, false. Bloom *is* a kind of foreigner and his habits of mind suggest a curiosity about the world and an interest in intellectual pursuits. Furthermore, he has this very day been sinned against – not just by his adulterous wife, but also by various anti-Semitic Dubliners, most notably the Citizen in the previous chapter – and we have not observed any particular sinning on his part (except, perhaps, the sin of impurity committed here). What we see, then, is not that Gerty's pre-packaged narratives fail to accurately describe the real, for that real is itself various, presenting no definitive interpretation of its meaning. Instead, the real provides a range of details out of which its meaning can be built. What "Nausicaa" shows us is how Gerty's pre-packaged desires structure her apprehension of reality in such a way as to correlate her *experience* of that reality with these internal desires.

Gerty's consciousness cannot then simply be dismissed as false. Rather, her interaction with Bloom is "an expression of … society's fundamental way of structuring human relationship[s];" it has a determinate relationship to the world in which she lives, one reinforced by the chapter's style.[55] Indeed, our only access to these events is through Gerty's consciousness; our sense of the objectivity of the scene is, thus, coterminous with her subjective perceptions, and so these perceptions themselves attain a certain amount of objectivity. The chapter's style fluctuates *between* subject and object, as much a part of the external world as it is of Gerty's interiority. There is not, here, a confrontation between a subject and an object world that either forms or is formed by that subject. Rather there is, once again, a common ground upon which the two meet. Furthermore, this common ground is not only found between Gerty's thoughts and the chapter's flowery prose, but, crucially, in the mythic parallel itself. For Gerty is not the only one to see a noble hero in Bloom's disheveled appearance. *This is, in fact, the central conceit of the novel.* How, we might ask, can we distinguish between these two modes of apprehension: Gerty's and that of the mythic method?

The key is in the distinction between production and consumption. The problem is not that Gerty's narratives are false. Rather, the problem is that she has so readily acceded to them. Gerty has failed to understand that central Joycean insight: the fact that, in the words of Hugh Kenner, "people live in stories that structure their worlds."[56] It is only by understanding this fact that we are able to attain any purchase on reality by asserting some form of control over these stories. The Odyssean parallel is one such assertion; its virtue is in its very imposition as a subjective way of reinterpreting the given world that, at the same time, replicates one of the main structural formations of that world.

Gerty, we have said, lacks control over this imposition of hero onto Bloom as it is granted to her by commodity culture. When we turn, however, to the relationship between religious imagery and sexual desire present in the chapter, we can view her actions in much the same light as we have just described Joyce's method. The entire scene takes place against the background of a religious retreat whose devotions to the Virgin Mary are periodically audible. Sexuality is thus intermingled with religion, even as earlier the descriptions of Gerty's physique – her hands "of finely veined alabaster" and "the waxen pallor of her face ... almost spiritual in its ivory-like purity" (*U* 340) – partake of the iconography of the Virgin. Again we can easily spot the joke – an undermining of the virginity of the Virgin – but we must also attend to what is radical in this union. For in this linkage of religion and sexuality, Gerty manages to articulate her desire within the terms she has been granted, an articulation which is a kind of *aufhebung* of the virgin/whore split, at once preserving and transcending its terms.

Furthermore, in those same descriptions that link sexuality to religion, there is a third term – namely commodity culture, the products of the woman's magazines through which Gerty attempts to remake her body into the image of desirability. In fact, desire itself seems, here, to be structured by that same commodity culture and so the primary opposition is less that of religion to sexuality and more one between religion and capitalism, an archaic/modern pair with extreme relevance for turn-of-the-century Ireland. The Irish, Joyce here suggests, are as much passive consumers of religious narratives as they are those of consumer capitalism. And each can be mobilized against the other, for just as Stephen's discussion of the epiphany used the conceptual force of religion to resist the reification of imperial commodity culture, so the desires unleashed by capital here confront the physical repressions associated with religious doctrine.

With the similarities between Stephen and Gerty we can see that the situation of the Irish transcends the seemingly stark divisions of gender and subject position. The counter-hegemonic process is structurally the same, whether one is a budding artist or a lovelorn teenager. In each case one must overcome the false binary between authenticity and collaboration, locating agency within the very structures of hegemonic control that seem most to prevent it, mobilizing the transcendent as a critique of the everyday and the everyday as a critique of what would transcend it. Irish community is, finally, to be found in the colonial situation itself, for all of the Irish are, like Stephen and Gerty, the servants of two masters.

By way of conclusion, then, I would like to turn to the communal structures that Joyce highlights in *Ulysses*, which will ultimately lead me back to the novel's form. For Joyce locates, within the Ireland of his day, certain utopian tendencies that he hoped would transcend both the colonial state from which he fled and the nationalist state he saw coming into being. To examine these tendencies I will turn, first, to "Wandering Rocks," before concluding with the novel's final sections.

COSMOPOLITAN IRELAND

"Wandering Rocks" is what Joyce called an *entr'acte*, a pause in the action that also marks a turn from the largely subjective determinations of the novel's first eight chapters to the objective structures of the remainder of the book.[57] Composed of eighteen short vignettes followed by a recapitulation of the previous scenes, the chapter is structure by two related journeys. The first is that of "The Superior, the Very Reverend John Conmee, S. J." (*U* 214); the second the viceregal calvalcade containing "William Humble, earl of Dudley," his Lady, and other prominent representatives of the British government in Ireland (*U* 246). Church and state – Rome and England – are shown here moving through the land they jointly rule. As is well known, Joyce's composition of this episode reached remarkable heights of meticulousness, maps of Dublin lined with different colored pens allowing him to mark precisely the moments when his characters would intersect with either of these two ruling forces. At the same time, however, this pinnacle of the novel's fidelity to the real is marked by two curious facts. The first: there was no viceregal procession on June 16, 1904. It is one of the few public events invented by Joyce, a fact that suggests a strong desire to represent the Irish in relation to both their imperial and religious masters. The second concerns the Odyssean parallel. In *The Odyssey*, the "Wandering Rocks" is not actually an episode at all. Rather, it is a peril avoided, a non-adventure, and surely part of the joke of Joyce's chapter is the way in which this procession fails to organize the polity in any unified manner and so is also a kind of non-adventure.

This fact, however, does not suggest, as Michael Tratner has argued, that the viceregal cavalcade is merely "a passing perception, something seen by all, but only one among many sights ... one institution that intersects with other institutions in many ways."[58] Instead, the very fact that Joyce takes the time to note such a range of reactions – and particularly those reactions that are not reactions, such as the "salute of Almidano Artifoni's sturdy trousers swallowed by a closing door" with which the chapter ends – suggests the presence of some more determinate relation to empire (*U* 249). The empire might not organize all of Dublin into a united polity, but it is a presence that requires some form of response; it is a point against which all of Dublin feels required to place itself. Some social institutions, we might say, are more determining than others.

Furthermore, the other salient formal device of the chapter – its repetition of certain scenes to illustrate the simultaneity of the characters' actions – suggests, in its emphasis on temporal and spatial continuity, the existence of all the characters in the shared communal space of the city, even as it suggests the multiple ways these citizens inhabit that city. The focus of the chapter, then, is not on the perceiving subject – we are not in the world of the *flâneur* – but rather on this communal space itself, on Dublin, crossed as it is by church and state. In this way "Wandering Rocks" manages to suggest both the objectivity of certain facts of Dublin life, while maintaining the freedom of individual response. The state is not so much one institution among many, as it is – along with the church – the background of time and space against which the multiple citizenry of Dublin takes shape. Church and state structure the lived reality of Dublin, but the ways in which they do so are as multiple as the citizens themselves.

The movement begun in "Wandering Rocks," whereby objective context takes precedence over subjective intention, is brought to its fruition in the novel's final chapters, where Joyce finally presents us with those events toward which the entire novel has been moving: the meeting of Stephen and Bloom and Bloom's homecoming. Instead of dramatizing these scenes, Joyce buries them within an avalanche of linguistic ingenuity, in chapters widely considered to constitute the dissolution of individual identity.[59] Thus, "Eumaeus" replaces narration with cliché, "Ithaca" speaks in the language of objectivity itself, and Molly's flowing monologue and ringing affirmations seem to present us with the novel's culmination: a subject without history, a betrayal without judgment. What these chapters represent, however, is not quite the destruction of the subject in favor of a world affirmed without critique. Rather, they demonstrate the overcoming of the individualistic subject by a subject communally constituted.

"Eumaeus," as I have suggested, is written in the language of cliché. As W. J. McCormack has demonstrated, the word cliché originates from print culture and thus describes "a production of language which is increasingly removed from the individual's control."[60] The language of "Eumaeus," however, is cliché of a particularly odd sort, for the loss of control it depicts is not, simply, the result of the rigidity of the received idioms through which the subject must express him/herself, an idea that would return us to Stephen's desire for pure expression. Rather, error in "Eumaeus" emerges through the chapter's most characteristic device: the misplaced modifier.

Typically these misplaced modifiers oscillate between Stephen and Bloom, as in the opening sentence: "Preparatory to anything else Mr Bloom brushed off the greater bulk of the shavings and handed Stephen the hat and ashplant and bucked him up generally in orthodox Samaritan fashion, which he very badly needed" (*U* 599). To understand how this form of language works, I would like to develop an insight gained from Nicholas Brown. For Brown, the error-language of "Eumaeus" forces the reader to construct the imaginary sentences at which the text was aiming. "By wallowing in a degraded language," Brown argues, "a language that must be negated before its content appears, 'Eumaeus' attempts to recover, from within the safety and complacency of an utterly reified language, the shock" of Bloom's desire to connect with Stephen.[61] Thus, pursuing Brown's line of thinking, we can see how the chapter's opening sentence requires us first to recognize the attribution of need to Bloom as a mistake, before realizing the greater truth this mistake reveals: Bloom's need to play the Samaritan is stronger than Stephen's need for his help.

A similar process occurs later in the chapter when we find Bloom offering a critique of Mulligan and then searching Stephen's face for a response: "The guarded glance of half solicitude, half curiosity, augmented by friendliness, which he gave at Stephen's at present morose expression of features did not throw a flood of light, none at all in fact, on the problem" (*U* 607). Again, for Brown, what is important here is the revelation of Bloom's need within a language so error-ridden as to seemingly preclude the expression of anything quite so intimate. What interests me, however, is less the truth content that can be rescued from error than the way the chapter's language produces meanings in excess of a relatively clear subjective intention. This excess is not simply a product of the objective structures of language, but rather occurs *through the subject's own deformations of that language*. Subjectivity, that is to say, leads beyond itself. What we find with the chapter's consistently misplaced modifiers is not just, or even primarily, subjective error but rather the possibility that multiple subjects might inhabit the linguistic position the narrating subject seeks to occupy. What the error-ridden language of the previous quotations discloses is that the common ground Bloom so movingly desires to find with Stephen *already exists*. Thus, in the above passage, as the "flood of light" oscillates between Bloom and Stephen, it becomes less important to locate which character will actually be able to illuminate the problem of Buck Mulligan. Instead, what is important is the hesitation itself, as knowledge emerges not from one subject or another, but from the space the two create together, a space that virtually defines the language of "Eumaeus" as it floats from subject to subject oscillating between the errors of subjective intention and the rigidity of objective structure. Community in Ireland is as much linguistic as it is conceptual.

Ulysses, that is to say, continually emphasizes the way communal structures of meaning are latent within the imposed discourses of language and culture, church and state, commodity and religion. Furthermore, it is from within these discourses themselves that the Irish generate the meaning of their social world. Thus as, C. L. Innes argues, the effect of *Ulysses*'s wealth of particular detail – details that would only be legible to a citizen of Dublin circa 1904 – is "not to make those sections meaningless to those who do not share the knowledge of Irish place and history; it is rather to create an awareness among Irish readers of a shared knowledge and history, over which they have authority and mastery, and which non-Irish readers must be taught."[62] *Ulysses* thus embodies and creates a sense of community around a particular form of "Irishness," one structured not around blood, but rather around shared cultures and public spaces, the kernel of truth present in Bloom's blundered definition of the nation: "[T]he same people living in the same place" (*U* 323).

At the same time, *Ulysses* addresses a different community, one that learns about Ireland through its reading of the novel. *Ulysses*, that is to say, is one event in the emergence of Ireland onto the international stage. It is, we might say a bit hyperbolically, itself a step out of Irish periphery. There are, then, at least two broadly defined reading communities for the book: Irish and non-Irish, local and "universal," national and cosmopolitan. Each of these communities emerges from Joyce's distinctive combination of transcendental reference and local detail, two moments of the way subjects inhabit the spaces in which they live. Crucially, these two moments are present within Irish reality itself, for a colonial country is, in some important sense, *always already* international, constructed, in the Irish case, via England and Rome. Cosmopolitanism, then, is present within the very heart of the nation itself. And this nation was itself coming into being as the novel was written, even as the city it depicts was being destroyed.[63] In its preservation of a city that had already passed away, *Ulysses* preserves a kind of alternative Dublin, one that has not yet become the Irish Free State from which Joyce distanced himself. If history is, in Blake's impatient phrase, "fabled by the daughters of memory," Joyce seeks to fable it differently (*U* 24). In his fable, the heroes are hybrid: a Hungarian Jew and a woman from Gibraltar.

Here we can return, at last, to the central event of the novel: Molly's infidelity. It represents, as I have already noted, a burlesque on that favorite theme of Irish history – shared by the Citizen and Mr. Deasy – the perfidy of women. Bloom, however, does not slaughter the suitors, but seems rather to suffer passively through Molly's actions, a fact that has led some critics to suggest that the book's ethics lie in this resignation. Yet, if there is an ethic here, it cannot be based on either Bloom's resignation or on the free-flowing desire of Molly's monologue, each of which would simply be another version of the denial of agency I have spent the bulk of this chapter critiquing. Instead, I would argue, Bloom's refusal to police his wife's sexuality rejects the mutual imbrication of racial and gendered discourses characteristic of the nationalist ethos of purity. It is, finally, a refusal to replicate the colonial relationship within his domestic space, a relationship Bloom refers to in "Eumaeus" through the revealingly oxymoronic phrase "mutual superiority," advocating instead "mutual equality" (*U* 629).

It is this mutuality that Joyce discloses at the end of the novel. Present linguistically in "Eumaeus," it is replicated by the object language of "Ithaca," a chapter modeled, as Hugh Kenner has shown, as much on the Catholic catechism as it is on Bloom's favorite periodical *Tit-Bits*, thus further reinforcing the way religion and commodity culture structure the world the Irish inhabit.[64] And it emerges, finally, in "Penelope" as the solution to a marital dilemma that is, simultaneously, an allegory for an Ireland that has continuously betrayed itself, and, at the same time, an ordinary marital dilemma.

Joyce's alternate version of the Irish nation is built as much upon the notion of mutuality as on the hybridity of his not-quite allegorical heroes, grounding its hopes of joining the community of nations in the fact that the community of nations is already present within Ireland. The dual frame of the novel – transcendental reference, local detail – returns once more as something immanent in the world Joyce was describing. *Ulysses* presents us with an imagined community, one that reflects a world from which it also seeks to preserve a critical distance. It represents, ultimately, a version of Jameson's "archeology of the future" – preserving a series of possibilities latent in a moment that had passed, pointing toward a future that had not yet come into being. The novel's dual temporality – its shifting reflections upon the recent past – is not, finally, a refusal of historical movement as such, but rather, a refusal to be satisfied with the historical movement that had occurred.

5

"Moments of Pride in England": Virginia Woolf and the forms of national subjectivity

BEAUTIFUL, BUT TOO VAST

The balance between the outer and the inner is, after all, a terribly precarious business. They depend upon each other with the utmost closeness.

– Virginia Woolf (*E* 3:109)

Clarissa Dalloway was clearly a woman who captured Virginia Woolf's imagination. Appearing most famously in the novel that bears her name, she is also a character in the short story from which that novel was born. Less celebrated is her presence in Woolf's first novel, *The Voyage Out*. The novel's focus is on Rachel Vinrace, who meets the Dalloways on board her father's ship, and although Clarissa and her husband Richard are relatively minor figures, they are important in the novel's architecture, insofar as Richard's kiss of Rachel marks a turning point in the plot, an early moment of sexual awakening tied, inescapably, to patriarchal social relations. The Dalloways, in this first appearance, are unrepentant imperialists, although this imperialism is consistently articulated through nationalist sentiments; for them there seems little distinction between the two. "Being on this ship," Clarissa declares, "makes it so much more vivid – what it really means to be English. One thinks of all we've done, and our navies, and the people in India and Africa, and how we've gone on century after century, sending out boys from little country villages ... it makes one feel as if one couldn't bear *not* to be English."[1]

It is particularly curious, then, to find Clarissa, several years and three novels later, advancing nearly the opposite position: "Love and religion! thought Clarissa ... How detestable, how detestable they are ... The cruelest things in the world, she thought, seeing them clumsy, hot, domineering, hypocritical, eavesdropping, jealous, infinitely cruel and unscrupulous ... Had she ever tried to convert any one herself? Did she not wish everybody merely to be themselves?"[2] How, we might ask, is it possible for Clarissa to support "sending out boys from little country villages" to "people in India and Africa" and yet wish that everybody could simply "be themselves"? The answer is obvious enough: these are two different novels, and so it makes little sense to construct imaginary continuities out of what are two distinct collections of words rather than two manifestations of some unitary person. The real question is not how can we reconcile Clarissa's seeming difference from herself, but rather why has Woolf decided here in *Mrs. Dalloway* not only to rescue Clarissa, but to make her the focus of the novel? For despite the shift in sentiment – Clarissa in 1928 providing a critique of the Clarissa of 1915 – Woolf did not substantially alter her character. Why would a writer generally prized for her critique of patriarchal culture spend so much time with characters such as Clarissa Dalloway who are, more or less, comfortably embedded within that culture?

Indeed, Clarissa stands in stark contrast to the heroine of *The Voyage Out*, who attempts, in the fictional South American colony of Santa Marina, to articulate some vision of "herself as a real everlasting thing, different from anything else, unmergeable, like the sea" (*VO* 75). The narrative, however, consists almost entirely of entanglements. Not only do the various British tourists with whom Rachel spends her time end up deftly re-creating English social relations in Santa Marina, but Rachel soon finds herself engaged to a man named Terence Hewet. "Our marriage," Terence declares, "will be the most exciting thing that's ever been done" (*VO* 281). Together they express "those beautiful but too vast desires ... for a world, such as their own world ... where people knew each other intimately ... and never quarreled" (*VO* 274). Inevitably, differences of opinion develop, creating distance rather than intimacy. "Perhaps I ask too much," Terence suggests, "Perhaps it isn't really possible to have what I want" (*VO* 285). For her part, Rachel "seemed to be able to cut herself adrift from him, and to pass away to unknown places where she had no need of him" (*VO* 285). What seems, at this stage of the novel, to be metaphor becomes all too real at the novel's end, as Rachel dies of an unspecified illness contracted in the South American jungle. Now, Terence realizes, they had "what they had always wanted to have, the union which had been impossible while they lived" (*VO* 334).

Critics have typically read Rachel's death as an indictment of the institution of marriage and the sacrifices it demands from its female participants, a version of the "too much" Terence felt he was asking of Rachel.[3] This idea is supported by Rachel's silent reverie after Terence's earlier outburst:

It seemed to her now that what he was saying was perfectly true, and that she wanted many more things than the love of one human being – the sea, the sky. She turned again and looked at the distant blue, which was so smooth and serene where the sky met the sea; she could not possibly want only one human being. (*VO* 285)

Seen through the closing lines of this passage, the novel seems to be a critique of the tyranny of patriarchal love, which prevents Rachel's inarticu-
late desires from bearing fruition. I want, however, to suggest a different
reading of these lines, for it is striking that when Rachel turns away from
Terence, she does so through metaphors of expansion: the "beautiful but
too vast desires" for a world of one's own, matched by the "unknown
places" to which she passes, the sea and the sky for which she longs.
Reading these desires within the context of a British colony suggests that
their expansiveness borrows something from the experience of empire.
The failure of the novel – the fact that Rachel's bold experiment to live a
life in opposition to her culture ends in death – might have as much to do
with the *form* of Rachel's desires as it does with the social order that would
prevent her from achieving their realization.

In fact, as I will argue below, *The Voyage Out* is as suspicious of Rachel's
need to be "different from anything else" as it is of the colonizing reach
of its patriarchal subjects. Critiquing Britain's imperialist expansion
seems to require, for Woolf, a critique of its analogously expansive subjects, whether that expansion takes the form of patriarchal domination
or an inexpressibly deep heart's core. Like Pound, then, Woolf seeks to
localize the falsely universalizing Western subject, but she cannot do so
by confronting that subject with cultural values that stand outside of it
in the manner of Pound's *Cantos*. For Woolf, as the daughter of empire,
seems to find it nearly impossible to distinguish engagement with other
cultures from domination. Instead, she imagines an England that will
combat its acquisitive impulses by rediscovering itself as local. The voyage
out, we might say, becomes the voyage in, as Woolf shifts her attention
from characters such as Rachel Vinrace, who desire to stand outside of
English society, to those like Clarissa Dalloway, Mrs. Ramsay, or the protagonists of *The Waves*, who have relatively secure places within it, even if
these places are also marked by discontinuity or what a Marxist vocabu-
lary would name contradiction.[4] Woolf, thus, presents a process similar to
the one I have located in Joyce's work, focusing her attention on the forms
of agency latent within even the most seemingly compromised members
of the British social system. And she will do so, like Eliot, by grounding
the unreal world she wishes to create within the real world that is before
her, revealing the common culture that underlies such seemingly disparate
figures as Clarissa Dalloway and Rachel Vinrace.

With this claim, we can begin to unfold what I take to be a dramatic
shift in Woolf's prose, from her first two novels, which revolve around
marriage plots and are relatively straight-forward in style, to her later

works, most of which rely on interior monologue and make a point of resisting the kind of dramatic events that structure the earlier works. Beginning with *Jacob's Room*, the emergent structure of feeling that occupies the *plot* of both *The Voyage Out* and *Night and Day* migrates into Woolf's *form*. A clue to the logic behind this shift comes from the end of *Night and Day*. Whereas *The Voyage Out*, as we have seen, ends in failure, *Night and Day* ends with a sense of possibility – albeit one laced with challenges embedded in Woolf's syntax – that points toward the project of the later novels. Here are Katharine Hilberry and Ralph Denham, the novel's newly engaged protagonists, contemplating their future:

She felt him trying to piece together in a laborious and elementary fashion fragments of belief, unsoldered and separate, lacking the unity of phrases fashioned by the old believers. Together they groped in this difficult region, where the unfinished, the unfulfilled, the unwritten, the unreturned, came together in their ghostly way and wore the semblance of the complete and the satisfactory. The future emerged more splendid than ever from this construction of the present. Books were to be written, and since books must be written in rooms, and rooms must have hangings, and outside the windows there must be land, and an horizon to that land, and trees perhaps, and a hill, they sketched a habitation for themselves.[5]

The process of crafting a unity out of cultural fragments is "laborious" and it takes place in "a difficult region" marked by a series of negations, each of which is present in a "ghostly way" and appears (although obviously enough, it is not) "complete and satisfactory." It is as if here, in all its incompleteness, we discover the *form* of a possible future that can be built out of the very incoherence of the present. Crucially, this future requires a habitation; it requires, above all, rooms and windows, land and trees, perhaps even a hill. Woolf, here, suggests something like the process I have located in *The Waste Land*; she seeks to make a currently unreal future into something real, concrete, habitable.

This future will not simply come about on its own, but rather will emerge from a laborious process requiring an agency capable of projecting the future out of a particular "construction of the present." Woolf thus lodges her abstractions in the everyday structures of the world we inhabit together. Her imagination, that is to say, is dominated by the local and the commonplace, the kitchen table that is the figure for Mr. Ramsay's philosophical endeavors, the shoes held out at the close of *Jacob's Room*, the party at the center of *Mrs. Dalloway*. Each of these moments demonstrates Woolf's investment in the way humans ground themselves in the object world and, further, how our grounding in the object world becomes one of the main ways we connect with each other. Reality emerges, for Woolf, from our coexistence in these local habitations.

Which is why Woolf never again, in a serious way, returned to the colonial background of her first novel, choosing instead to remain within the local context of United Kingdom.[6] Yet the lessons learned from *The Voyage Out* reverberate throughout her whole career, as Woolf retreats from the expansiveness of her earliest protagonists and attempts, instead, to "find palatable ways to express her affinity for England and to assert the value of English traditions."[7] Woolf, that is to say, is as invested in what *Jacob's Room* calls "the chasms in the continuity of our ways" as she is in the continuity disclosed by the "supreme mystery" that Mrs. Dalloway claims is "simply this: here was one room; there another"[8] (*MD* 124, 125). Indeed, this distinction between continuity and discontinuity is itself already contained in Mrs. Dalloway's comment where the emphasis seems to fall as much on the way one room turns into another as it does on their separation. In this hesitation, we find Woolf's understanding of a continuity that is itself marked by disjunction, built out of temporary meeting points that construct common ground out of a pair of shoes or a dinner to honor a fallen friend.

The force of this conception only becomes clear, however, when we consider the imperial context within which Woolf wrote, where to be British was also to be imperial, where indeed, the very constitution of the British subject – as countless postcolonial scholars have shown – was dependent upon events that took place elsewhere.[9] The British national subject was stretched across time and space and, as a result, constantly fashioning forms of continuity for itself as a counter to the discontinuities produced by empire. I will call this discontinuous subject the "free trade subject," permeable on all sides, open to all around it. Curiously enough this is the form of Woolfian subjectivity critics most commonly valorize. However, alongside the Woolf who deconstructs the "gigantic falsehood" of personality, we must also attend to the Woolf invested in tradition, whose "route towards innovation came not through rejecting the literary past but through drawing upon it."[10] Subjectivity in Woolf, that is to say, mirrors the back and forth of a British subject constituted by both its imperial adventures and its attempts to recenter itself within a continuous national history.

In what follows, I will describe Woolf's construction of an alternative genealogy for the nation, one motivated by a critique of the forms of subjectivity produced by the expansive appropriations of imperialism. Here, we can build upon the link between imperial and domestic discourses suggested by the structure of Woolf's first novel, for the critique of the subject that scholars have continuously located in Woolf's prose must be thought alongside the structures of empire that produce those subjects, a linkage best seen in Clarissa Dalloway, who, I will argue, represents the height of imperial subjectivity and, for that very reason, the best place for Woolf to begin her reimagining of the British nation. Bourgeois subjectivity itself – constituted by the desire to transcend the social order – becomes the barrier to the realization of the egalitarian community toward which Woolf's novels point. Instead, the beginnings of this community, the basis upon which Woolf feels it can be grounded, lie in the realm of national culture.

To make this argument, I will first examine the free trade subject in *Mrs. Dalloway* before turning to Woolf's investment in the literary tradition – in particular, her lifelong fascination with the travel voyages of Richard Hakluyt. Then I will return to *The Voyage Out*, a novel Woolf layers with references to Elizabethan literature, in order to understand how it critiques the too vast desires of its heroine by connecting them to the structures of the British Empire, both past and present.

FREE TRADE SUBJECTS

To think about oneself is, of course, to think about a great many other things and
people too;   – Virginia Woolf (*E* 2:75)

The relationship between the nation and the construction of the subject has recently come under productive scrutiny via the work of transnational studies. Laura Doyle, for instance, has claimed that "the fundamentally dialectical approach" of transnational studies "opens the way to a fresh consideration of the human or existential subject of history."[11] Drawing on both Merleau-Ponty and Frantz Fanon, Doyle develops a notion of the subject as fundamentally other-directed: "To be an embodied subject," Doyle writes,

is to be already double, to belong already to the world of others as well as self, and to arrive at one's own visibility and audibility together with others ... I move across this hinge of myself ... perceiving from the outside what I also sense from the inside, arriving at myself via an object-body that *belongs* to the realm of a material, onlooking orders of others.[12]

As this subject is constituted by its relation to others, so too is the nation: "Nations do exist, but as transnations or internations; they share a 'tilted' structure of orientation to other nations that is dialectical and dyadic yet also multiple and circumferential or horizontal."[13]

As this last claim demonstrates, Doyle is working within a critical tradition that has long recognized a relationship between capitalism, the bourgeois construction of the subject and the structure of the nation-state. The nation, as in Franco Moretti's influential account, helps to bound the limitless and potentially destabilizing energies of subjective transformation unleashed by industrial capital, while positing itself as the social space within which capitalism's abstract and isolated subjects find their common ground.[14] Self-legislating subjects are grounded in isolated nation-states; other-directed subjects are born out of transnations. This division, however, is immediately complicated when we consider the subject of empire. For an empire is certainly a kind of "transnation," but one that definitively lacks the equality and openness Doyle seeks from her embodied subjects. Indeed, imperial subjectivity might be just as implicated in the world outside itself as the transnational subject Doyle describes. Consider, in this light, the famous scene in *Mrs. Dalloway*, where we observe the novel's protagonist gazing at herself in the mirror:

How many million times had she seen her face, and always with the same imperceptible contraction! She pursed her lips when she looked in the glass. It was to give her face point. That was her self – pointed; dartlike; definite. That was her self when some effort, some call on her to be her self, drew the parts together, she alone knew how different, how incompatible and composed so for the world only into one centre, one diamond, one woman ... (*MD* 36)

This moment condenses in miniature Woolf's vision of subjectivity: a face composed to meet the faces that we meet, stitched together from innumerable possible selves into a temporary coherence for social purposes. Here we find Woolf the critic of the various ideologies that frame and construct subjects, prime among them gender, social position, and familial relations. Yet this way of stating the case is too simple, relying as it does on an untenable opposition between the social – conceived of as a realm of constraint and falsehood – and the individual, imagined as the place of freedom, flux, and possibility. Instead, Woolf presents us with a subject that is permeated, at all levels, with the social, and a social world that is, in turn, deeply subjective. Thus, we observe Mrs. Dalloway, walking through the streets of London, considering the fact that someday she will no longer be:

Did it matter that she must inevitably cease completely; all this must go on without her; did she resent it; or did it not become consoling to believe that death ended absolutely? but that somehow in the streets of London, on the ebb and flow of things, here, there, she survived, Peter survived, lived in each other, she being part, she was positive, of the trees at home; of the house there, ugly, rambling all to bits and pieces as it was; part of people she had never met; being laid out like a mist between the people she knew best, who lifted her on their branches as she had seen the trees lift the mist, but it spread ever so far, her life, herself. (*MD* 9)

Even after her death, Clarissa thinks, she will remain in the streets of London, just as her old friend Peter survives in her, and this presence will extend to those she will never meet; it will extend, that is to say, beyond the boundaries of personal relations to become something objective, external, present in the world as a force that transcends her particular subjectivity. Subjects in Woolf are complicated sites of interaction, composed of experiences that are present and not-present, histories both personal and transpersonal. They are permeable, open to the scoring of those famous atoms that "fall upon the mind in the order in which they fall" (*E* 3:33). The self-legislating subject of bourgeois liberalism – the ground of its own autonomous authority – is, for Woolf, "a gigantic falsehood," for "to think about oneself is, of course, to think about a great many other things and people too" (*E* 1:169, 2:75).

In contrast to the self-legislating subject, tied to the form of the nation-state, we find, in Woolf, what I have called the free trade subject, born out of the structures of the British Empire. Here we can turn to the late Giovanni Arrighi's magisterial *The Long Twentieth Century* and its description of Britain's "free-trade empire." Britain's rise to power, Arrighi argues, came from turning a "fundamental geopolitical handicap in the continental power struggle *vis-à-vis* France and Spain into a decisive competitive advantage in the struggle for world commercial supremacy."[15] Even as France and Spain were busy annihilating each other on the continent, Britain used its navy – a necessity for the defense of a small island nation – to seek out other markets, "channeling [its] energies and resources towards overseas expansion, while the energies and resources of its European competitors were locked up in struggle close to home."[16] The result was a tremendous influx of capital that could be sent back to invest in the colonial project: "The recycling of imperial tribute extracted from the colonies into capital invested all over the world enhanced London's comparative advantage as a world financial center."[17] London became the territorial mediation for capital that flowed in and out of Britain's ever-expanding imperial market and this continual flow became the basis of Britain's free-trade empire. Between "the mid-1840's to 1931, Britain unilaterally kept its domestic market open to the products of the whole world," thus creating "world-wide networks of dependence on, and allegiance to, the expansion and health of the United Kingdom."[18] British imperialism, that is to say, was constituted by the permeability of its borders and London was the center of this structure.

It is this permeability of national borders that is reflected in the permeability of Woolf's subject, a fact particularly evident when the subject is Clarissa Dalloway, strolling through the streets of an imperial London Woolf associated with cosmopolitanism. "To say that a man is a Londoner," Woolf writes in a 1905 article entitled "Literary Geography," "implies only that he is not one of the far more definite class of countrymen; it does not stamp him as belonging to any recognised type" (*E* 1:33). Thackeray, she continues, is rightly called a "cosmopolitan; with London for a basis he traveled everywhere; and it follows that the characters in his books are equally citizens of the world" (*E* 1:33). If Londoners can travel everywhere, so too is there "scarcely a ship on the seas that does not come to anchor in the Port of London in time" (*E* 5:275). This last quotation comes from an essay entitled "The Docks of London," one of six essays Woolf wrote for *Good Housekeeping* that, as Jeanette McVicker has persuasively argued, illustrate the constitutive relationship between the ships that arrive in the port of London, the dismal factories that exist on the river's banks, the streets of consumption within the capital, and the domestic homes where these goods are consumed.[19] Linking these essays to the description of Thackeray's characters allows us to see the way this imperial structure creates the indistinct subjectivity of the cosmopolitan Londoner.

It would be possible to rest here, declaring Woolf's simultaneous assault on the realist novel and its accompanying bourgeois subject as signs of her complicity with her imperial moment. There is more to the story than this, however, for there is another aspect of Woolf that is as invested in those fictions of continuity I have aligned with the nation as she is in their deconstruction. Consider, in this light, Septimus Warren Smith, the character Woolf "intended to be [Clarissa's] double" (*E* 4:549). Septimus is, of course, a shell-shocked WWI veteran. Having gone to France "to save an England which consisted almost entirely of Shakespeare's plays and Miss Isabel Pole in a green dress walking in a square," he returns unable to connect to his surroundings in any meaningful way (*MD* 84).

Perhaps the most dramatic rendering of Septimus's difference from those around him comes early in the novel in a scene depicting the passing of a motorcar, which seems to house "a face of the very greatest importance" (*MD* 13). "Every one," Woolf tells us, "looked at the motor car" (*MD* 14) and although most people here find "greatness" and think "of the majesty of England, of the enduring symbol of the state," Septimus sees a world "about to burst into flames" (*MD* 16, 15). No sooner does the crowd constitute itself around this empty symbol than a new entertainment emerges: A plane flies by writing words in the sky. These words, it soon becomes clear, are an advertisement. Septimus, however, thinks "they are signaling to me" (*MD* 21). He tries to shut his eyes, "[b]ut they beckoned; leaves were alive; trees were alive. And the leaves being connected by millions of fibres with his own body, there on the seat, fanned it up and down; when the branch stretched, he, too, made that statement. The sparrows fluttering ... were part of the pattern" (*MD* 22).

There are many ideas to tease out of this particular sequence. The first is how neatly Woolf has demonstrated the relationship between empire and capital, depicting a symbol of British national greatness transformed into an advert, even as England itself was shifting from direct conquest to economic forms of imperialism. The scene also vividly captures the empty center at the heart of political symbols – the barely glimpsed and never verified hint of "greatness" being enough to constitute a modern crowd defined by its open admiration of this cipher. Clearly, this is a critique of both the mob mentality of contemporary mass culture as well as of the threat of demagoguery built into the very structure of democracy. What is less obvious, however, until one attends to the role of Septimus in this scene, is the potentially positive quality of the community so constituted. For the defining feature of Septimus's reality is that there are no crowds to share in his visions. Septimus, like Clarissa before him, feels his subjectivity in the trees. He finds himself, as she does, connected with things outside of him, but the external world does not reflect this connection back to him. Clarissa, that is to say, has her own clearly defined supports and although these supports of class, nation, and gender come under critique in the novel, this critique can only extend so far. Boundless subjectivity can be *too* boundless and the image of this negative freedom is Septimus: Cut off from the world around him, he lives in a world of private meaning, which is to say, no world at all. *Septimus is the unbounded liberal subject, freed from its anchor in the common world of the nation.* The most injured subject in Woolf, then, is simultaneously the one most characteristic of the self-legislating bourgeois, unable to connect his impressions to anything resembling a common purpose, unable, that is to say, to totalize.

Septimus, it seems, has walked straight out of *The Waste Land* for his world is fundamentally unreal.[20] Importantly, he has been wounded into this condition by the state. Initially inspired by Shakespeare, he has now learned a dispiriting truth: "How Shakespeare loathed humanity – the putting on of clothes, the getting of children, the sordidity of the mouth and the belly! This was now revealed to Septimus; the message hidden in the beauty of words. The secret signal which one generation passes, under disguise, to the next is loathing, hatred, despair" (*MD* 86).[21] On the one hand, Septimus has uncovered the hidden secret of English nationalism – how it is built upon violence and repression – and so he has overthrown the pieties of an English nationalist tradition happy to send him off to slaughter in the battlefields of France. On the other hand, Septimus has nothing with which he can replace this tradition. Some grounding in the object world is needed, some form of tradition is necessary, although this tradition must not replicate the various injustices of a British nationalism intimately intertwined with imperialism. How to bound the free trade subject, thus reining in its acquisitive impulses, without returning to the pieties of a hypocritical nationalist tradition?

Woolf's answer to this question puts her squarely within the modernist recuperation of tradition I have been describing, for even though she is clear about the need for women writers to reject "the very form of the sentence ... made by men" for "it is too loose, too heavy, too pompous for a woman's use," she also advises a young poet to think of "yourself ... [as] a poet in whom live all the poets of the past" (*E* 5:32, 5:309). Despite the difference of both gender and generation that separates Woolf from her literary predecessors, she is, as a number of critics have argued, not nearly as isolated from the literary tradition as she at times seems to suggest.[22] Indeed, Woolf comes quite close to articulating the argument of "Tradition and the Individual Talent," where Eliot was determined to assert the relevance of the literary tradition for a present age that feels its distinction too acutely. Consider the following remarks from a 1916 essay entitled "Hours in the Library":

No age of literature is so little submissive to authority as ours, so free from the dominion of the great; none seems so wayward with its gift of reverence, or so volatile in its experiments. It may well seem ... that there is no trace of school or aim in the work of our poets and novelists. But the pessimist ... shall not persuade us that our literature is dead ... Whatever we may have learnt from reading the classics we need now in order to judge the work of our contemporaries ... But if we need all our knowledge of the old writers in order to follow what the new writers are attempting, it is certainly true that we come from adventuring among new books with a far keener eye for the old. (*E* 2:59)

The classics help us judge even works of such striking novelty that they appear aimless, and yet these same adventurous works allow for a deeper appreciation of the old. As in Eliot's famous proclamation, tradition becomes a way to understand one's present moment, not as a standard by which to be judged, but as a flexible set of texts that produce continuity out of discontinuity, that are created out of the dialectical tension between what they share and the ways in which they diverge. Literary objects are thus deeply historical for Woolf, via their connection to those that have come before them. Culture, for Woolf, as for all of the writers in my study, becomes a site of negotiation, as the quarrel over the meaning of the present takes place, in part, through a particular construction of the past to which it is indebted. Woolf thus demonstrates the persistence of the past as well as its adaptability.

We can see, then, why Woolf went to such pains to connect the imperial voyage of her first novel to those Elizabethan voyages of discovery she found so enticing in Richard Hakluyt's *Traffics and Discoveries*. Woolf's insistence that *The Voyage Out* be understood by way of Elizabethan England produces a complex set of relationships between England's literary past, its imperial present, and the possibilities for a different future. For with this gesture, Woolf simultaneously connects present-day empire to its origins, while also suggesting how a return to those origins might allow us to imagine an alternative historical tradition. As with Clarissa Dalloway, then, a transformation of England must emerge from within the nation itself, as Woolf attempts to discern what potential there might be in the subject's ability to engage with the world around her, even as she seeks to rein in the flux and immediacy of imperial subjectivity through what she once described as the "control" of tradition (*E* 4:278). Expressive subjectivity is, in this way, returned to its historical grounds. To pursue this claim further, I will now turn to Woolf's lifelong investment in Hakluyt.

CHRONICLES OF UNCERTAINTY

Although Woolf's work contains all the usual signs of empire – characters heading to or returning from India – she produced few explicit considerations of the topic. This general absence makes a short text like "Thunder at Wembley" all the more interesting. A signed piece in the *Nation & Athenaeum*, "Thunder at Wembley" is a review of the wildly popular British Empire Exhibition of 1924 and 1925. In what seems a foreshadowing of the structure of *The Waves*, Woolf's essay counters imperial display with the power of nature. "It is nature," she begins, "that is the ruin of Wembley" (*E* 3:410). No sooner is this asserted, however, than we find ourselves in one of Woolf's characteristically mixed descriptions of the middle classes. "They say, indeed, that there is a restaurant where each diner is forced to spend a guinea upon his dinner," Woolf declares, which is, apparently, shocking. Since there will obviously be no "champagne, plovers' eggs or peaches" at Wembley, there can be nothing worthy of such an amount. All that is likely to be for sale is ham and bread, which should cost the "mediocre sum" of "six and eightpence." This mediocre sum is then tied to all the mediocre objects on display, each of which leads Woolf to observe that "one can imagine better; one can imagine worse" (*E* 3:411). Neither opulent nor cheap, the exhibition disappoints through the poverty of its imagination: "But then, just as one is beginning a little wearily to fumble with those two fine words – democracy, mediocrity – Nature asserts herself where one would least look to find her – in clergymen, school children, girls, young men, invalids in bath-chairs" (*E* 3:411). Woolf's gaze turns here from the spectacle of imperial display to the crowds who are its intended audience. "How," she asks, "with all this dignity of their own, can they bring themselves to believe in that?" (*E* 3:412). Hardly straightforward up to this point, the essay here takes a curious turn, for this last remark, called a "cynical reflection, at once so chill and so superior," is attributed to a "thrush" let into the exhibition by "some grave oversight on the part of the Committee" (*E* 3:412). We are back to the natural world, the thrush in league with the "livid" sky that unleashes a downpour that ends Woolf's piece with an echo of its opening: "The Empire is perishing; the bands are playing; the Exhibition is in ruins. For that is what comes of letting in the sky" (*E* 3:413).

This contradictory text seems, on the one hand, to put its faith in the dignity of the crowd, while yet, at the same time, marking this democratic crowd as mediocre. Indeed, this linkage of the two terms aligns Woolf with her modernist peers in their simultaneously elitist and progressive critique of the emerging phenomenon of modern mass culture here constituted by its relationship to imperial display. But why should this perspective be attributed to the thrush? The complication of the piece comes, in other words, from its suggestion that although human nature and the natural world are aligned in their critique of empire, it is only the thrush that knows it. The crowd, for all its dignity, remains duped by imperial pageantry. In aligning the thrush with the sky, Woolf describes a form of consciousness in tune with the world around it; in connecting it to human nature, she suggests that this same form of attunement might be possible for the crowd as well. Nature points the way for a humanity that *might* realize its dignity by rejecting the mediocrity of imperial display but has not yet done so.

I would like to contrast this text's anticipation of an anti-imperial populace, to a much smaller crowd present in a 1919 essay called "Reading."

The essay begins in a library, but quickly Woolf travels, through one of her favorite books, Richard Hakluyt's *Principal Navigations, Voyages, and Discoveries of the English Nation*, into the distant past.[23] Referring to English merchants as "the vanguard of civilisation" (*E* 3:148), Woolf describes a scene that could have taken place in any of the numerous contact zones Hakluyt's book unveils:

> Here they are, three or four men from the west of England set down in the white landscape with only the huts of savages near them, and left to make what bargains they can and pick up what knowledge they can.... Strange must have been their thoughts; strange the sense of the unknown; and of themselves, the isolated English, burning on the very rim of the dark, and the dark full of unseen splendours. (*E* 3:147)

What Woolf's image emphasizes is the radical alterity of the situation in which the English find themselves, a difference that encourages self-reflection. Exploring the New World becomes as much a process of self-discovery as of territorial conquest, one urged on by unfamiliar surroundings.

This scene will replay itself in all of Woolf's writings on Hakluyt, which consistently praise his work for its "great theme of adventure and discovery" that reveals the "largeness of [Elizabethan] imaginations" (*E* 1:121).[24] As with Woolf's critique of the realist novel, this investment in Hakluyt clearly demonstrates her complicity with the project of empire, as her metaphorization of these imperial voyages as figures for imaginative exploration replicates the original colonial violence by sublimating it. Yet, as before, I am concerned less to argue that Woolf's feminist voyages build themselves upon colonial ones than to delve further into these voyages themselves. For when we actually look at Hakluyt's anthology, what is most striking about it is the vast ideological range of the texts it collects. Woolf's reading of the text as displaying a "largeness of imagination" is both naïve and yet, in some basic way, compelling as a reading of the colonial encounters Hakluyt's work includes.

Hakluyt's anthology, I want to suggest, offers something like what Myra Jehlen has called "history before the fact." Jehlen's interest is in a curious moment in John Smith's *General Historie of Virginia*, where he describes a coronation ceremony involving the Algonquian Chief Powhatan. The incoherence of Smith's story, according to Jehlen, calls into question the assumption that his text can be read solely as an ideological support for the imperial project: "The self-deconstructing tendency of the coronation passage reflects its historical indeterminancies. Smith is uncertain about his situation, meaning that he is neither sure what the story unfolding around him is, nor how to tell it."[25] Smith's narrative is thus understood as a "chronicle of uncertainty" written from a moment where "alternatives coexist."[26] In a similar fashion, Hakluyt's text is simultaneously complicit in the empire it will help bring about, and yet written from a moment that cannot know this historical telos.

Indeed, as many scholars of Hakluyt have suggested, the sheer variety of reports he includes – along with a range of other materials including ships' logs, lists of commodities and maps – tends to complicate his explicit aim for the volume: the promotion of a distinctly British empire that might compete directly with the Spanish. Its distinction was to be its exclusive focus on economics, for Hakluyt, as Richard Helgerson has argued, "thinks in economic terms," his most significant innovation being "his understanding of England as an essentially economic entity, a producer and consumer of goods."[27] At the same time, Hakluyt's reports "come from the partial experience of individual mariners and traders," making his text an important part of the modern ethos "that redefines truth not by tradition but by experience, not holistically but individually, each man his own author."[28] Hakluyt, that is to say, is a figure of an emergent bourgeoisie. Against the aristocrats, he speaks for the merchants, positioning them as key players in a national dialogue. Yet what is crucial is precisely the notion of "emergent," for the overall effect of the text is something like that created by modernist principles of montage: "For the most part, the interaction of these various discourses and of the different sorts of people responsible for them is left to happen in the reader's mind by the force of juxtaposition."[29] What is, in the backward glance of history, part of modernity's simultaneous turn toward individual experience and the potential testing of that experience against others, is perhaps more accurately apprehended without such telos as a kind of early modern perspectivalism, as a number of distinct views fail to add up to any consistent hegemonic narrative.

What is crucial for my discussion of Woolf is the sheer range of issues embedded in Hakluyt's anthology, which, in turn, opens up several different ways of assessing Woolf's lifelong interest in his work. On the one hand, the anthology brings together a variety of experiences and encounters with other cultures that are not easily subsumed into the hierarchies characteristic of the racialized imperialism of nineteenth and twentieth-century Europe. At the same time, the book suggests an incipient narrative of globalization, imagined by Helgerson as a version of the League of Nations – that is to say, an international system of nation-states conceived as equals and working in their mutual economic interest – but which we also know to be a continuance of the imperial project through the structures of international capital.[30] It seeks, that is to say, to create common ground out of a range of diverse experiences, even as it suggests how the experience of imperialism was part of a crucial moment in the shaping of the modern subject: the shift away from the authority of tradition to that of personal observation. Hakluyt's anthology thus stands at the beginning of a process Woolf hopes the spectators of "Thunder at Wembley" might finally see come to an end.

Woolf's recourse to Hakluyt is, then, an attempt to think back to empire's origins. Returning to this originary moment of English empire, Woolf imagines an alternative history, one laced with a range of possible futures. Hakluyt becomes, in this reading, one of those cultural resources the modernists continually mobilized to attack present day problems, for as Woolf notes in the essay "Reading," from which this discussion of Hakluyt comes, "one is tempted to impute to the dead the qualities which we find lacking in ourselves" (*E* 3:149). Importantly, what allows for this form of projection is precisely the relationship Woolf perceives between Hakluyt's moment and her own: "To know that it was all founded on hard truth, that the voyagers were substantial Elizabethan seamen, and that the whole makes a consecutive chapter of English history checks the tendency which we feel towards a vague enthusiasm, but founds it on a real and permanent basis" (*E* 1:121).

This "real and permanent" basis is, clearly enough, the continuity embedded in English history. Hakluyt is relevant to Woolf *because* he is both English and imperial, and it his Englishness that becomes the basis for Woolf's critique of imperial subjectivity in *The Voyage Out*.[31] Layered with explicit references to Hakluyt and Elizabethan literature, Woolf reins in the *content* of her novel – a journey to South America – by circumscribing it formally, suggesting a return to a chastened version of Englishness that, nevertheless, cannot extricate itself from its imperial context.

A FINE, CLOSELY-WOVEN SUBSTANCE

They agreed to accept this ideal [of the Angel in the House], because for reasons I cannot now go into – they have to do with the British Empire, our colonies, Queen Victoria, Lord Tennyson, the growth of the middle class and so on – ... <a real relationship> between men and women was then unattainable.

– Virginia Woolf[32]

The Voyage Out begins with an image of London, as Woolf follows Rachel's aunt and uncle, Helen and Ridley Ambrose, walking toward the docks where her father Willoughby Vinrace's ship is moored:

As the streets that lead from the Strand to the Embankment are very narrow, it is better not to walk down them arm-in-arm. If you persist, lawyers' clerks will have to make flying leaps into the mud; young lady typists will have to fidget behind you. In the streets of London where beauty goes unregarded, eccentricity must pay the penalty, and it is better not to be very tall, to wear a long blue cloak, or to beat the air with your left hand. (*VO* 3)

London here performs a normalizing function, one that corresponds to the needs of its two allegorical modern types: the lawyer's clerk and the lady typist. The Ambroses, however, defy such requirements, leaving a trail of "angry glances" from those who "had appointments to keep, and drew a weekly salary," glances that they fail to observe (*VO* 3). This ability clearly comes from their shared privilege, but it also has a gendered specificity: Ridley is engaged in "thought" while Helen, worried about leaving her children, feels "sorrow" (*VO* 3).

Gradually Helen breaks out of her mood, long enough to observe the city around her:

She knew how to read the people who were passing her; there were the rich who were running to and from each others' houses at this hour; there were the bigoted workers driving in a straight line to their offices; there were the poor who were unhappy and rightly malignant ... When one gave up seeing the beauty that clothed things, this was the skeleton beneath. (*VO* 5)

Whereas the individual resentments of the men and women inconvenienced by the Ambrose's self-absorption were invisible, here the various passersby become legible at a larger level of analysis, that of social class. The skeleton beneath London is social stratification. What makes the city readable is the native's ability to locate each of its citizens in the social order.

Once out at sea, however, this social legibility takes on a different cast. England appears to be "a shrinking island in which people were imprisoned" while the ship gains "an immense dignity" (*VO* 24). "She was," Woolf continues, speaking of the ship,

an inhabitant of the great world, which has so few inhabitants, traveling all day across an empty universe, with veils drawn before her and behind. She was more lonely than the caravan crossing the desert; she was infinitely more mysterious ... The sea might give her death or some unexampled joy, and none would know of it ... for as a ship she had a life of her own. (*VO* 24–5)

Mysterious, unknown, separate from the world, and described with the full complement of Orientalist images, the ship at sea stands in direct opposition to the cramped streets of London. Legibility, from this new vantage, appears as imprisonment.

This contrast between a known England and an infinite colonial space is developed in one of the novel's set piece descriptions of the Santa Marina landscape. Rachel is sitting on the edge of a cliff with her soon to be fiancé, Terence Hewet:

> Looking the other way, the vast expanse of land gave them a sensation which is given by no view, however extended, in England; the villages and the hills there having names, and the farthest horizon of hills as often as not dipping and showing a line of mist which is the sea; here the view was one of infinite sun-dried earth ... Perhaps their English blood made this prospect uncomfortably impersonal and hostile to them, for having once turned their faces that way they next turned them to the sea, and for the rest of the time sat looking at the sea ... It was this sea that flowed up to the mouth of the Thames; and the Thames washed the roots of the city of London. (*VO* 194)

The contrast between the English landscape, as knowable as London, and the infinite earth of Santa Marina could not be clearer. English blood, however, feels more comfortable looking toward the sea, for the sea leads back, in an image straight out of *Heart of Darkness*, to the city with which the novel begins.

The novel, we might say, understands totality – the structure of a world system that connects the mysterious periphery to its imperial center – even if the characters do not. Woolf, insists, here, upon the relationship between colonial and domestic spaces, which has several important consequences for the structure of the novel. The first is to suggest that the British view of Santa Marina is just that: a British view. Thus, the discourse of infinity seems less an ontological claim about the openness of peripheral space than a claim about how this appears to the British eye. The mystery of South America is produced from the perspective of legible London, even as the image of London as a prison is generated by oceanic expansiveness. We cannot simply valorize expansiveness over imprisonment, then, for the infinite is generated by imperial adventure. The truth emerges from the totality that contains both of these concepts.

At the same time, this emphasis on totality forces us to connect Rachel's individual journey to its imperial setting. Indeed, as I have already suggested, Woolf goes to considerable lengths to underline this relationship, primarily through a repeated pattern of references to Elizabethan voyages of discovery, which connects her twentieth-century travel narrative with those at the very origin of the British Empire.[33] We are told early on that Rachel's "mind was in the state of an intelligent man's in the beginning of the reign of Queen Elizabeth" (*VO* 26). Santa Marina, meanwhile, is in a similar position: "[I]n arts and industries the place is still much where it was in Elizabethan days" (*VO* 80). Willoughby Vinrace's ship, too, is analogous to those of the Renaissance that had once landed on Santa Marina's shores, even as his name recalls that of the sixteenth-century explorer Sir Hugh Willoughby, himself anthologized in Hakluyt.[34]

Woolf develops these connections further in an abbreviated history of the colony. "Three hundred years ago," Woolf writes, "five Elizabethan barques had anchored where the *Euphrosyne* now floated" (*VO* 79). No sooner had the Elizabethan ships landed than they met a number of Spanish galleons. Immediately a "fight ensued ... The Spaniards, bloated with fine living upon the fruits of the miraculous land, fell in heaps; but the hardy Englishmen, tawny with sea-voyaging ... despatched the wounded, drove the dying into the sea, and soon reduced the natives to a state of superstitious wonderment" (*VO* 79–80). Despite this early success, the British did not keep hold of Santa Marina, as it was eventually retaken by the Spanish, which seems to be the reason for its curious lack of historical progress. Only in the last ten years, Woolf concludes, had the British returned to found the little colony in which the novel takes place. Woolf's narrative goes some way to explaining the seemingly static history of the South American colony, creating a continuity of imperial relations, by linking what we might call Willoughby Vinrace's "informal empire" to the original conquest of Santa Marina.[35] Rachel Vinrace is quite literally the daughter of an empire that stretches back three hundred years.

Yet, as we have already seen, Woolf tended to associate Elizabethan England with a wideness of imagination and an openness to possibility. Her suggestion, then, that both Santa Marina and Rachel are somehow Elizabethan is not, simply, a form of primitivism or a way to enforce Rachel's lack of intelligence as critics have often claimed.[36] Rather, Woolf is here highlighting the continuity of imperial relations, even as she is attempting to return to this earlier moment to recapture something of the newness of discovery, a feeling that she imagines existed before the discourses of both empire and gender were codified. In this sense, the Elizabethan rhetoric highlights a transformative possibility that is itself inseparable from the colonial relations Woolf seeks to alter.

The contrast to the sense of possibility is Richard Dalloway's version of "continuity," a term that leads directly to a "vision of English history ..."

which went steadily from Lord Salisbury to Alfred, and gradually enclosed, as though it were a lasso that opened and caught things, enormous chunks of the habitable globe" (*VO* 42, 42–43). What has enabled the English to achieve this imperial success, Richard explains to Rachel, is their adherence to a single ideal: "Unity. Unity of aim, of dominion, of progress. The dispersion of the best ideas over the greatest area" (*VO* 55). Progress, unity, and continuity all unite in a vision of benign imperial expansiveness. Here we encounter the mirror-image of Septimus. On the one hand, a subject who cannot connect his individual impressions to the world around him. On the other, a man entirely unable to recognize the difference between the two. In each case, the subject is all.

Rachel counters this vision of imperial unity with an emergent structure of feeling that, for this precise reason, she can barely articulate. The issue, appropriately enough, concerns the fate of working women. Richard describes what he calls the best achievement of his life – that "owing to me some thousands of girls in Lancashire … can spend an hour every day in the open air" (*VO* 56). Acknowledging that his activities in London have, indeed, benefited some, Rachel nevertheless wonders about "the mind of the widow – the affections" those areas of life, which his practical, reform-minded policies "leave untouched" (*VO* 57). Richard disagrees, asserting that one's spiritual outlook is affected by material things. "I can conceive no more exalted aim," he declares, than "to be the citizen of the Empire" for the state is "a complicated machine; we citizens are parts of that machine" (*VO* 57). Rachel's understanding, however, falters. She cannot seem to connect living bodies with Dalloway's discourse of social machinery. She "was haunted by absurd jumbled ideas – how, if one went back far enough, everything perhaps was intelligible; everything was in common; for the mammoths who pastured in the fields of Richmond High Street had turned into paving stones and boxes full of ribbons, and her aunts" (*VO* 58). "It's the way of saying things, isn't it," she concludes, "not the things" (*VO* 59).

Dalloway's "way of saying things" is undermined here not only by his forceful kiss of Rachel, but by the mechanistic metaphors that he employs. Against Dalloway's image of the state as a machine, Rachel offers a more fluid sense of social connection; against the abstractions of telic history, Rachel offers the power of the everyday; and against an acquisitive individualism she harkens back to a time when "everything was in common." We might say that she operates at two distinct levels. The first connects events in the present-day with those of the distant past, but without the discourse of progress Dalloway articulates. The second emphasizes the local against the high-minded abstractions Dalloway refuses to connect to his tyrannizing behavior.

The pivot of Rachel's argument concerns her aunts, a point she will develop in conversation with Hewet. Observing that while "she always submitted to her father, just as [her aunts] did," Rachel notes that it was, nevertheless, "her aunts who influenced her really; her aunts who built up the fine, closely woven substance of their life at home" (*VO* 201). Here we can see the beginnings of Woolf's eventual fascination with figures such as Mrs. Ramsay and Clarissa Dalloway, for whom a party is "an offering; to combine, to create" (*MD* 119). What I want to suggest here is that Rachel is inarticulately groping toward something like the counter-discourse Enrique Dussel has located in a "Hispanic, Renaissance, and humanist modernity" opposed to the "solipsistic subjectivity, without community" characteristic of an ultimately victorious Anglo-Germanic modernity.[37] Read as a version of modernity's "counter-discourse" – and through the novel's repeated references to the Renaissance – Rachel's vision of her aunts suggests Woolf's attempt to reimagine modernity at its origins, in the hopes of constructing a social order capable of valuing the inner-lives of widows and the "closely woven substance" of domestic life.

Why, then, does the novel shut the door on this sense of possibility by killing Rachel? The answer comes from Rachel's own complicity with the imperial relationship she here seeks to avoid, a complicity that reveals itself in two ways. First, as we have already seen, Rachel is animated by a desire to become a "real everlasting thing, different from anything else" (*VO* 75). She seeks, like Stephen Dedalus, to express her soul in "unfettered freedom," seeks, that is to say, something like the unrestrained subjectivity Dalloway here expresses. Furthermore, if Dalloway is linked to empire through both his vision of historical progress and his acquisitive attitude, Rachel is linked to empire through her need to enter into the minds of the subjects around her, a need she instinctively resists when it is imposed upon her by Hewet but unconsciously replicates in her conversation with Dalloway.

Woolf, here, takes seriously the idea of determination and the impossibility of standing outside of a social order one seeks to resist as no character in the novel can be said to be free from the stain of imperialism. As with Joyce, Woolf instead locates resistance within hegemony itself. We can begin with Dalloway's notion of "continuity," for despite its link to empire, continuity is also the "real and permanent basis" that connects Woolf to Hakluyt. Woolf, that is to say, is invested in a particular form of continuity, although it must be one that privileges neither the lassoing of the globe nor the seemingly related impulse to enter the minds of widows. Against these two interrelated forms of imperial expansion, Woolf offers a vision of the local that preserves sexual difference, interiority, and something akin to Edmund Burke's famous "rights of an Englishman." To understand how this works, we must delve a bit more deeply into the novel's investigation of the "woman question," and what will eventually become a full-blown critique of the notion of sympathy, as Woolf suggests that what binds us together as humans is not our ability to enter into each other's imaginative lives, but rather the objective structures in which we live.

THE LIMITS OF SYMPATHY

Always to have sympathy, always to be accompanied, always to be understood would be intolerable.   – Virginia Woolf (*E* 4:320–1)

The "woman question," according to Wendy Brown, is neither interesting nor good, but arises, instead, because of the liberal conception of equality as sameness, what Pericles Lewis calls, "the mistaken tendency, inherited from the Enlightenment, to understand political concepts (liberty and equality) as resulting from natural attributes of human beings."[38] Lewis is here describing the quarrel between Edmund Burke and the French Revolution, one that is deeply relevant for Woolf's conception of the English nation. Burke famously claimed to prefer the "rights of an Englishman" to the abstract rights of the French Revolution, and in doing so seemed to naturalize the various prejudices and entitlements of English tradition over and against a universal conception of justice. Yet as Hannah Arendt notes, the condition of stateless peoples in the twentieth century offers "an ironical, bitter, and belated confirmation" of Burke's argument, for those who are stateless would certainly prefer the rights of an Englishman to those useless human rights which they, nevertheless, still maintained.[39] The point, here, is not necessarily to agree with Burke, but to notice how his formulation opens up a critical question about equality. If equality is imagined to be an inherent human quality, what are the possibilities for allowing differences to persist, particularly in social formations such as the nation-state used to manage those differences? Bringing Arendt into the conversation allows us to see how the notion of equality as sameness permeates both gendered and imperial discourse, so that what Brown identifies as the central ideological tenet of gender relations is also the constitutive question of colonialism. Thus, of all the characters who ruminate on the "woman question" in *The Voyage Out*, the most insightful might be Rachel's friend Helen, who decides that she has been too harsh about women. "I must," she writes in a letter back home, "retract some of the things I have said against them. If they were properly educated I don't see why they shouldn't be much the same as men – as satisfactory I mean; though, of course, very different" (*VO* 86).

In direct contrast, Hewet maintains that distinctions between the sexes are overrated. Rachel has been insulted by Hewet's friend St. John Hirst, and failing to find the words to explain herself, she declares in exasperation that "[i]t's no good; we should live separate; we cannot understand each other; we only bring out what's worst" (*VO* 142). Hewet, in response, "brushed aside her generalisation as to the natures of the two sexes, for such generalisations bored him and seemed to him generally untrue" (*VO* 142). At first, this dismissal seems positive, Hewet insistent that men and woman can, in fact, understand one another, and so when he begins declaring his desire for women to express themselves, we are initially sympathetic. "Just consider," Hewet says, "it's the beginning of the twentieth century, and until a few years ago no woman had ever come out by herself and said things at all" (*VO* 200). It has always been "the man's view that's represented" and so he turns to Rachel to ask her ideas about the matter (*VO* 201). Somehow, though, despite the fact that his "determination to know ... gave meaning to their talk," it also "hampered her" (*VO* 201).

A similar moment occurs later on, after the two are engaged. Rachel is playing the piano, and Terence is attempting to write. He interrupts Rachel to express some generalizations about sexual difference and then waits expectantly for Rachel to respond. Instead, she returns to her music and "again neglected this opportunity of revealing the secrets of her sex" (*VO* 275). We must view with suspicion, then, Hewet's desire to write a book "about Silence ... the things people don't say," for Rachel seems particularly invested in keeping these things to herself, refusing Hewet's efforts to mine what the novel early on calls "untapped resources, things to say as yet unsaid" (*VO* 204, 17).[40] With this turn of phrase, Woolf links the effort to excavate the unsaid with an extractive impulse particularly apt for the conquest of South America. Hewet's efforts to plumb the depths of Rachel's subjectivity and disclose the common human nature that lies within – an impulse we have already seen Rachel embody in her critique of Dalloway's material reforms – is understood here as a form of colonial expansion.

Rachel's counter-discourse, then, is not the answer to the imperial subjectivity Dalloway represents. For by seeking to inhabit the minds of the widows, Rachel engages in an act of sympathetic imagination that Woolf consistently critiqued throughout her career. Mr. Ramsay, for instance, goes about his days working his way through the philosophical alphabet – he is at the moment stalled at Q – and demanding sympathy from his wife: "It was sympathy he wanted, to be assured of his genius, first of all, and then to be taken within the circle of life, warmed and soothed, to have his senses restored to him, his barrenness made fertile, and all the rooms of the house made full of life."[41] Mrs. Ramsay, of course, obliges, providing the domestic comfort that supports his public labor, although Woolf is clear that this "rapture of successful creation" is not without its toll (*TTL* 38). "Immediately" after Mr. Ramsay leaves, "Mrs. Ramsay seemed to fold herself together, one petal closed in another, and the whole fabric fell in exhaustion upon itself" (*TTL* 38). Despite the obvious effort of such work, Mrs. Ramsay dismisses its importance: "[W]hat she gave the world, in comparison with what he gave, [was] negligible" (*TTL* 39).

Such is the rule of gender, that even Lily Briscoe, the unattached artist, feels the pressure to perform its socially prescribed duties, being forced to "renounce the experiment – what happens if one is not nice to that young man there" under the pressure of Mrs. Ramsay's sociability (*TTL* 92). Mr. Ramsay is capable of making such demands even at his approach. "Let him be fifty feet away," Lily thinks, "let him not even speak to you, let him not even see you, he permeated, he prevailed, he imposed himself" (*TTL* 149). For his part, Mr. Ramsay feels an "enormous need" that "urged him, without being conscious what it was, to approach any woman, to force them, he did not care how, his need was so great, to give him what he wanted: sympathy" (*TTL* 150, 150–1). Therefore, when Mr. Ramsay comes upon Lily painting, she again tries her experiment, hoping that "this insatiable hunger for sympathy, this demand that she should surrender herself up to him entirely ... should leave her ... before it swept her down in its flow" (*TTL* 151). Sympathy, in Lily's account, requires the surrender of herself, in order to satisfy the demands Mr. Ramsay makes upon her.

What is perhaps most striking about this scene is Woolf's use of the word need. Mr. Ramsay, the rational philosopher operating in the public sphere, is dominated by his emotions; he is neither self-sufficient nor, it turns out, particularly rational. Instead, he is driven by emotional demands for inter-subjective comfort. It is as if the very force of his own subjectivity creates the need to find support from others. Woolf here dramatizes the *fiction* of bourgeois self-sufficiency as she reveals the wound at the heart of masculine subjectivity. Men, that is to say, are hardly the universal subjects they purport to be. To be a man, in Woolf's world, is to be marked by particularity. In this way, Woolf suggests, it is not only women or outsiders who are marked by difference. These are simply the subjects who are aware of their condition. *Subjectivity itself is the injured state.*[42]

Which returns us to Septimus Warren Smith. I have already suggested how Septimus is an inverted vision of bourgeois subjectivity, so self-legislating as to entirely efface the common world in which he exists. As such, he represents a kind of parodic confirmation of what liberal subjectivity hopes for itself. Septimus represents the realization of the self-sufficiency Mr. Ramsay can only hope for a self-sufficiency mirrored in Rachel and Terence's desire to create a world of their own. Furthermore, his status as a shell-shocked veteran reveals the historical circumstances behind this particular identity-formation. Woolf thus gives us both the self-legislating subject and its historical underpinnings, showing both its falsity and yet the way that falsity is, nevertheless, experienced as truth.

Framed this way, we can see that subjectivity in Woolf is always *fundamentally* historical. Thus, the opening gesture of *Mrs. Dalloway*: Clarissa, throwing open her French windows in London and immediately finding herself back in the village of Bourton where she spent her youth with Peter Walsh, Sally Seton, and her eventual husband. The present-day Clarissa is as constituted by those events of the past as she is by her current surroundings. In an important sense she is nothing other than the accumulation of those particular historical experiences, her subjectivity, despite Woolf's famed stream-of-consciousness, never emanating from some deep heart's core such as Hewet seeks to excavate, but rather represented in relation to events both past and present. In this way, Woolf opens up the hermetically sealed subject not only to the world around it but also to the historical process of its shaping. Sympathy fails in its chief goal – the creation of a common world – because it is structured around subjects that remain sealed off from that world, whereas the common world is there all along, *in the very structure of subjectivity itself.* Common worlds emerge in Woolf through shared histories, like those that bind the subjects in *Mrs. Dalloway* or the protagonists of *The Waves* or the historically grounded rights of Burke's Englishmen.

Aligning this notion with Burke, however, opens up one last problem that we must address: if communities only emerge from local ties – as the critique of the expansive subject suggests – we seem to have shut ourselves off from ever understanding those who are different from us. Shared histories, in this formulation, function exactly as self-legislating subjects. Revealing the truth of the historical formation of seemingly transcendent subjectivity seems only to make the transformation of that subjectivity that much harder. As a way of examining this last issue, I want to conclude with Woolf's 1930 essay, "Memories of a Working Women's Guild."

Woolf's text describes herself listening to a series of speeches by the guild's members. Although she is in agreement with their proposals, "a weight of discomfort was settling" in her mind: "All those questions, I found myself thinking ... which matter so intensely to the people here ... leave me, in my own blood and bones, untouched. If every reform they demand was granted this very instant it would not matter to me a single jot. Hence my interest is merely altruistic" (*E* 5:178). This altruism, furthermore, is of the mind "but the mind was without a body" (*E* 5:178). It was, that is to say, sympathy Woolf was feeling, but a sympathy that was without an actual shared interest that can only originate, for Woolf, from shared material and social circumstances. Thus, her failure to pretend to be "Mrs Giles of Durham City" founders on the fact that "one's body had never stood at the wash tub; one's hands had never wrung and scrubbed and chopped up whatever the meat may be that makes a miner's dinner" (*E* 5:179). Side-stepping the tell-tale sign of condescension – surely Woolf was capable of discovering the contents of a miner's dinner – I want to highlight Woolf's claim that true understanding emerges only from shared circumstances that are situated, local, and embodied – a version of her attempt to restrict imperial subjectivity to its national origins.

Trying to overcome her "aesthetic sympathy, the sympathy of the eye and of the imagination, not of the heart and of the nerves," Woolf then turns to accounts of these women's lives written by the women themselves (*E* 5:182). Here she seems to fair better, and yet the condescension noted above does not go away, as Woolf marvels at the women's "indomitable" faces, which demonstrate "that human nature is so tough that it will take such wounds ... and survive them" (*E* 5:185). That someone as sophisticated as Woolf could produce the standard "triumph of the human spirit" narrative out of the lives of working women, while simultaneously declaring that "no working man or woman works harder with his hands or is in closer touch with reality than a painter with his brush or a writer with his pen" is stunning (*E* 5:182). What is more interesting is that Woolf here replicates exactly the critique Rachel levels at Richard Dalloway, whose reforms fail to touch the minds of widows. And yet what is obvious enough, is that the working women Woolf addresses would likely prefer their extra hour of rest to all of her sophisticated appreciation of their story-telling abilities. Richard Dalloway seems to win the argument.

On the one hand, then, the emphasis that we only know from our own subject positions is extremely salutary, insofar as it operates as a check on the universalizing impulses of imperial subjectivity. On the other hand, it is not clear how confining our understanding to shared physical circumstances can ever produce anything like true understanding. Woolf, that is to say, seems to enforce the limits of sympathy so strictly as to end up effacing any possibility for allegiances across social position. All subjectivity must be rooted in place, all attempts at understanding invasive and prone to a misuse of the other. Ultimately, it becomes so difficult to disentangle subjectivity from location that it is not entirely clear whether the difference matters at all. If understanding is only possible through the self or through the shared set of circumstances that produces that self it remains remarkably limited. How, then, is it possible for two such disparate subjects as Clarissa Dalloway and Septimus Warren Smith to be doubles of each other? Are not their circumstances so totally opposed as to negate any common ground between them?

Septimus famously intrudes upon Clarissa's party, and as she hears of his death she repeats the lines of *Cymbeline* that have been running through her head all day: "Fear no more the heat of the sun" (*MD* 182). Septimus, too, had considered these very same lines shortly before throwing himself out of the window. Shakespeare, it seems, is the common ground between Septimus and Clarissa. The way out of historically crafted – and therefore class-specific – subjectivities is through the "real and permanent basis" of culture. That this cultural artifact means different things to these two individuals is, itself, a crucial part of its power. A common culture brings diverse subjects together, becoming the medium through which they can articulate their distinct histories within a shared horizon of meaning, a real and permanent basis upon which to attempt to forge historically grounded ties. National culture, considered as the site for the struggle for hegemony, becomes, for Woolf, the only place for an England that must retreat from its imperial ambitions.

Writing as she does more securely from the heart of empire than Joyce, Eliot or Pound, while at the same time feeling herself, continually, to be outside of its most basic forms of privilege, Woolf is much more sensitive than they are to the perils of cosmopolitan subjectivity. Confining her perspective to England and its literary tradition, Woolf risks a certain kind of nativism, and yet, at the same time, suggests that the transformations in social relations she desires will not come from an England that continues to inflict itself on the world. They must, instead, emerge from within England itself. Connecting Dalloway's imperial subjectivity to Hewet's seemingly more benign version, demonstrating the fragility that occurs when subjects are unmoored from their common habitations in a shared culture, Woolf critiques the form of subjectivity constitutive of a British nationalism that was, simultaneously, imperial. But she does so not by positing any outside to this subjectivity. For one's five hundred pounds might come from an aunt who dies in Bombay – and there's always Clarissa Dalloway to be dealt with, standing there at the novel's end.

Coda: The Edwardian lumber room

Writing in 1920 about "Imperfect Critics," T. S. Eliot made one of his rare direct references to imperialism:

Romanticism ... leads its disciples only back upon themselves. George Wyndham had curiosity, but he employed it romantically, not to penetrate the real world, but to complete the varied features of the world he made for himself. It would be of interest to divagate from literature to politics and inquire to what extent Romanticism is incorporate in Imperialism. (*SW* 31–2)

These lines offer us some insight into "The Love Song of J. Alfred Prufrock." Often described as a dramatic monologue, "Prufrock" is perhaps more accurately understood as a romantic lyric that desires the situatedness characteristic of drama. The poem begins with a gesture toward companionship: "Let us go then, you and I." No sooner is this "you" addressed, however, than his/her one attempt to participate in the conversation is brushed aside: "Oh, do not ask, 'What is it?' / Let us go and make our visit" (*CP* 3). Paralyzed by indecision, Prufrock cannot even eat a peach, let alone approach a woman whose intentions he might misunderstand. His anxieties, that is to say, only lead back upon themselves; his simultaneous inability to express himself in the external world *and* connect with other subjects leads to a rejection of the real world. Instead, he lives in a world of his own making. Read through the lens of the quotation above, Prufrock's inability to give in to what *The Waste Land* calls "the awful daring of a moment's surrender," emerges as the solipsism inherent in both the romantic and imperial world views. If we take Eliot's claim seriously, the effort to overcome imperialism is, in part, the effort to overcome the self-contained subjectivities it creates and engage in the real world. Since this world was an imperial one, overcoming imperialism means, paradoxically, acknowledging its determining power.

Writing a few years after Eliot, Virginia Woolf does just that, beginning a 1925 essay on Renaissance literature, *The Elizabethan Lumber*

Room, with her old friend Hakluyt. Calling his anthology, "not so much a book as a great bundle of commodities loosely tied together," Woolf goes on to describe both the contents of this "emporium" and its origins: "[T]his jumble of seeds, silks, unicorns' horns, elephants' teeth, wool, common stones, turbans, and bars of gold, these odds and ends of price-less value and complete worthlessness, were the fruit of innumerable voyages, traffics, and discoveries to unknown lands" (*E* 4:53). "All this," Woolf continues, "the new words, the new ideas, the waves, the savages, the adventures, found their way naturally into the plays which were being acted upon the banks of the Thames" (*E* 4:55–6). "Thus," she concludes, "we find the whole of Elizabethan literature strewn with gold and silver" (*E* 4:56). The spoils of imperial conquest, Woolf explicitly argues, make themselves felt in literary representation.

Now Woolf is making this claim about the Renaissance, but her ability to see the connections between imperial adventure and literary accumula-tion is, I would submit, a function of her own historical moment. As we have seen, this moment was dominated by a particular kind of economic crisis: that of overaccumulation. Perhaps no modernist poem thematizes this issue more directly than Pound's "Portrait d'une Femme." Most often understood as an anti-feminist critique, "Portrait d'une Femme" is largely a poem about accumulation. Its subject is "person of some interest," a salon woman who collects both ideas and objects, but whose main asset seems to be the time she is able to spend patiently awaiting the arrival of something of value.[1] Although her guests take "strange gain away," this gain is as unproductive as the woman herself, consisting only of a:

> Fact that leads nowhere; and a tale or two,
> Pregnant with mandrakes, or with something else
> That might prove useful and yet never proves,

The anti-feminist critique – the suggestion that a woman must be bio-logically productive in order to be useful – is here but one example of the general problem of unproductive labor. The accumulation of ideas and objects leads, over time, to a form of interest that somehow fails to be useful.

The poem's opening line – "Your mind and you are our Sargasso Sea" – situates this problem within the framework of the British Empire. The Sargasso Sea, of course, is home to the Bermuda triangle, which explains the basic structure of Pound's metaphor, but it is also the sea through which English ships traveled to reach their Caribbean colonies. The ideas the woman collects, as well as the treasures described later on in the poem, are thus, in part, the spoils of empire. Her failure to circulate them – to realize the value they contain – is analogized by Pound as a failed imperial adventure, a ship lost on the journey from periphery to center.

Now we have seen Pound describe his own poetic works as the result of imperial conquest before, as in the 1912 poem "Epilogue," which begins "I bring you the spoils, my nation, / I, who went out in exile, / Am returned to thee with gifts" (*CEP* 209).[2] Thus, the ringing conclusion of "Portrait" – "No! there is nothing! In the whole and all, / Nothing that's quite your own." – tells us as much about Pound himself as it does the woman that is its subject. Clearly the author of "Epilogue" was worrying about the return he might be able to make on his own poetic investments. How, "Portrait" seems to ask, it is possible to realize the value contained in the accumulation of culture? When framed in terms of accumulation, the solutions Pound will later develop – circulation, a journey to the East – seem suspiciously like those of imperial capital itself.

And so do the aesthetic solutions of all of my principal writers. Joyce, building his description of Dublin out of materials from elsewhere; Eliot, seeking to overcome the unreality of an imperial city through a series of fragments torn from their original contexts; Woolf, countering imperial fictions of progress with the continuity of national culture; Pound, constructing a world culture an incipient globalization was busy producing. Each of these forms of culture is, necessarily, conditioned by the imperial world it seeks to resist; each risks, as years of criticism outlining modernism's complicity with imperialism demonstrates, being mistaken for the culture that determines it. With this critique I am largely in agreement. Indeed, one of the central claims of this book has been that the term modernism is best used for the literary forms that arise from the accumulation of capital and culture that only occurs in the centers of empire. Modernism, that is to say, is entirely complicit with empire, but it is precisely by virtue of this complicity that its aesthetic structures are able to gain purchase on the world that informs them. To think otherwise is to hold to a naïve view of the autonomy of literature, one that imagines some utopian outside to the structures of imperial capital.

This, finally, is an argument that emerges from within the literature I have been discussing. The solutions to the problems of history can only come from history itself. They cannot be found in the too vast desires of a colonial space, or in the construction of a private language shorn of the effects of the marketplace. They are not to be understood through a paraphrase of the classics or in the decisions and revisions of an infinitely vast interiority. Time and again, modernism points to the world outside it.

The writers in this study, of course, saw this world differently from one another, but some common themes are present throughout their works: a distrust of expressive subjectivity, an interest in communal structures of meaning, and an emphasis on the cultural tradition as the place from which one might resist an increasingly commodified world alongside an interest in transforming that tradition to better suit the needs of the present. Perry Anderson has grounded this revolutionary impulse in the precarious social order out of which modernism arose, one that contained a range of possible futures unknowable at the time.[3] Modernism, in this account, straddles two worlds: an old one that was dying and a new one struggling to be born. However, it does so without the backward glance through which its faith in the power of art cannot help but seem excessive. Often misread as a form of aesthetic autonomy, this faith arises instead from the opposite impulse, from the belief that art is so intimately enmeshed within the social order from which it arises that it cannot help but change along with that world. "Artists," Ezra Pound argued in 1934, "are the race's antennae. The effects of social evil show first in the arts" (*SP* 229). We are a far cry, here, from Shelley's unacknowledged legislators. Less the view that art transforms the world, modernism's revolutionary desire emerges from an understanding of totality, of the connections between culture and politics, art and economics, privilege and perspective.

Pound struggled all his life to represent this totality, viewing his inability to do so as a kind of personal failing. "I am not a demi-god," he famously wrote in one of the unfinished fragments of *The Cantos*, "I cannot make it cohere" (CXVI: 810). Thus, *The Cantos* do not so much conclude as stop. The same can be said for any number of modernist texts. Clarissa Dalloway standing at the stairs; Stephen Dedalus going forth to encounter "for the millionth time the reality of experience;" the pair of shoes dangling at the close of *Jacob's Room*. Each of these endings, despite critical clichés about organic wholes, are startlingly inconclusive. Even Eliot's claim that the repetition of "Shantih" at *The Waste Land*'s end is "formal," serves only to emphasize its provisional nature. Modernist literature is filled with conclusions that fail to conclude, that hover on the brink of a transformative change the literature itself fails to supply. No accumulation of culture, these endings seem to suggest, can replace an encounter with the real world itself. The representation of blocked subjectivities, of those who fail to actualize their cultural accumulation in the world, is not an endorsement of that form of subjectivity, but rather a critique of its persistent need to remake the world in its own image.

Western capital, as we have already seen, betrays a similar desire, eradicating traditional ways of life in favor of an all-encompassing capitalist modernity. By insisting that works of the past have value and demanding that we encounter them in all their objectivity, modernist literature resists an imperial world with which it was intimately intertwined, insisting on the distinction between the accumulation of culture and the accumulation of capital, even as it acknowledges the constitutive relationship between the two. For the modernist subject's alienation from the world is the very mark of his/her formation by that world. Alongside the impulse to totalize, then, modernism registers the inability to do so adequately, the failure, that is to say, of its subjects to accurately map the world solely through the power of their own minds. This failure cannot, however, prevent us, like Prufrock, from encountering the reality of experience. Instead, we are called upon to act with the openness of a Molly Bloom, whose final words assent to a future whose shape she cannot hope to know.

Notes

INTRODUCTION: IMPERIAL STRUCTURES OF FEELING

1 James Joyce, *Dubliners* (New York: Penguin, 1967), 43 hereafter referred to parenthetically as *D*.

2 Ibid., 42.

3 Melba Cuddy-Keane, *Virginia Woolf, the Intellectual, and the Public Sphere* (Cambridge: Cambridge University Press, 2003), Alex Davis and Lee Jenkins, eds., *The Locations of Literary Modernism* (Cambridge: Cambridge University Press, 2000), Paul Peppis, *Literature, Politics, and the English Avant-Garde: Nation and Empire, 1901–1918* (Cambridge: Cambridge University Press, 2000), Lawrence Rainey, *Revisiting the Waste Land* (New Haven, CT: Yale University Press, 2005), Vincent B. Sherry, *The Great War and the Language of Modernism* (New York: Oxford University Press, 2003).

4 Douglas Mao and Rebecca L. Walkowitz, "The New Modernist Studies," *PMLA* 123, no. 3 (2009): 737 and Laura Doyle and Laura A. Winkiel, "Introduction: The Global Horizons of Modernism," in *Geomodernisms: Race, Modernism, Modernity*, ed. Laura Doyle and Laura A. Winkiel (Bloomington: Indiana University Press, 2005), 3.

5 Friedman has written a series of essays on this topic. This quotation comes from "Periodizing Modernism: Postcolonial Modernities and the Space/ Time Borders of Modernist Studies," *Modernism/Modernity* 13, no. 3 (2006): 433. See also "Definitional Excursions: The Meanings of *Modern/Modernity/ Modernism*," *Modernism/Modernity* 8, no. 3 (2001) and "Modernism in a Transnational Landscape," *Paideuma* 32, no. 1–3 (2003).

6 Doyle and Winkiel, "Introduction," 6.

7 Douglas Mao and Rebecca L. Walkowitz, "Introduction: Modernisms Bad and New," in *Bad Modernisms*, ed. Douglas Mao and Rebecca L. Walkowitz (Durham, NC: Duke University Press, 2006). The Howe quotation comes from the "Introduction" to his edited volume *Literary Modernism*. Both Howe and Huyssen are quoted on page 5.

8 Mao and Walkowitz, "Introduction: Modernisms Bad and New," 6.

9 Friedman, "Definitional Excursions," 493.

10 Ibid., 494.

11 T. S. Eliot, *The Sacred Wood* (New York: University Paperbacks, 1964), 52, hereafter referred to parenthetically as *SW*.

12 Virginia Woolf, *The Essays of Virginia Woolf: Volume One: 1904–1912*, ed. Andrew McNeillie, 5 vols., vol. 1 (New York: HBJ, 1986), 126–7, hereafter referred to parenthetically as *E* followed by volume number: page number.

13 Works in this vein include edited collections by Richard Begam and Michael Valdez Moses, eds., *Modernism and Colonialism: British and Irish Literature, 1899–1939* (Durham, NC: Duke University Press, 2007), Howard J. Booth and Nigel Rigby, eds., *Modernism and Empire* (Manchester: Manchester University Press, 2000) and Anthony L. Geist and José B. Monleón, eds., *Modernism and Its Margins: Reinscribing Cultural Modernity from Spain and Latin America* (New York: Garland Publishing Inc., 1999). See also works by Melba Cuddy-Keane, "Modernism, Geopolitics, Globalization," *Modernism/Modernity* 10, no. 2 (2003), Joshua Esty, *A Shrinking Island: Modernism and National Culture in England* (Princeton, NJ: Princeton University Press, 2004), Simon Gikandi, "Preface: Modernism in the World," *Modernism/Modernity* 13, no. 3 (2006), *Writing in Limbo: Modernism and Caribbean Literature* (Ithaca, NY: Cornell University Press, 1992) and Jahan Ramazani, "Modernist Bricolage, Postcolonial Hybridity," *Modernism/Modernity* 13, no. 3 (2006), "A Transnational Poetics," *American Literary History* 18, no. 2 (2006).

14 The standard account of primitivism in its relationship to imperialist discourse is, of course, Marianna Torgovnick, *Gone Primitive: Savage Intellects, Modern Lives* (Chicago: The University of Chicago Press, 1990).

15 Dipesh Chakrabarty, "Universalism and Belonging in the Logic of Capital," *Public Culture* 12, no. 3 (2000): 668, 669, 670.

16 For more on this rift, see the essays in Crystal Bartolovich and Neil Lazarus, eds., *Marxism, Modernity, and Postcolonial Studies* (Cambridge: Cambridge University Press, 2002), particularly Bartolovich's introduction, as well as the excellent, book-long discussion of the topic that unites the various essays in Neil Larsen, *Determinations* (New York: Verso, 2001).

17 Georg Lukács, *History and Class Consciousness*, trans. Rodney Livingstone (Cambridge, MA: The MIT Press, 1971), 83.

18 Karl Marx, *Communist Manifesto*, ed. Frederic L. Bender (New York: Norton, 1988), 59.

19 Fredric Jameson, "Third-World Literature in the Era of Multinational Capitalism," *Social Text* 15 (1986): 78. This way of construing form is also behind the basic modernist view that the forms of Victorian literature cannot serve as vehicles for engaging the modern world. Those older forms had outlived their use and became part of "the objective situation" that the modernists sought to overturn.

20 Raymond Williams, *Marxism and Literature* (New York: Oxford University Press, 1977), 133, *Politics and Letters* (London: Verso, 1981), 168. For an excellent discussion of Williams's phrase and its critical afterlife, see Kevis Goodman, *Georgic Modernity and British Romanticism* (Cambridge: Cambridge University Press, 2004), particularly 1–16.

21 Williams, *Marxism and Literature*, 125. The italics are Williams's.

22 Ibid., 130.

23 Ibid.
24 See Pascale Casanova, *The World Republic of Letters*, trans. M. B. DeBevoise (Cambridge, MA: Harvard University Press, 2004).

1 E. J. Hobsbawm, *The Age of Empire 1875–1914* (New York: Pantheon Books, 1987), 10. There is, of course, a lively debate about the specific components of the Age of Empire. Anthony Brewer provides a helpful survey of the Marxist tradition that includes the dependency and world systems theory of writers such as Andre Gunder Frank, Immanuel Wallerstein, and Samir Amin (among others). See Anthony Brewer, *Marxist Theories of Imperialism: A Critical Survey* (London: Routledge & Kegan Paul, 1980). The debate about the British Empire has been invigorated by the work of Peter Cain and A. G. Hopkins, who have shifted the focus from industrialization to the rise of finance and commercial services and, in doing so, have argued for the links between an older aristocratic order and the emerging capitalist one, a synthesis they dub "gentlemanly capitalism." See Peter J. Cain and A. G. Hopkins, *British Imperialism, 1688–2000*, 2nd ed. (New York: Longman, 2002). Cain and Hopkins's work is particularly valuable for understanding how emergent social forms simultaneously defeat and incorporate older social forms. The category of service, however, is a slippery one and difficult to untangle from commodity production and, finally, industrialization itself. For details see Ronald M. Chilcote, ed., *The Political Economy of Imperialism: Critical Appraisals* (Boston, MA: Kluwer Academic Publishers, 1999); Raymond E. Dumett, ed., *Gentlemanly Capitalism and British Imperialism: The New Debate on Empire* (New York: Longman, 1999). I address the Marxist tradition of Lenin, Bukharin, Hilferding, and Luxemburg in more detail later in this chapter..
2 Hobsbawm, *Age of Empire*, 13, 62.
3 Ibid., 63.
4 Ibid., 64.
5 Hobsbawm writes "The word ... first entered politics in Britain in the 1870s, and was still regarded as a neologism by the end of that decade. It exploded into general use in the 1890s.... In short, it was a novel term devised to describe a novel phenomenon" (*Age of Empire*, 60).
6 V. I. Lenin, *Imperialism* (New York: International Publishers, 1939), 89.
7 From J. S. Mill, *Representative Government*, cited in J. A. Hobson, *Imperialism: A Study* (London: George Allen & Unwin Ltd., 1905), 5.
8 Ibid., 6.
9 Ibid., 245.
10 Ibid., 145.
11 Ibid.
12 See Fredric Jameson, "Modernism and Imperialism," in *The Modernist Papers* (New York: Verso, 2007).

13 Nikolai Bukharin, *Imperialism and World Economy* (New York: Monthly Review Press, 1973), 35.

14 Ibid., 23, 25.

15 Ibid., 21.

16 "Capitalism in its full maturity also depends in all respects on non-capitalist strata and social organizations existing side by side with it." See Rosa Luxemburg, *The Accumulation of Capital*, trans. Agnes Schwarzschild (New York: Routledge, 2003), 345.

17 Hobsbawm, *Age of Empire*, 31.

18 James Clifford, *The Predicament of Culture: Twentieth-Century Ethnography, Literature, and Art* (Cambridge, MA: Harvard University Press, 1988), 3.

19 Ibid., 5.

20 Bill Brown, *A Sense of Things: The Object Matter of American Literature* (Chicago: University of Chicago Press, 2003), 5, 12. A similar question is taken up in Douglas Mao, *Solid Objects: Modernism and the Test of Production* (Princeton, NJ: Princeton University Press, 1998). As will become clear, I am sympathetic to the impulse in modernism to treat the object outside of the subject's dominance – as well as to the notion that objects might be experienced through an emotion that "must be something like love" (4) – but I still believe the commodity relation to be the most important structuring principle of the historical period I am analyzing. Mao's study, then, while fascinating in itself, is focused on a fundamentally different problem than mine.

21 Brown, *A Sense of Things*, 12 (ellipsis Brown's).

22 Theodor W. Adorno and Walter Benjamin, *The Complete Correspondence, 1928–1940*, ed. Henri Lonitz, trans. Nicholas Walker (Cambridge, MA: Harvard University Press, 2001), 130.

23 Ezra Pound distinguishes three types of goods: "1. Transient: fresh vegetables, luxuries, jerry-built houses, fake art, pseudo books, battleships; 2. Durable: well constructed buildings, roads, public works, canals, intelligent afforestation; 3. Permanent: scientific discoveries, works of art, classics. That is to say these latter can be put in a class by themselves, as they are always in use and never consumed; or they are, in jargon, 'consumed' but not destroyed by consumption." See Ezra Pound, "The State," in *Selected Prose 1909–1965*, ed. William Cookson (New York: New Directions, 1973), 214–15, hereafter referred to parenthetically as *SP*.

24 The list could continue. Wallace Stevens consistently described poetry as an interaction between imagination and reality. William Carlos Williams too spoke of imagination, but produced "The Red Wheelbarrow." Gertrude Stein could be said to push her concrete interest in language to the point of pure imaginative abstraction.

25 Rob Shields, "Fancy Footwork: Walter Benjamin's Note on Flânerie," in *The Flâneur*, ed. Keith Tester (New York: Routledge, 1994), 66.

26 Ibid., 67.

27 Ibid., 74.

28 Walter Benjamin, *The Arcades Project*, trans. Howard Eiland and Kevin McLaughlin (Cambridge, MA: The Belknap Press of Harvard University Press, 1999), 3.

29 The first quotation is from Walter Benjamin, *Illuminations*, ed. Hannah Arendt, trans. Harry Zohn (New York: Schocken Books, 1968), 165. The second can be found in Michael Jennings, "On the Banks of a New Lethe: Commodification and Experience in Benjamin's Baudelaire Book," *boundary 2* 30, no. 1 (2003): 97.

30 Benjamin's quotation is in *The Arcades Project*, 7. The second quotation is from Rosalind H. Williams, *Dream Worlds: Mass Consumption in Late Nineteenth-Century France* (Berkeley: University of California Press, 1982), 58.

31 Thomas Richards, *The Commodity Culture of Victorian England: Advertising and Spectacle, 1851–1913* (Stanford, CA: Stanford University Press, 1990), 3.

32 Ibid., 4, 17.

33 Ibid., 3,1.

34 Williams, *Dream Worlds*, 64.

35 Ibid., 65.

36 Richards, *Commodity Culture*, 5. The idea that "the definite social relation between men … assumes here, for them, the fantastic form of a relation between things" is Marx's. See Karl Marx, *Capital, Volume I*, trans. Ben Fowkes (New York: Penguin Books, 1990), 165. There is, of course, a relatively wide-ranging literature that reads the expansion of commodity culture as an expansion of freedom. Victoria de Grazia's *Irresistible Empire*, for instance, argues that consumption is a "matter of choices freely exercised" and contrasts a European world where "aristocratic customs … continued to make sumptuary habits a source of social division" to an American commodity culture that "acted much like the French and Bolshevik Revolutions in overthrowing old regimes that proved incapable of reform and were obstructive and reactionary." See Victoria de Grazia, *Irresistible Empire: America's Advance through Twentieth-Century Europe* (Cambridge, MA: Harvard University Press, 2005), 237, 9, 11. The ideological content of this argument hardly requires critique.

37 Richards, *Commodity Culture*, 121.

38 Walter Benjamin, *Charles Baudelaire*, trans. Harry Zohn (New York: Verso, 1997), 55.

39 Ibid.

40 Karl Marx, *Capital, Volume 1*, trans. Samuel Moore, Edward Aveling, and Ernest Untermann (Chicago: Charles H. Kerr & Company, 1912), 82. Ben Fowkes's 1976 translation, which is generally more readable than Moore's 1912 text, has the commodity *emerging* – a word that fails to capture the performative and active nuances of the German verb *auftreten,* reflected in Moore's *step forth.*

41 Mary Gluck, "The *Flâneur* and the Aesthetic Appropriation of Urban Culture in Mid-19th-Century Paris," *Theory, Culture & Society* 20, no. 5 (2003): 54.

42 Ibid., 63.
43 Ibid., 63, 61.
44 Ibid., 74.
45 Ibid., 77.
46 Ibid., 72.
47 E. J. Hobsbawm, *The Age of Capital: 1848–1878* (New York: Charles Scribner's Sons, 1975), 99–100.
48 Both Joyce and Pound explicitly credited Flaubert with introducing a new spirit in letters, whereas Eliot not only quotes Baudelaire in the "Burial of the Dead," but also quite clearly takes up the Baudelairean persona of the *flâneur* in his early poems. The *flâneur* is present in *Mrs. Dalloway* both in the novel's eponymous hero – privileged consumer of all that London has to offer – and in Septimus Warren Smith, whose suicide underlines the dark side of the dislocations that produce such figures of metropolitan privilege. Pound, for his part, reimagines the *flâneur* as a Provençal troubadour, bringing home poetic spoils from his ethnographic wanderings. Joyce's combination of Bloom and Odysseus can be seen as a return to Gluck's popular *flâneur*, even as he uncovers the common meanings embedded in the cityscape legible to its colonial citizens. In each of these cases, the ahistorical *flâneur* is returned to the world that surrounds him.
49 Nevertheless, it is still worth noting what is the most consistent feature of the scholarship about Britain's relationship to 1848: namely, why the revolutions that occurred in Europe did not occur in Great Britain. The answers to this, typically found in the scholarship on Chartism and its aftermath, vary from the uneven nature of British industrial development – producing the so-called labor aristocracy, a group of artisan workers more aligned to the bourgeois values of independence than a more fully proletarianized working class might be – to the complacency of the British middle classes – co-opted by financial reforms made possible by the increased exploitation of the colonies – to the repressive apparatus of the British state that actively suppressed potential revolutionary movements. I have found the work of Margot C. Finn and Miles Taylor helpful in summarizing the main issues in the critical literature. See Margot C. Finn, *After Chartism: Class and Nation in English Radical Politics, 1848–1874* (Cambridge: Cambridge University Press, 1993), in particular the introduction and Miles Taylor, "The 1848 Revolutions and the British Empire," *Past and Present* 166, no. 146–180 (2000), "Rethinking the Chartists: Searching for Synthesis in the Historiography of Chartism," *The Historical Journal* 39, no. 2 (1996). Although these arguments are all of interest, what is important for my purposes is that the exact same issues surrounding the relationship between the bourgeoisie and the proletariat animate nineteenth-century English discourse. Thus, the Reform Act of 1832 can be seen as a half-measure by which the state sought to prevent the vast majority of the working class from participating in democracy, even as the century-long battle over the Corn Laws is largely a struggle between the landed estates and the various members of the bourgeoisie – merchants,

financiers – who stood to gain from free trade, with the working class caught in the middle. Nineteenth-century England might not offer the spectacle of revolution, but it nevertheless reveals the extent to which class division became the explicit subject of political conflict across Europe. My decision to focus on the revolutions in France, then, is based both on the large body of Marxist inflected scholarship that has attached this moment to the birth of modernism and the manifest importance of Baudelaire and Flaubert, the two writers most often associated with 1848, to each of my principal authors.

50 Fredric Jameson, *A Singular Modernity: An Essay on the Ontology of the Present* (New York: Verso, 2002), 166.

51 Roberto Schwarz, *A Master on the Periphery of Capitalism: Machado De Assis*, trans. John Gledson (Durham, NC: Duke University Press, 2002), 119.

52 Ibid.

53 Karl Marx, "The Eighteenth Brumaire of Louis Bonaparte," in *Marx's 'Eighteenth Brumaire' (Post)Modern Interpretations*, ed. Mark Cowling and James Martin (Sterling, VA: The Pluto Press, 2002), 22.

54 Ibid., 19.

55 Neil Larsen, *Modernism and Hegemony: A Materialist Critique of Aesthetic Agencies* (Minneapolis: University of Minnesota Press, 1990), 22.

56 Ibid., 23.

57 Ibid., xxiv.

58 Ibid.

59 Karl Marx, *Grundrisse*, trans. Martin Nicolaus (New York: Penguin Books, 1973), 460.

60 Hannah Arendt, *The Origins of Totalitarianism* (New York: Harcourt Brace & Company, 1979), 126.

61 Ibid., 125.

62 Ibid., 135.

63 Ibid.

64 Ibid., 157.

65 Brewer, *Marxist Theories of Imperialism*, 81.

66 Ibid., 81–2.

67 Ibid., 82.

68 Rudolf Hilferding, *Finance Capital: A Study of the Latest Phase of Capitalist Development*, ed. Tom Bottomore, trans. Morris Watnick and Sam Gordon (Boston, MA: Routledge & Kegan Paul, 1981), 301.

69 Brewer, *Marxist Theories of Imperialism*, 97.

70 What is crucial to note is that this does not represent the betrayal of some existing historical agency, but rather a turn away from increased participation at precisely the moment when society is promising to become more egalitarian.

71 Arendt, *Origins*, 143.

72 Ibid., 147.

73 Marx, "The Eighteenth Brumaire," 23.

74 Marx, *Communist Manifesto*, 57.
75 This famous phrase – where Marx proposes to answer how a "grotesque medi-ocrity came to play a hero's part" – is from the preface to the first German edition of *The Eighteenth Brumaire*, which is inexplicably left out of Cowling and Martin's otherwise excellent 2002 edition.
76 Karl Marx, *The Class Struggles in France (1848–1850)* (New York: International Publishers, 1964), 72.
77 Ibid.
78 The literature on this topic is enormous. Bob Jessop and Paul Wetherly pro-vide complementary summaries of the major participants. See Bob Jessop, "The Political Scene and the Politics of Representation: Periodising Class Struggle and the State in the *Eighteenth Brumaire*," in *Marx's 'Eighteenth Brumaire': (Post)Modern Interpretations*, ed. Mark Cowling and James Martin (Sterling, VA: The Pluto Press, 2002) and Paul Wetherly, "Making Sense of the 'Relative Autonomy' of the State," in *Marx's 'Eighteenth Brumaire': (Post) Modern Interpretations*, ed. Mark Cowling and James Martin (Sterling, VA: The Pluto Press, 2002).
79 Jessop, "The Political Scene," 181.
80 On the general tendency of capitalist social formations to separate the eco-nomic from the political see Ellen Meiksins Wood, *Empire of Capital* (New York: Verso, 2003).
81 In fact, it is more accurate to say that the modern state *needs* to preserve the interests of the capitalist class, in order to preserve its own relative auton-omy. Paul Wetherly argues that since the state requires revenue but does not own the means of production, it can only generate money through taxation, which, in turn, requires those who own the means of production – the capit-alist class – to generate wealth. The state is thus compelled to provide a stable social structure to aid this accumulation of capital, all of which tends to align the interests of a formally autonomous state with those of the capitalist class. Wetherly's argument, then, is a nice specification of the way "relative autonomy" is itself a structure that supports the bourgeoisie's interests. See Wetherly, "Making Sense of the 'Relative Autonomy' of the State."
82 Jessop, "The Political Scene," 181.
83 The classic Marxist account of the struggle for hegemony is, of course, Gramsci's. See Antonio Gramsci, *Selections from the Prison Notebooks*, trans. Quintin Hoare and Geoffrey Nowell Smith (New York: International Publishers, 1971).
84 Georg Lukács, *The Historical Novel*, trans. Hannah Mitchell and Stanley Mitchell (Middlesex: Penguin Books, 1961), 205.
85 Ibid., 206.
86 Ibid., 209, 208.
87 Ibid., 215, 216.
88 Ibid., 220.
89 Larsen, *Modernism and Hegemony*, xxv, xiv. Although it is certainly fair to say that Adorno represents the most rigorous philosophical defense of

modernism available, it is questionable whether he can stand in for modernism as a whole. Furthermore Adorno does not argue for an ontological crisis in the concept of representation itself, but rather for the necessity of negation in a specific historical situation where culture has become commodity. The problem, for Adorno, is less about the evacuation of historical agency, then, than about the way capital appropriates various seemingly oppositional subjective postures and, in the process, negates their critical purchase.

90 Ibid., 29.
91 Ibid., 22.
92 Ibid., 25.
93 Larsen, *Determinations*, 58.
94 Ibid., 61.
95 Ibid., 62.
96 Ibid., 64.
97 Gayatri Chakravorty Spivak, "Can the Subaltern Speak?" in *Marxism and the Interpretation of Culture*, ed. Cary Nelson and Lawrence Grossberg (Chicago: University of Illinois Press, 1988), 287. For a critique of the tendency in postcolonial theory to refer to an undifferentiated notion of "the West," see Neil Lazarus, "The Fetish of 'the West' in Postcolonial Theory," in *Marxism, Modernity and Postcolonial Studies*, ed. Crystal Bartolovich and Neil Lazarus (Cambridge: Cambridge University Press, 2002).
98 Spivak, "Can the Subaltern Speak?" 275.
99 Ibid., 308, 291.
100 Ibid., 286, 287.
101 Ibid., 288–9.
102 Schwarz, *A Master on the Periphery*, 120.
103 Ibid., 120, 121.
104 This feature of modernism has long been recognized, although not necessarily connected to its origins in the conditions of capital. Hugh Kenner's *The Pound Era*, for instance, contains the following sentence on its first page: "James' world of discourse teems with inverted commas, the words by which life was regulated having been long adrift, and referable only, with lifted eyebrows, to usage, his knowledge of her knowledge of his knowledge of what was done." See Hugh Kenner, *The Pound Era* (Berkeley: University of California Press, 1973), 3.
105 Larsen, *Modernism and Hegemony*, 4.
106 Jameson, "Third-World Literature," 78.
107 The phrase "unseizable forces" comes from *Jacob's Room*, in a paragraph that aptly catches both Woolf's aspiration to totality and her sense of its impossibility: "It is thus that we live, they say, driven by an unseizable force. They say that the novelists never catch it; that it goes hurtling through their nets and leaves them torn to ribbons. This, they say, is what we live by – this unseizable force." See Virginia Woolf, *Jacob's Room* (New York: Harcourt Brace Jovanovich, 1960), 156. For a characteristic statement from

Ezra Pound, we can turn to the following quotation from the 1913 essay "Patria Mia": "Sismondi said that one studies the past so as to learn how to deal with the present or something of that sort, I forget his exact phrasing" (*SP* 125).

108 Charles Altieri, "'Preludes' as Prelude: In Defense of Eliot as Symboliste," in *T. S. Eliot: A Voice Descanting*, ed. Shyamal Bagchee (New York: St. Martin's Press, 1990), 4.

109 T. S. Eliot, *Selected Essays* (New York: Harcourt, Brace & World, Inc., 1964), 374.

110 T. S. Eliot, *Collected Poems, 1909–1962* (New York: Harcourt, Brace & World, Inc., 1963), 14, hereafter referred to parenthetically as *CP*.

111 See Phillipe Lacoue-Labarthe and Jean-Luc Nancy, *The Literary Absolute: The Theory of Literature in German Romanticism*, trans. Philip Barnard and Cheryl Lester (Albany: State University of New York Press, 1988), for details.

112 Section IV begins: "His soul stretched tight across the skies / That fade behind a city block, / Or trampled by insistent feet / At four and five and six o'clock;" (*CP* 14).

113 Peter Osborne, *The Politics of Time: Modernity and the Avant-Garde* (New York: Verso, 1995), 145.

114 Jameson, *A Singular Modernity*, 215.

2 *THE WASTE LAND* AND THE UNREAL CENTER OF CAPITALIST MODERNITY

1 Allyson Booth, "Sir Ernest Shackleton, Easter Sunday & the Unquiet Dead in T. S. Eliot's *Waste Land*," *Yeats Eliot Review* 16, no. 2 (1999): 28.

2 Ibid. The contiguity of these two events was not lost on Shackleton. Eager to avoid appearing to have taken men away from the war effort, he spends considerable time in his preface justifying his journey, and dedicates the book "To my comrades who fell in the white warfare of the south and on the red fields of France and Flanders" (Booth 29).

3 John A. McClure, *Late Imperial Romance* (New York: Verso, 1994), 10.

4 For an excellent account of the birth of the so-called third world out of the structures of imperialism, see Mike Davis, *Late Victorian Holocausts: El Nino Famines and the Making of the Third World* (New York: Verso, 2001).

5 That *The Waste Land* is a poem of imperialism has been suggested before, although the arguments have tended to diagnose Eliot as either for or against Empire. Thus, David Trotter has argued for certain discursive similarities between the apocalyptic vision of *The Waste Land* and that of the New Imperialists, suggesting that Eliot regards with excitement what imperialists approached with suspicion. See David Trotter, "Modernism and Empire: Reading *the Waste Land*," *Critical Quarterly* 28, no. 1 & 2 (1986). In sharp contrast, Paul Douglass finds the poem to be based on an "aesthetic of empire." See Paul Douglass, "Reading the Wreckage: De-Encrypting

Eliot's Aesthetics of Empire," *Twentieth Century Literature* 43, no. 1 (1997). In support of this argument, Douglass adduces Eliot's 1924 letter to the *Transatlantic Review*, where he claimed that he was "all for empires," but fails to quote the phrase immediately following: "[E]specially the Austro-Hungarian Empire," which surely ironizes Eliot's initial statement. See T. S. Eliot, "A Letter," *Transatlantic Review* 1, no. 1 (1924): 95. Recently, Declan Kiberd has made the same mistake, although it is only one of many, including adducing Eliot's essay on Virgil – written in 1951 – as an example of his "critical essays in the 1920s" that supposedly show that he "had no scruples about the imperial project." See Declan Kiberd, "Postcolonial Modernism," in *Modernism and Colonialism: British and Irish Literature, 1899–1939*, ed. Richard Begam and Michael Valdez Moses (Durham, NC: Duke University Press, 2007), 270. In 1979, Eleanor Cook found in the poem the suggestion of the British Empire's inevitable decline. Her articulation of this argument through the work of John Maynard Keynes has recently been developed by Michael Levenson. See Eleanor Cook, "T. S. Eliot and the Carthaginian Peace," *ELH* 46, no. 2 (1979) and Michael Levenson, "Does *The Waste Land* Have a Politics?," *Modernism/Modernity* 6, no. 3 (1999). I draw on each of these articles for helpful information but my emphasis on form and mediation takes me away from their investment in Eliot's "position." For an excellent discussion of *The Four Quartets* in relation to Britain's imperial decline, see Esty, *A Shrinking Island*.

6 T. S. Eliot, *The Waste Land: A Facsimile and Transcript of the Original Drafts Including the Annotations of Ezra Pound*, ed. Valerie Eliot (New York: Harcourt Brace & Company, 1971), 3. For the original quotation, see Joseph Conrad, *Heart of Darkness*, ed. Robert Kimbrough (New York: W.W. Norton & Company, 1988), 68.

7 Conrad, *Heart of Darkness*, 12.

8 Jameson, "Modernism and Imperialism," 160.

9 Ibid., 152, 157. Though Jameson is quite clear that he is describing a metropolitan perspective, he has still come under criticism for this focus. See, for instance, the essays in Booth and Rigby, eds., *Modernism and Empire*.

10 Ibid., 157.

11 Ibid., 160.

12 Ronald Bush has written eloquently on this topic. See Ronald Bush, "The Presence of the Past: Ethnographic Thinking/Literary Politics," in *Prehistories of the Future: The Primitivist Project and the Culture of Modernism*, ed. Elazar Barkan and Ronald Bush (Stanford, CA: Stanford University Press, 1995), 33. His argument is supported by an uncollected essay entitled "The Beating of a Drum" in which Eliot argues against the idea that dance originated in an attempt to mimic some supernatural power: "It is equally possible to assert that primitive man acted in a certain way and then found a reason for it. An unoccupied person, finding a drum, may be seized with a desire to beat it; but unless he is an imbecile he will be unable to continue beating, and thereby satisfying a need (rather than a 'desire') without finding a reason for

doing so." Rationalization follows instinct here in what Eliot seems to think is a universal quality. See T. S. Eliot, "The Beating of a Drum," *The Nation and the Athenaeum*, October 6 1923, 12.

13 Eliot explains that despite finishing the "first draft of my dissertation in 1916," he never finished the requirements for the degree. See T. S. Eliot, *Knowledge and Experience in the Philosophy of F. H. Bradley* (New York: Columbia University Press, 1964), 9, hereafter referred to parenthetically as *KE*.

14 Eliot's focus on the inter-subjective attempt to conjure up a common world of meaning has led various critics to align his thought with neo-pragmatism in general, and the work of the late Richard Rorty in particular. Of these the most compelling is Richard Shusterman, *T. S. Eliot and the Philosophy of Criticism* (London: Duckworth, 1988). Shusterman makes an excellent case for Eliot's interest in historical contingency, although it is doubtful that Eliot ever "maintained a non-foundational, non-absolutist, pragmatic view of human knowledge" (3). Furthermore, Eliot's claim that "if you have a definite ideal for society, then you are right to cultivate what is useful for the development and maintenance of that society, and discourage what is useless and distracting" is a far cry from Rorty's notion of truth as "what works" Eliot, *Selected Essays*, 458.

15 Here we find the central difference between Eliot and Bergsonian vitalism, for Eliot is less interested in the finite center itself, than in the process by which these centers create a common world out of their seeming detachment from that world. Despite never writing about Bergson at any great length, Eliot made numerous remarks about him in his prose that make clear his general opposition to what he once called the "thuriferous ju-ju" of Bergsonian intuition. See T. S. Eliot, "Books of the Quarter," *The New Criterion*, October 1926, 757. A year later, he phrased his objections more forcefully: "The Bergsonian time doctrine ... reaches the point of a *fatalism* which is wholly destructive. It is a pure naturalism." In the "fluid world" of vitalism, Eliot continued, "everything must be admired because nothing is permanent." See T. S. Eliot, "Mr. Middleton Murry's Synthesis," *The Monthly Criterion*, October 1927, 346, 347. Eliot here associates the primitivism of "ju-ju" – defined by the Oxford English Dictionary as "a fetish" and dated to 1894 – with historical determinism, as each seems to eviscerate both critical judgment and human agency. For a thorough discussion of Eliot's relationship to Bergson that takes a different position, see Donald J. Childs, *From Philosophy to Poetry: T. S. Eliot's Study of Knowledge and Experience* (London: The Athlone Press, 2001).

16 Quoted as the epigraph to Eliot, *The Waste Land: A Facsimile*, 1.

17 Altieri, "'Preludes' as Prelude," 19.

18 Ibid., 10.

19 Joseph McLaughlin, *Writing the Urban Jungle: Reading Empire in London from Doyle to Eliot* (Charlottesville: University Press of Virginia, 2000), 169. McLaughlin suggestively situates Eliot's poetic production in relation to London's cosmopolitan makeup, but his analysis rests on an insufficiently

mediated sense of the relationship between capitalism and subjectivity, as in the following claim: "People, as well as commodities and capital, were becoming increasingly international and cosmopolitan as cultural identity, like currency, became less fixed and more variable" (171).

20 *The Isle of Dogs* is also a lost play by Ben Jonson and Thomas Nashe that was suppressed by Elizabethan authorities, leading to a stay in jail for its playwrights. The phrase thus manages to correlate England's imperial present with its cultural past. I thank Travis Williams for this observation.

21 Cook, "T. S. Eliot and the Carthaginian Peace," 341.

22 Ibid., 342.

23 Levenson, "Does *The Waste Land* Have a Politics?" 9, 7.

24 Eliot, *The Waste Land: A Facsimile*, 43.

25 Moishe Postone, "Anti-Semitism and National Socialism," in *Germans and Jews since the Holocaust: The Changing Situation in West Germany*, ed. Anson Rabinbach and Jack Zipes (New York: Holmes & Meier, 1986), 311.

26 Ibid., 310.

27 Michael North, *The Political Aesthetics of Yeats, Eliot, and Pound* (New York: Cambridge University Press, 1991), 95.

28 Maud Ellmann, "The Imaginary Jew: T. S. Eliot and Ezra Pound," in *Between 'Race' and Culture: Representations of 'the Jew' in English and American Literature*, ed. Bryan Cheyette (Stanford, CA: Stanford University Press, 1996), 93.

29 Rainey's interest is "with the kind of order which is dictating the composition of the poem: that order is fundamentally contingent and retrospective. It is not, in other words, an order being achieved as the realization of a plan or program." See Rainey, *Revisiting the Waste Land*, 43. Although I am in sympathy with Rainey's argument, his textual approach is fundamentally a biographical one – a history of Eliot's decisions and revisions – whereas I am interested in the historical structures to which the poem responds.

30 Levenson, "Does *The Waste Land* Have a Politics?" 8.

31 Keynes, quoted in Levenson, 8.

32 Eliot's interest in India has been read mostly through the lens of comparative philosophy. Works include Cleo McNelly Kearns, *T. S. Eliot and Indic Traditions* (Cambridge: Cambridge University Press, 1987) and Vinod Sena and Rajiva Verma, eds., *The Fire and the Rose: New Essays on T. S. Eliot* (Delhi: Oxford University Press, 1992).

33 Davis, *Late Victorian Holocausts*, 9.

34 Ibid., 312.

35 Ibid., 174.

36 The process also worked the other way around, as India became a prime dumping ground for British goods, which, in turn, resulted in the deindustrialization of colonial lands. Davis writes: "The deindustrialization of Asia via the substitution of Lancashire cotton imports for locally manufactured textiles reached its climax only in the decades after the construction of the Crystal Palace" (294). This period coincides with the rise of German and American

industry. England's loss of its industrial prominence was masked, then, by its ability to force its colonies to absorb a "surplus of increasingly obsolescent and noncompetitive industrial exports" (298). Thus, even though the "coerced levies of wealth from India and China were not essential to the rise of British hegemony" – for this Davis credits the transatlantic trade in slaves and commodities – "they were absolutely crucial in postponing its decline" (296).

37 "There is considerable evidence, moreover, that in pre-British India before the creation of a railroad-girded national market in grain, village-level food reserves were larger, patrimonial welfare more widespread, and grain prices in surplus areas better insulated against speculation. (As we have seen, the perverse consequence of a unitary market was to export famine, via price inflation, to the rural poor in grain-surplus districts)" (Davis 285).

38 Ibid., 285.

39 Ibid., 280.

40 See Spivak, "Can the Subaltern Speak?" As should be clear, the success of this movement – like Pound's similar vexed interest in China – is up for debate. However, the impulse of the poem, here, is one of openness rather than appropriation.

41 Eliot's note reads "'Datta, dayadhvam, damyata' (Give, sympathize, control)." The standard translation of *Damyata*, however, is "self-control." The *Norton Anthology* glosses the passage as follows: "The Hindu fable referred to is that of gods, men, and demons each in turn asking of their father Prajapati, 'Speak to us, O Lord.' To each he replied with the one syllable '*DA*,' and each group interpreted it in a different way: '*Datta*,' to give alms; '*Dayadhvam*,' to have compassion; '*Damyata*,' to practice self-control." M. H. Abrams and Stephen Greenblatt, eds., *The Norton Anthology of English Literature*, 7th ed., vol. 2 (New York: W.W. Norton & Company, 2000), 2382.

42 This passage has become something of a critical crux for the poem, although it is generally conceded that the word "invited" explains its distinction from the scene with the typist. Hugh Kenner writes: "Unlike the rider, who may dominate his horse, the sailor survives and moves by cooperation with a nature that cannot be forced; ... If dominance compels response, control invites it: and the response comes 'gaily.' But – 'would have': the right relationship was never attempted." See Hugh Kenner, *The Invisible Poet: T. S. Eliot* (New York: McDowell, Obolensky, 1959), 177.

43 Rainey, *Revisiting The Waste Land*, 120.

44 Thomas Kyd, *The Spanish Tragedy*, ed. J. R. Mulryne (New York: W. W. Norton & Company, 1989), IV.i.174–8.

45 Kenner, *The Invisible Poet*, 180.

46 Richard Drain, "*The Waste Land*: The Prison and the Key," in *The Waste Land in Different Voices: The Revised Version of Lectures Given at the University of York in the Fiftieth Year of the Waste Land*, ed. A.D. Moody (London: Edward Arnold, 1974), 32.

47 Eliot, *Selected Essays*, 65.

48 Ibid., 67.

49 The phrase appears in both Swinburne's "Itylus," which begins "Swallow, my sister, O sister swallow" and Tennyson's "The Princess," Canto IV, 76 – "O Swallow, Swallow, flying, flying south" – and following.

3 COSMOPOLITAN KULCHUR: *THE CANTOS* AS WORLD LITERATURE

1 From the essay "The Renaissance" in Ezra Pound, *Literary Essays of Ezra Pound*, ed. T. S. Eliot (New York: New Directions, 1968), 218, hereafter referred to parenthetically as *LE*.

2 Hobsbawm, *Age of Empire*, 79.

3 Ibid.

4 Ibid., 144.

5 Hobson, *Imperialism*, 6.

6 Ibid., 67.

7 Georg Simmel, "The Metropolis and Mental Life," in *The Sociology of Georg Simmel*, ed. Kurt H. Wolff (London: The Free Press, 1950), 411.

8 Ibid.

9 Ibid., 411, 411–12.

10 Ibid., 416.

11 Ibid., 419.

12 Ibid.

13 Pound argued that money "*ought* to be the representation of something solid," and most often defined it as "a certificate of work done within a system" (*SP* 443, 311). He thus railed against the view of "Paterson, the founder of the 'Bank of England' [who] told his shareholders that they would profit because 'the bank hath profit on the interest of all the moneys which it creates out of nothing'" (*SP* 290). Money's abstract exchangeability leads to a loss of particularity that Pound felt infected all of society: "You can probably date any Western work of art by reference to the ethical estimate of usury prevalent at the time of that work's composition; the greater the component of tolerance for usury the more blobby and messy the work of art" (*SP* 76). The single best account of Pound's economics remains Peter Nicholls, *Ezra Pound: Politics, Economics and Writing* (London: Macmillan, 1984). See also Andrew Parker, "Ezra Pound and the 'Economy' of Anti-Semitism," in *Postmodernism and Politics*, ed. Jonathan Arac (Minneapolis: University of Minnesota Press, 1986), Richard Sieburth, "In Pound We Trust: The Economy of Poetry/the Poetry of Economics," *Critical Inquiry* 14, no. 1 (1987), and Leon Surette, *Pound in Purgatory: From Economic Radicalism to Anti-Semitism* (Urbana: University of Illinois Press, 1999).

14 Ezra Pound, *The Cantos of Ezra Pound* (New York: New Directions, 1986), II.6. Further references to *The Cantos* will refer parenthetically to canto number followed by the page.

15 Teodolinda Barolini, "Bertran De Born and Sordello: The Poetry of Politics in Dante's *Comedy*," *PMLA* 94, no. 3 (1979): 398.

16 Christine Froula, *To Write Paradise: Style and Error in Pound's Cantos* (New Haven, CT: Yale University Press, 1984), 155.

17 Charles Altieri, *Painterly Abstraction in Modernist American Poetry: The Contemporaneity of Modernism* (Cambridge: Cambridge University Press, 1989), 308.

18 There would seem little to add to the conversation about Pound's politics. His anti-Semitism is indisputable, despite the oft-trotted out passages where he offers what is, at best, an ambiguous critique of anti-Semitism. See, for instance, the essay "What is Money for?" where Pound writes: "At this point, and to prevent the dragging in of red-herrings, I wish to distinguish between prejudice against the Jew as such and the suggestion that the Jew should face his own problem" (*SP* 299). It should hardly need saying that the effort to distinguish his critique from prejudice is negated by referring to usury as the Jew's "own problem," not to mention the use of the word "jewspapers" in the preceding sentence. Pound's fascist commitments are less clear. He does betray a career-long interest in the heroic individual, particularly the heroic *political* individual, and although he often associated the artist with the worker, and in this way deflated inherited notions of the exceptional artistic genius, he also tended to view Mussolini as an artist claiming that any true estimate of *Il Duce* must start "from his passion for construction. Treat him as *artifex* and all the details fall into place. Take him as anything save the artist and you will get muddled with contradictions." Ezra Pound, *Jefferson and/or Mussolini* (New York: Liveright Publishing, 1936), 34. For judicious estimations of Pound's politics, see Tim Redman, *Ezra Pound and Italian Fascism* (Cambridge: Cambridge University Press, 1991) and Surette, *Pound in Purgatory*. The case for the prosecution is made in Robert Casillo, *The Genealogy of Demons: Anti-Semitism, Fascism, and the Myths of Ezra Pound* (Evanston, IL: Northwestern University Press, 1988). A nuanced and intelligent version of the anti-Pound argument – one that refrains from sentences that begin "Like Hitler, Pound" – can be found in Paul Morrison, *The Poetics of Fascism: Ezra Pound, T. S. Eliot, Paul de Man* (New York: Oxford University Press, 1996).

19 Slavoj Žižek has made this link most forcefully in his essay "Multiculturalism, or the Cultural Logic of Multinational Capital," and similar claims have been made by Timothy Brennan, David Palumbo-Liu and E. San Juan, Jr. See Timothy Brennan, *At Home in the World: Cosmopolitanism Now* (Cambridge, MA: Harvard University Press, 1997), particularly 155–162, David Palumbo-Liu, "Multiculturalism Now: Civilization, National Identity, and Difference before and after September 11th," *boundary 2* 29, no. 2 (2002), E. San Juan, Jr., *Racism and Cultural Studies: Critiques of Multiculturalist Ideology and the Politics of Difference* (Durham, NC: Duke University Press, 2002) and Slavoj Žižek, "Multiculturalism, or, the Cultural Logic of Multinational Capitalism," *New Left Review* I, no. 225 (1997).

20 The only sustained consideration of Pound's multicultural poetics is in Joon-Hwan Kim, *Out of the "Western Box": Towards a Multicultural Poetics in the Poetry of Ezra Pound and Charles Olson* (New York: Peter Lang Publishing,

2003). Kim's book is sympathetic to Pound, but argues that since Pound's "multicultural poetics aimed to reconstruct Western culture," they serve only to assimilate "the Other ... into the grand Odyssean-Dantean narrative of emancipation through [Pound's] Enlightenment rationality," a problem Charles Olson somehow seems to avoid (82, 83). Here, Kim manages simultaneously to underestimate Pound's critique of the Enlightenment and overemphasize the need to overthrow all vestiges of Enlightenment thinking.

21 Stanley Fish gives an excellent account of this problem, although his solution – "inspired adhockery" – is as unsatisfactory as it is predictable. See Stanley Fish, "Boutique Multiculturalism, or Why Liberals Are Incapable of Thinking About Hate Speech," *Critical Inquiry* 23, no. 2 (1997).

22 Ulrich Beck, Seyla Benhabib and Vijay Prashad, among others, have made this argument. See Ulrich Beck, "The Cosmopolitan Society and Its Enemies," *Theory, Culture & Society* 19, no. 1–2 (2002), Seyla Benhabib, "The Liberal Imagination and the Four Dogmas of Multiculturalism," *Yale Journal of Criticism* 12, no. 2 (1999) and Vijay Prashad, *Everybody Was Kung Fu Fighting: Afro-Asian Connections and the Myth of Cultural Purity* (Boston: Beacon Press, 2001). Rey Chow argues that the fetish of difference is itself dependent upon a post-structuralist logic and that this dependence undoes the ubiquitous rhetoric of resistance that marginalized ethnicities often claim against a theory seen to be irremediably Eurocentric. See Rey Chow, "The Interruption of Referentiality: Poststructuralism and the Conundrum of Critical Multiculturalism," *The South Atlantic Quarterly* 101, no. 1 (2002).

23 The first phrase is from Beck, "The Cosmopolitan Society and Its Enemies," 37 and is echoed by Prashad, *Everybody Was Kung Fu Fighting*, 61 and San Juan, *Racism and Cultural Studies*, 198. The second is from Fish, "Boutique Multiculturalism," 382.

24 Hence, the United Colors of Benetton. This much-discussed ad campaign, and an apologetic discussion of it in the journal *Postcolonial Studies* (3.3), form the core of Crystal Bartolovich's essay on the relationship between Marxism and postcolonial studies, particularly around the categories of diversity and political economy. See Bartolovich, "Introduction." The argument about diversity as a symptom of global capitalism comes from Žižek, "Multiculturalism."

25 Benhabib nicely summarizes this point: "'The culture wars' are, in my view, unintelligible unless we understand more clearly how culture has become a ubiquitous synonym for identity, as well as an identity-marker and differentiator ... What is novel is that social and political groups forming around such identity-markers plead for special recognition from the state and its agencies in the name of their cultural specificity." Benhabib, "The Liberal Imagination," 401.

26 San Juan, *Racism and Cultural Studies*, 9.

27 Cary Wolfe, "Ezra Pound and the Politics of Patronage," *American Literature* 63, no. 1 (1991): 27, 30.

28 "As a value, the commodity is an equivalent; as an equivalent, all its natural properties are extinguished." Marx, *Grundrisse*, 141. "The transformation

of the commodity into exchange value does not equate it to any particular commodity, but expresses it as equivalent, expresses its exchangeability relation, *vis-à-vis* all other commodities." Marx, *Grundrisse*, 144.

29 John Guillory, *Cultural Capital: The Problem of Literary Canon Formation* (Chicago: University of Chicago Press, 1993), 308. For the discussion of what Guillory calls the "double discourse of value," see 269–340.

30 Of course, Pound's career was long and complicated and there are obvious differences between the early Pound – who spent most of his time talking about poetry – and the later Pound, who was more overtly concerned with economics and ultimately descended into anti-Semitic rancor. Yet, as any scholar working on Pound can attest, both of these concerns are present in all phases of a body of work that is often quite contradictory, even within the same time period. This fact makes constructing a developmental timeline out of Pound's creative output a somewhat quixotic endeavor. To this end, I have emphasized concerns that I find common to all periods of his work. Nevertheless, the bulk of the prose I address comes from the 1910s and 1920s and when I turn to later texts – such as 1938's *Guide to Kulchur* – I have done so to highlight these continuities.

31 Ezra Pound, *Guide to Kulchur* (New York: New Directions, 1970), 8.

32 T. S. Eliot, "Notes Towards the Definition of Culture," in *Christianity and Culture* (New York: Harvest/HBJ, 1968), 127.

33 See Emily Apter, "Global *Translatio*: The 'Invention' of Comparative Literature, Istanbul, 1933," *Critical Inquiry* 29, no. 2 (2003), Jonathan Arac, "Anglo-Globalism," *New Left Review*, no. 16 (2002), Djelal Kadir, "To World, to Globalize – Comparative Literature's Crossroads," *Comparative Literature Studies* 41, no. 1 (2004) and Efrain Kristal, "Considering Coldly: A Reply to Franco Moretti," *New Left Review*, no. 15 (2002). Moretti has, in turn, replied to his critics in Franco Moretti, "More Conjectures," *New Left Review*, no. 20 (2003).

34 Franco Moretti, "Conjectures on World Literature," *New Left Review*, no. 1 (2000): 58.

35 Ibid.

36 Ibid., 68.

37 Apter, "Global Translatio," 256.

38 Quoted in Froula, *To Write Paradise*, 145.

39 Christine Froula, "The Beauties of Mistranslation: On Pound's English after *Cathay*," in *Ezra Pound & China*, ed. Zhaoming Qian (Ann Arbor: University of Michigan Press, 2003), 61.

40 Hugh Kenner, "Introduction," in *Ezra Pound: Translations* (New York: New Directions, 1963), 9.

41 Benjamin, *Illuminations*, 81.

42 Eric Hayot provides an excellent summary of the debate, which asks whether Pound's interest in China is a replication of, or challenge to, existing Orientalist discourse. See Eric Hayot, "Critical Dreams: Orientalism, Modernism, and the Meaning of Pound's China," *Twentieth Century*

Literature 45, no. 4 (1999). An expanded version of this argument can also be found in Eric Hayot, *Chinese Dreams: Pound, Brecht, Tel Quel* (Ann Arbor: University of Michigan Press, 2004). A surprising number of Pound's critics, from Wai-Lim Yip onward, have argued that his poems capture the "spirit" of the originals, despite many obvious "howlers," and the alarming fact that he knew no Chinese. Zhaoming Qian has even shown how Pound's interpretations have been supported by recent Chinese language scholarship, a point also made by Feng Lan in his book on Pound's Confucianism. See Feng Lan, *Ezra Pound and Confucianism: Remaking Humanism in the Face of Modernity* (Toronto: University of Toronto Press, 2005), Zhaoming Qian, *Orientalism and Modernism: The Legacy of China in Pound and Williams* (Durham, NC: Duke University Press, 1995), and Wai-Lim Yip, *Ezra Pound's Cathay* (Princeton, NJ: Princeton University Press, 1969). What emerges from this recent scholarship is a more nuanced picture of the way *Cathay* both conforms to certain Western stereotypes of the East – as, for instance, in the argument of Barry Ahearn – and yet, at the same time, represents an advance over the domestication of earlier Victorian translations such as those by Herbert Giles. See Barry Ahearn, "*Cathay*: What Sort of Translation?" in *Ezra Pound & China*, ed. Zhaoming Qian (Ann Arbor: University of Michigan Press, 2003). Two excellent recent discussions of Pound and China can be found in Christopher Bush, *Ideographic Modernism: China, Writing, Media* (Oxford: Oxford University Press, 2010), Josephine Nock-Hee Park, *Apparitions of Asia: Modernist Form and Asian American Poetics* (Oxford: Oxford University Press, 2008). What I hope to add to this discussion is a consideration of the political economy of Pound's interest in China.

43 Froula, "The Beauties of Mistranslation," 51.

44 Ibid., 60.

45 Ibid., 60, 61.

46 Ibid., 61. The distinction between "represent" and "bring into being" is admittedly a crucial one. It situates Pound in the orbit of Kant's *Third Critique*, where the *sensus communis aestheticus* is either revealed or created by the subjective universality of aesthetic judgment. This argument is replayed within Pound criticism by Charles Altieri's criticism of Michael André Bernstein for failing to understand the futurity of Pound's tribe. See Altieri, *Painterly Abstraction*, 474, n.8.

47 Although Paul Morrison's argument that in the poem a "Dantean or Confucian commitment to proper names … [ultimately] emerges triumphant" provides a compelling account of the content of the later Cantos, it fails to address the simple and yet important fact that the poem remains "at sea" even in its final line, still negotiating the various cultures of its polyglot form. See Morrison, *The Poetics of Fascism*, 19.

48 The word "botched," of course, comes from Section V of "Hugh Selwyn Mauberley": "There died a myriad, / And of the best, among them, / For an old bitch gone in the teeth, / For a botched civilization." See Ezra Pound, *Personae*, (New York: New Directions, 1990), 188.

49 Ezra Pound, *Collected Early Poems*, ed. Michael King (New York: New Directions, 1976), 209, hereafter referred to parenthetically as *CEP*. This metaphor can also be found in the poem "Purveyors General," which asks for praise from the "Home-Stayers" for "We, that through all the world / Have wandered seeking new things / And quaint tales" (*CEP* 61–2).

50 Hence Pound's somewhat cryptic reference to Eliot in the opening of Canto VIII: "These fragments you have shelved (shored)." Pound here suggests that Eliot's poem fails to circulate its various cultural fragments. His shoring is a form of shelving that cuts off poetry from any public utility.

51 These ideas are quite familiar to students of Pound as they appear in a variety of disguises: in Imagism's "direct treatment of the 'thing'" (*LE* 3) with its concomitant assertion that "the natural object is always the *adequate* symbol" (*LE* 5); in the 1912 claim that "it is not until poetry lives again 'close to the thing' that it will be a vital part of contemporary life" (*SP* 41); and in a 1934 description of the "ideogrammic method" as "the examination and juxtaposition of particular specimens – e.g. particular works, passages of literature" (*LE* 61).

52 Ezra Pound, *The Spirit of Romance* (New York: New Directions, 1968), 5.

53 Roland Barthes, "The Reality Effect," in *French Literary Theory Today: A Reader*, ed. Tzvetan Todorov (Cambridge: Cambridge University Press, 1982), Bill Brown, *The Material Unconscious: American Amusement, Stephen Crane & the Economics of Play* (Cambridge, MA: Harvard University Press, 1996), Fredric Jameson, "The Realist Floor-Plan," in *On Signs*, ed. Marshall Blonsky (Baltimore, MD: Johns Hopkins, 1985).

54 The translation from Flaubert is from Carroll F. Terrell, *A Companion to the Cantos of Ezra Pound* (Berkeley: University of California Press, 1993), 30. Pound has substantially rearranged the phrases from Flaubert's original.

55 Jameson, "The Realist Floor-Plan," 373. Gustave Flaubert, *Three Tales*, trans. Robert Baldick (New York: Penguin, 1986), 7.

56 Jameson, "The Realist Floor-Plan," 379.

57 Ibid., 383.

58 Jameson writes: "I believe that the symbolic and iconographic readings which have been proposed of the temple … correspond to a nostalgia for meaning … a high modernist longing for symbolic unification which seeks to convert the work of art into an immense organic totality, most frequently under the sign of 'myth.'" Ibid., 382.

59 Ibid., 383.

60 "poor old Homer blind, / blind as a bat, / Ear, ear for the sea-surge; / rattle of old men's voices" (VII.24). Where Canto VII has "rattle" Canto II reads "murmur." The obscure point here is that despite his blindness, Homer wrote out of direct observation.

61 Altieri, *Painterly Abstraction*, 474, n. 8. Altieri is here arguing against Michael André Bernstein. See note 45. The phrase "tale of the tribe" is from Pound, *Guide to Kulchur*, 194.

62 Froula, *To Write Paradise*, 4. The phrase "a record of struggle" is also from Pound, *Guide to Kulchur*, 135.

63 Pound, *Personae*, 3.

64 In *Gaudier-Brzeska* Pound writes "In the 'search for oneself,' in the search for 'sincere self-expression,' one gropes, one finds some seeming verity. One says 'I am' this, that, or the other, and with the words scarcely uttered one ceases to be that thing." See Ezra Pound, *Gaudier-Brzeska: A Memoir* (New York: New Directions, 1970), 85. The crucial point is that sincerity is not, for Pound, a way of expressing an interior state; it is, rather, an objective criterion of the accuracy of perception, a distinction, that is to say, between sincerity of content and sincerity of form. Hence the anecdote of the Russian correspondent, who tells Pound, "I see, you wish to give people new eyes, not to make them see some new particular thing" (*Gaudier-Brzeska*, 85). Altieri summarizes this aspect of Pound well – "Art expresses, not worlds or selves, but ways of seeing and arranging the world" – although he goes on to argue for the abstract quality of these ways of seeing, whereas I focus on their emergence from specific situations. See Altieri, *Painterly Abstraction*, 299, and chapter 8 generally.

65 Judith Butler, "Universality in Culture," in *For Love of Country?* ed. Joshua Cohen (Boston: Beacon Press, 1996), 48.

66 Ibid., 51.

67 Ibid.

68 Zhaoming Qian, "Painting into Poetry: Pound's Seven Lakes Cantos," in *Ezra Pound & China*, ed. Zhaoming Qian (Ann Arbor: University of Michigan Press, 2003), 72.

69 Qian, "Painting into Poetry," 90. For further details on the screen book, see Sanehide Kodama, *American Poetry and Japanese Culture* (Hamden, CT: Archon, 1984), esp. 105–120.

70 Qian, "Painting into Poetry," 91.

71 Qian notes this shift to a "pre-World War II Euro-American context," with Pound becoming "a Westerner seeking a way out of political chaos," but does not elaborate (91). My reading of the Canto's end can be seen as a specification of the context to which Qian only gestures.

72 Moretti, "Conjectures," 62, 61.

73 Ibid., 55.

74 Quoted in Angela J. Palandri, "The 'Seven Lakes Canto' Revisited," *Paideuma* 3 (1974): 51.

4 TURNING CONSUMPTION INTO PRODUCTION:
ULYSSES AND THE CONSTRUCTION OF
POSTCOLONIAL AGENCY

1 James Joyce, *Ulysses* (New York: Random House, 1961), 7, 14, hereafter referred to parenthetically as *U*.

2 Declan Kiberd, "James Joyce and Mythic Realism," in *Inventing Ireland* (Cambridge, MA: Harvard University Press, 1996), 347, 346, 347.

3 Georg Lukács, "The Ideology of Modernism," in *The Meaning of Contemporary Realism* (London: Merlin Press, 1963), 18. Franco Moretti agrees with this

assessment, although not with Lukács's dismissal: "Joyce is telling us that all days are the same: this devastates – to Lukác's [sic] dismay – historical and 'literary' perspective ... and with it the idea of historical 'progress.'" See Franco Moretti, "The Long Goodbye: *Ulysses* and the End of Liberal Capitalism," in *Signs Taken for Wonders: Essays in the Sociology of Literary Forms* (London: NLB, 1983), 263. The phrase "mythical method" can be found in T. S. Eliot, "Ulysses, Order, and Myth," *The Dial* (1923): 483.

4 Thus, M. Keith Booker argues that "Lukács' criticism of Joyce ... may ... be accurate" but he "fails to take into account Joyce's position as a postcolonial writer." Nicholas Brown claims that *Ulysses* is a text in which "any sense of historical movement is foreclosed." Enda Duffy remarks that "Dublin in *Ulysses* is a place without any center of viable political power and hence ... without any real possibility that the city could exist as the site of a viable community." Emer Nolan locates Joyce's ambivalent relationship to nationalism in the vexed politics of his time, suggesting that "writing about nationalism is by necessity deformed in contemporary conditions." See M. Keith Booker, *Ulysses, Capitalism, and Colonialism: Reading Joyce after the Cold War* (Westport, CT: Greenwood Press, 2000), 118, Nicholas Brown, *Utopian Generations: The Political Horizon of Twentieth-Century Literature* (Princeton, NJ: Princeton University Press, 2005), 37, Enda Duffy, "Disappearing Dublin: *Ulysses*, Postcoloniality, and the Politics of Space," in *Semicolonial Joyce*, ed. Derek Attridge and Marjorie Howes (Cambridge: Cambridge University Press, 2000), 49 and Emer Nolan, *James Joyce and Nationalism* (London: Routledge, 1995), 68.

5 In the seminal essay "Ireland, Saints and Sages," Joyce claims that it is "rather naïve to heap insults on England for her misdeeds in Ireland. A conqueror cannot be causal, and for so many centuries the Englishman has done in Ireland only what the Belgian is doing today in the Congo Free State." See James Joyce, *The Critical Writings of James Joyce*, ed. Ellsworth Mason and Richard Ellmann (Ithaca, NY: Cornell University Press, 1989), 166. England, in Joyce's estimation, "was as cruel as she was cunning. Her weapons were, and still are, the battering-ram, the club, and the rope" (166). Joyce also discusses the development of underdevelopment: "Ireland is poor because English laws ruined the country's industries, especially the wool industry, because the neglect of the English government in the years of the potato famine allowed the best of the population to die from hunger" (167). As for the Irish, Joyce argues that "the English came to Ireland at the repeated request of a native king" and that "parliamentary union was not legislated at Westminster but at Dublin, by a parliament elected by the vote of the people of Ireland" (162).

6 Brown, *Utopian Generations*, 39. The phrase about the literary tradition is from Franco Moretti, *The Way of the World: The Bildungsroman in European Culture*, trans. Albert Sbragia (New York: Verso, 2000), 242.

7 Cheryl Herr, *Joyce's Anatomy of Culture* (Chicago: University of Illinois Press, 1986), 167.

8 Enda Duffy, *The Subaltern 'Ulysses'* (Minneapolis: University of Minnesota Press, 1994), 156.

9 Marx, *Capital, Volume I*, 163.

10 Garry Leonard, *Advertising and Commodity Culture in Joyce* (Gainesville: University Press of Florida, 1998), 13.

11 David Lloyd, *Anomalous States: Irish Writing and the Post-Colonial Moment* (Durham, NC: Duke University Press, 1993). For more on the peculiarity of the Irish colonial situation, see the excellent work of Joe Cleary both "Misplaced Ideas? Locating and Dislocating Ireland in Colonial and Postcolonial Studies," in *Marxism, Modernity and Postcolonial Studies*, ed. Crystal Bartolovich and Neil Lazarus (Cambridge: Cambridge University Press, 2002) and "Toward a Materialist-Formalist History of Twentieth-Century Irish Literature," *boundary 2* 31, no. 1 (2004). The specificity of the Irish situation is also reflected in Irish historiography, which has shifted back and forth from reading the Irish as imperialism's victims to some of its most willing partners. For a helpful overview of this material see Seamus Deane, "Introduction," in *Nationalism, Colonialism, and Literature* (Minneapolis: University of Minnesota Press, 1990).

12 Mary C. King, "Hermeneutics of Suspicion: Nativism, Nationalism, and the Language Question in 'Oxen of the Sun'," *James Joyce Quarterly* 35, no. 2–3 (1998): 351.

13 As Jeremy Hawthorn has shown, "nearly every Marxist account of 'Ulysses' written in the 1930s commented upon the fact that its characters belong to the petty-bourgeoisie," as if this was a problem rather than an accurate description of the social order of colonial Dublin. See Jeremy Hawthorn, "'Ulysses,' Modernism and Marxist Criticism," in *James Joyce and Modern Literature*, ed. W. J. McCormack and Alistair Stead (Boston, MA: Routledge and Kegan Paul, 1982), 113.

14 Lukács, "The Ideology of Modernism," 43, 21.

15 Ibid., 18, 21.

16 Georg Lukács, "Franz Kafka or Thomas Mann," in *The Meaning of Contemporary Realism* (London: Merlin Press, 1963), 78.

17 Enda Duffy reads this claim as "deeply ironic given the 1916 destruction" of the city. See Duffy, "Disappearing Dublin," 45.

18 This fact, noted by many critics, is stated succinctly by Trevor L. Williams who argues that in *Portrait* there "is never any doubt that the artist, like every other human being, is being 'produced' by a specific social context." See Trevor L. Williams, "Dominant Ideologies: The Production of Stephen Dedalus," in *James Joyce: The Augmented Ninth*, ed. Bernard Benstock (Syracuse, NY: Syracuse University Press, 1988), 312.

19 Cleary, "Toward a Materialist-Formalist History," 208.

20 Ibid., 208–9.

21 Ibid., 210.

22 The term "scientific discovery" comes from Eliot, "Ulysses, Order, and Myth," 482. The latter two phrases are Ezra Pound's, and they are as perceptive as they are undeveloped.

23 Williams, *Dream Worlds*, 3.

24 Much of this work is marred by an ideological investment in commodity culture itself, imagined, as in Garry Leonard's work, as a form of

"popular culture" that resists "all 'official' metanarratives," recording instead a "history of the now." See Leonard, *Advertising and Commodity Culture in Joyce*, xi.

25 Duffy, *The Subaltern 'Ulysses'*, 69.

26 Ibid., 155.

27 See Anne McClintock, *Imperial Leather: Race, Gender and Sexuality in the Colonial Contest* (New York: Routledge, 1995) and Richards, *Commodity Culture*.

28 Quoted in McClintock, *Imperial Leather*, 207.

29 Ibid., 43.

30 Ibid., 207.

31 Richards, *Commodity Culture*, 121.

32 Ibid., 121–3.

33 McClintock, *Imperial Leather*, 30.

34 See Vincent J. Cheng, *Joyce, Race, and Empire* (Cambridge: Cambridge University Press, 1995), particularly chapter 2. Cheng builds on the work of L. Perry Curtis, *Apes and Angels; the Irishman in Victorian Caricature* (Washington, DC: Smithsonian Institution Press, 1971).

35 According to Seamus Deane, Arnold "provided the Irish revival with one of its most cherished opinions about the utilitarian English spirit's incapacity to deal with the wild freedom of the imaginative Celt." See Seamus Deane, "'Masked with Matthew Arnold's Face': Joyce and Liberalism," in *James Joyce: The Centennial Symposium*, ed. Morris Beja (Chicago: University of Illinois Press, 1986), 11. The key Arnold texts are Matthew Arnold, "The Incompatibles," in *Complete Prose Works Vol. 9*, ed. R. H. Super (Ann Arbor: University of Michigan Press, 1977), and "On the Study of Celtic Literatures," in *Complete Prose Works Vol. 3*, ed. R. H. Super (Ann Arbor: University of Michigan Press, 1960). A powerful revision of Joyce's relationship to the Irish Revival can be found in Gregory Castle, *Modernism and the Celtic Revival* (Cambridge: Cambridge University Press, 2001). Joyce, Castle argues, "was critical of [the Celtic Revival] but did not repudiate it, and precisely in this way he succeeded in redefining it" (9).

36 It is, of course, nothing new to assert that Joyce rejected the common ground upon which Irish nationalism and British imperialism met. Indeed, the cosmopolitan Joyce has long been enshrined in the scholarship, animating the work of such luminaries as Richard Ellmann and Hugh Kenner, and representing a continuation of Joyce's self-enforced exile from his homeland. Recent criticism, however, has returned Joyce to the island from which he fled, reading in his work an adherence to the basic structures of Irish nationalist historiography, finding ambivalence or allegiance where once there seemed only to be rejection. A helpful summary of this nationalist turn is provided in Marjorie Howes and Derek Attridge, "Introduction," in *Semicolonial Joyce*, ed. Derek Attridge and Marjorie Howes (Cambridge: Cambridge University Press, 2000). Major works include Duffy, *The Subaltern 'Ulysses,'* Fredric Jameson, "*Ulysses* in History," in *James Joyce: A*

Collection of Critical Essays, ed. Mary T. Reynolds (Englewood Cliffs, NJ: Prentice Hall, 1993), Kiberd, "James Joyce and Mythic Realism," David Lloyd, "Adulteration and the Nation," in *Anomalous States: Irish Writing and the Post-Colonial Moment* (Durham, NC: Duke University Press, 1993) and Nolan, *James Joyce and Nationalism*. See also the work of Seamus Deane, including "Introduction," "Joyce and Nationalism," in *James Joyce: New Perspectives*, ed. Colin MacCabe (Bloomington: Indiana University Press, 1982), and "'Masked with Matthew Arnold's Face'." This critical oscillation between an apolitical cosmopolitanism and a politicized nationalism is, in my view, not simply a choice of critical perspective but something produced by *Ulysses* itself.

37 Patrick McGee, *Joyce Beyond Marx: History and Desire in Ulysses and Finnegans Wake* (Gainesville: University Press of Florida, 2001), 187.

38 Eliot, "Ulysses, Order, and Myth," 483.

39 Max Horkheimer and Theodor W. Adorno, *Dialectic of Enlightenment: Philosophical Fragments*, ed. Gunzelin Schmid Noerr, trans. Edmund Jephcott (Stanford, CA: Stanford University Press, 2002), 37.

40 See Timothy Brennan, "The National Longing for Form," in *Nation and Narration*, ed. Homi K. Bhabha (New York: Routledge, 1990).

41 Horkheimer and Adorno, *Dialectic of Enlightenment*, xviii.

42 Ibid., 1.

43 Theodor W. Adorno, *Negative Dialectics*, trans. E. B. Ashton (New York: Continuum, 1992), 320.

44 Horkheimer and Adorno, *Dialectic of Enlightenment*, 35.

45 Theodor W. Adorno, *Critical Models: Interventions and Catchwords*, trans. Henry W. Pickford (New York: Columbia University Press, 1998), 6.

46 Benjamin writes: "The dialectic of commodity production in advanced capitalism: the novelty of products – as a stimulus to demand – is accorded an unprecedented importance. At the same time, 'the eternal return of the same' is manifest in mass production." See Benjamin, *The Arcades Project*, 331. The reference to "shared work" comes from Benjamin's letter to Adorno dated 1 December, 1932. See Adorno and Benjamin, *The Complete Correspondence*, 21.

47 Deane, "Joyce and Nationalism," 181.

48 See, for instance, Homi Bhabha, "Signs Taken for Wonders: Question of Ambivalence and Authority under a Tree Outside Delhi, May 1817," in *The Location of Culture* (New York: Routledge, 1994).

49 From Adorno's letter to Benjamin, dated 2 August 1935 – 4 August 1935. See Adorno and Benjamin, *The Complete Correspondence*, 105.

50 James Joyce, *A Portrait of the Artist as a Young Man* (New York: Viking Press, 1964), 212, hereafter referred to parenthetically as *P*.

51 Flaubert had written, in his March 18, 1857 letter to Mademoiselle Leroyer de Chantepie: "The artist must be in his work as God is in creation, invisible and all-powerful; one must sense him everywhere but never see him." See Gustave Flaubert, *The Letters of Gustave Flaubert: 1830–1857*, trans. Francis Steegmuller (Cambridge, MA: Belknap Press of Harvard, 1980), 230.

52 James Joyce, *Stephen Hero* (New York: New Directions, 1963), 27, hereafter referred to parenthetically as *SH*. This development is typical as *Stephen Hero* tends to make explicit what, in the much shorter text of *Portrait*, is merely implied.

53 There is in this phrase a further irony, for in between "the language of memory" and the realization that he has misquoted Nash, a "louse crawled over the nape of his neck" (*P* 233). Joyce is here allowing the physical world to deflate Stephen's intellectual pretension, even as he shows that Stephen's very thoughts are structured, in ways he seems not to notice, by the world around him.

54 Garry Leonard, *Advertising and Commodity Culture in Joyce* (Tampa: University Press of Florida, 1998), 3.

55 Knapp, *Literary Modernism and the Transformation of Work* (Evanston, IL: Northwestern University Press, 1988), 140.

56 See Kenner, *The Pound Era*, 39.

57 This division is not absolute, but certainly the first four chapters of the novel are the most conventional, remaining within the basic parameters of stream of consciousness. "Lotus-Eaters" and "Laestrogonians" also proceed from Bloom's subjective state. With "Hades," I am on shakier ground, and "Aelous" represents the first appearance of what David Hayman has called the arranger, the presence that announces itself as self-consciously shaping the narrative of the novel. Nevertheless, it is still true that the stylistic determinations of these chapters pale in comparison to those of "Sirens" or "Cyclops," to say nothing of "Oxen of the Sun," or of the book's final three chapters, each of which moves towards the subject's ultimate dissolution.

58 Michael Tratner, *Modernism and Mass Politics: Joyce, Woolf, Eliot, Yeats* (Stanford, CA: Stanford University Press, 1995), 186.

59 That Molly's subjectivity is boundless is among the most standard tropes of Joyce criticism. Fredric Jameson has discussed Eumaeus and Ithaca as presenting "the centred but psychologised subject and the reified object" respectively. Calling the chapters the most boring parts of the novel, he reads Joyce as forcing "us to work through in detail everything that is intolerable about this opposition," and so moving toward "the construction of a form of discourse from which the subject – sender or receiver – is radically excluded." See Jameson, "*Ulysses* in History," 157. Nicholas Brown reads "Eumaeus" and "Ithaca" in terms of a Heideggerian inflected notion of reification, arguing that "the subjective-error language of 'Eumaeus' fumbles for the object, while the rigors of 'Ithaca' reach from objectivity to the subject." See Brown, *Utopian Generations*, 41.

60 McCormack, "James Joyce, Cliche and the Irish Language," in *James Joyce: The Augmented Ninth*, ed. Bernard Benstock (Syracuse, NY: Syracuse University Press, 1988), 329.

61 Brown, *Utopian Generations*, 50.

62 C. L. Innes, "Modernism, Ireland and Empire: Yeats, Joyce and Their Implied Audiences," in *Modernism and Empire*, ed. Howard J. Booth and Nigel Rigby (New York: Manchester University Press, 2000), 151.

63 "In the very years that Dublin was being represented with an intense attention to detail in *Ulysses*, swathes of the real city center were being destroyed." See Duffy, "Disappearing Dublin," 37.

64 Hugh Kenner, *Ulysses* (Baltimore: Johns Hopkins University Press, 1987), 145.

5 "MOMENTS OF PRIDE IN ENGLAND": VIRGINIA
WOOLF AND THE FORMS OF NATIONAL
SUBJECTIVITY

1 Virginia Woolf, *The Voyage Out* (New York: Penguin Books, 1992), 42, hereafter referred to parenthetically as *VO*.

2 Virginia Woolf, *Mrs. Dalloway* (New York: Harcourt Inc., 2005), 123, hereafter referred to parenthetically as *MD*.

3 Christine Froula, who has written the definitive essay from this perspective, concludes that "Neither the strength nor the resources of Rachel's desire are equal to the powerful cultural currents that oppose it, however, and the history of Woolf's heroine ends not in triumph but in death." See Christine Froula, "Out of the Chrysalis: Female Initiation and Female Authority in Virginia Woolf's *The Voyage Out*," *Tulsa Studies in Women's Literature* 5, no. 1 (1986): 63.

4 There are, to be sure, important exceptions to this remark, notably, the artist figures Lily Briscoe and Miss La Trobe, as well as the suicides Septimus Warren Smith and Rhoda from *The Waves*. Nevertheless, even when the focus is not squarely on such acculturated subjects as Clarissa Dalloway, they are hardly treated with the heavy satire of Woolf's first two novels. Clearly something was to be salvaged and praised in these women that Woolf had previously overlooked.

5 Virginia Woolf, *Night and Day* (New York: Penguin, 1975), 470.

6 The obvious exception is *Orlando*, although here the investigation of other cultures is subsumed into a narrative focusing on continuities and discontinuities within the English nation.

7 Esty, *A Shrinking Island*, 86.

8 Woolf, *Jacob's Room*, 96.

9 Of the many works in this tradition, I have found particularly helpful Ian Baucom, *Out of Place: Englishness, Empire, and the Locations of Identity* (Princeton, NJ: Princeton University Press, 1999), and Simon Gikandi, *Maps of Englishness* (New York: Columbia University Press, 1996).

10 The phrase "gigantic falsehood" comes from Woolf's essay "The Memoirs of Sarah Bernhardt" (*E* 1: 169), while the second quotation is from Jane de Gay, *Virginia Woolf's Novels and the Literary Past* (Edinburgh: Edinburgh University Press, 2006), 2. Gillian Beer makes a similar point, claiming that Woolf "did not simply reject the Victorians and their concerns, or renounce them. Instead she persistingly rewrote them." See Gillian Beer, *Arguing with the Past: Essays in Narrative from Woolf to Sidney* (New York: Routledge, 1989), 140.

11 Laura Doyle, "Toward a Philosophy of Transnationalism," *Journal of Transnational American Studies* 1, no. 1 (2009): 1.
12 Ibid., 6.
13 Ibid., 11.
14 See Moretti, *The Way of the World*.
15 Giovanni Arrighi, *The Long Twentieth Century: Money, Power and the Origin of Our Times* (New York: Verso, 1994), 51.
16 Ibid.
17 Ibid., 54.
18 Ibid., 55.
19 See Jeanette McVicker, "'Six Essays on London Life': A History of Dispersal, Part I," *Woolf Studies Annual* 9 (2003) and "'Six Essays on London Life': A History of Dispersal, Part II," *Woolf Studies Annual* 10 (2004).
20 Several critics have noticed the connections between these two figures but in entirely different contexts. See Raphael Ingelbien, "They Saw One They Knew: Baudelaire and the Ghosts of London Modernism," *English Studies* 88, no. 1 (2007), Erwin R. Steinberg, "*Mrs. Dalloway* and T. S. Eliot's Personal Waste Land," *Journal of Modern Literature* 10, no. 1 (1983).
21 Although the passage continues to note authors outside of the English tradition – "Dante the same. Aeschylus (translated) the same" – Septimus's primary focus throughout is on Shakespeare who, as we have already seen, was along with Miss Isabel Pole, one of the main reasons he chose to fight in the war (*MD* 86). The national connection thus, in my view, far outweighs the gesture toward cosmopolitanism.
22 As Susan Stanford Friedman persuasively argues, Woolf's tendency to view herself as an outsider has more to do with an enabling posture – Woolf "screening her uncommonness behind the mask of the 'common reader'" – than with the complexities of her simultaneously privileged and oppressed social position. See Susan Stanford Friedman, *Mappings: Feminism and the Cultural Geographies of Encounter* (Princeton, NJ: Princeton University Press, 1998), 115. Scholars who have addressed Woolf's relation to the literary tradition include the aforementioned Gillian Beer and Jane de Gay as well as the path-breaking Beverly Ann Schlack, *Continuing Presences: Virginia Woolf's Use of Literary Allusion* (University Park: Pennsylvania State University Press, 1979).
23 Woolf is here referring to R. H. Evans's five volume edition of 1809–1812 entitled *Hakluyt's Collection of the Early Voyages, Travels and Discoveries of the English Nations* although she also owned and made notes in the eight volume *Everyman* edition of 1907–08. Woolf wrote about Hakluyt on numerous occasions. He appears in two separate essays entitled "Traffics and Discoveries," written in 1906 and 1918 (*E* 1:120–124; 2:329–36), the "Elizabethan Lumber Room" published in the first *Common Reader* in 1925 (*E* 4:53–61), and the essay "Reading" under discussion here (*E* 3:141–161), as well as in scattered remarks throughout her writings on Elizabethan literature. Details on her reading editions can be found in the headnotes accompanying each essay in McNellie and Clark's five volume edition of Woolf's essays.

24 This praise appears virtually unchanged in the work of Woolf's critics, for whom her investment in Hakluyt has become commonplace, oft-mentioned but rarely investigated in any depth. We can let Christine Froula's comment stand in for any number of critics: "[Hakluyt's] voyages of discovery endow [Woolf's] own metaphysical voyages toward new 'lands' and 'civilizations' from *The Voyage Out* on." See Christine Froula, *Virginia Woolf and the Bloomsbury Avant-Garde: War, Civilization, Modernity* (New York: Columbia University Press, 2005), 17. Although Froula acknowledges (in a footnote) the imperial context, she does not develop the argument.

25 Myra Jehlen, "History before the Fact: Or, Captain John Smith's Unfinished Symphony," *Critical Inquiry* 19, no. 4 (1993): 688.

26 Ibid., 691, 692.

27 Richard Helgerson, *Forms of Nationhood: The Elizabethan Writing of England* (Chicago: University of Chicago Press, 1992), 163, 165.

28 The first quotation is from Helgerson, *Forms of Nationhood*, 165. The second comes from T. J. Cribb, "Writing up the Log: The Legacy of Hakluyt," in *Travel Writing and Empire: Postcolonial Theory in Transit*, ed. Steve Clark (New York: Zed Books, 1999), 103.

29 Helgerson, *Forms of Nationhood*, 179.

30 Helgerson writes: "His book makes it possible to imagine an England not merely competing with Spain for the same prize of universal dominance, but opposing itself to empire and working instead to construct a world of distinguishable and sovereign economic entities – that is, a world of nation-states – capable of entering into relations of trade with commercial England. Pushed by the need to differentiate England from tyrannical and Catholic Spain, Hakluyt's text moves toward an anti-imperialist – indeed, anti-colonialist – logic of economic and cultural nationalism." See Helgerson, *Forms of Nationhood*, 187.

31 I am in fundamental agreement, then, with Carey Snyder who finds that the novel "begins to trace the contours of a scaled-back version of Englishness, one that is anchored in everyday customs and artifacts." See Carey Snyder, "Woolf's Ethnographic Modernism: Self-Nativizing in *The Voyage Out* and Beyond," *Virginia Woolf Studies Annual* 10 (2004): 83. I find it hard, however, to see this as a result of "showing the strangeness of Englishness when viewed from another vantage," since the novel systematically forecloses anything other than an English perspective on Englishness. (91).

32 The quotation comes from a speech Woolf gave in January 1931 to the London/National Society for Women's Service. A typescript of the speech appears in Virginia Woolf, *The Pargiters*, ed. Mitchell A. Leaska (New York: Harvest/HBJ, 1977). The line in question appears on page xxx. The angle brackets indicate an insertion made by Woolf.

33 Several scholars have remarked on the general connection between *The Voyage Out* and Hakluyt's *Traffics and Discoveries*. By far the most detailed is Alice Fox, "Virginia Woolf at Work: The Elizabethan *Voyage Out*," *Bulletin of Research in the Humanities* 84 (1981). See also Alice Fox, *Virginia Woolf and*

the *Literature of the English Renaissance* (Oxford: Clarendon Press, 1990), particularly chapter 2.

34 Sir Willoughby, who died in 1554 exploring the Norwegian Sea, appears three times in Hakluyt. Twice he is referenced in passing. The third appearance is a ten-page excerpt from his notes, remarkable for being almost entirely devoid of incident.

35 Numerous details reinforce the imperial subtext of Willoughby's enterprise. One of the first rooms Helen and Rachel enter contains "the kind of lamp which makes the light of civilisation across dark fields to one walking in the country" (*VO* 12). Willoughby himself, "loved his business and built his Empire" despite occasionally having to deal with "wretched little natives who went on strike and refused to load his ships" (*VO* 16, 180). The phrase "informal empire" refers, of course, to the pursuit of empire by economic rather than direct formal conquest. The term seems to have been coined by the historian C. R. Fay in 1934, although it was brought to prominence in 1953 in two famous articles, one by John Gallagher and Ronald Robinson and the other by H. S. Ferns. See H. S. Ferns, "Britain's Informal Empire in Argentina, 1806–1914," *Past and Present* 4, no. 1 (1953), John Gallagher and Ronald Robinson, "The Imperialism of Free Trade," *The Economic History Review New Series* 6, no. 1 (1953). As Ferns and others have shown, British investment in South America was considerable. According to Irving Stone, "During the first ninety years of Latin American independence, that is, from the 1820's until the outbreak of World War I, British investors supplied more long-term capital to this region than did any other group of foreign investors." See Irving Stone, "British Long-Term Investment in Latin America, 1865–1913," *The Business History Review* 42, no. 3 (1968): 311.

36 As many critics have shown, Woolf revised the novel to make Rachel less intelligent and less sure of herself. For details, see Fox, "Woolf at Work," Elizabeth Heine, "The Earlier Voyage Out," *Bulletin of Research in the Humanities* 82, no. 3 (1981). The point of this revision, in my view, is to further highlight how ripe for transformative change she is, and to suggest the same possibilities for British culture.

37 Enrique Dussel, "Beyond Eurocentrism: The World-System and the Limits of Modernity," in *The Cultures of Globalization*, ed. Fredric Jameson and Masao Miyoshi (Durham, NC: Duke University Press, 1998), 14, 17.

38 See Wendy Brown, *States of Injury: Power and Freedom in Late Modernity* (Princeton, NJ: Princeton University Press, 1995), particularly chapter 6, and Pericles Lewis, *Modernism, Nationalism and the Novel* (Cambridge: Cambridge University Press, 2000), 62–3. Lewis's comment occurs by way of a discussion of Hannah Arendt, and is really no more than a way station toward his critique of the "false transcendent constructs" by which liberalism seeks to replace religion and natural law (63).

39 Arendt, *Origins*, 299. This argument is, by now, somewhat familiar through Giorgio Agamben's elaboration of the "state of exception." See, in particular, chapter 2 of Giorgio Agamben, *Homo Sacer: Sovereign Power and Bare*

Life, trans. Daniel Heller-Roazen (Stanford, CA: Stanford University Press, 1998) and the entirety of *State of Exception*, trans. Kevin Attell (Chicago: University of Chicago Press, 2005). I prefer Arendt's more historically grounded account than the abstract metaphysics of Agamben's biopower.

40 Similarly, Clarissa Dalloway finds the "little independence" that exists between herself and Richard to be the reason she is glad not to have married Peter: "[W]ith Peter everything had to be shared; everything gone into. And it was intolerable" (*MD* 7).

41 Virginia Woolf, *To the Lighthouse* (New York: Harcourt, Inc., 1981), 37, here-after referred to parenthetically as *TTL*.

42 With this phrase, I am riffing on the central thesis of Brown's *States of Injury*. For Brown, identity politics – itself simply a particular version of liberal subjectivity – "discursively entrenches the injury-identity it denounces," thus transforming a "historical effect of power" into an ontological claim about one's essential nature. See Brown, *States of Injury*, 21. Identities, in this account, are essentially reifications of history.

CODA: THE EDWARDIAN LUMBER ROOM

1 "Portrait d'une Femme" can be found in *Personae*, 57–8.
2 See the discussion in Chapter 3.
3 See Perry Anderson, "Marshall Berman: Modernity and Revolution," in *A Zone of Engagement* (New York: Verso, 1991).

Works Cited

Abrams, M. H., and Stephen Greenblatt, eds. *The Norton Anthology of English Literature*. 7th ed. Vol. 2. New York: W. W. Norton & Company, 2000.

Adorno, Theodor W. *Critical Models: Interventions and Catchwords*. Translated by Henry W. Pickford. New York: Columbia University Press, 1998.

———. *Negative Dialectics*. (1966). Translated by E. B. Ashton. New York: Continuum, 1992.

Adorno, Theodor W., and Walter Benjamin. *The Complete Correspondence, 1928–1940*. Translated by Nicholas Walker. Edited by Henri Lonitz. Cambridge, MA: Harvard University Press, 2001.

Agamben, Giorgio. *Homo Sacer: Sovereign Power and Bare Life*. Translated by Daniel Heller-Roazen. Stanford, CA: Stanford University Press, 1998.

———. *State of Exception*. Translated by Kevin Attell. Chicago: University of Chicago Press, 2005.

Ahearn, Barry. "*Cathay*: What Sort of Translation?" In *Ezra Pound & China*, edited by Zhaoming Qian, 31–48. Ann Arbor: University of Michigan Press, 2003.

Altieri, Charles. *Painterly Abstraction in Modernist American Poetry: The Contemporaneity of Modernism*. Cambridge: Cambridge University Press, 1989.

———. "'Preludes' as Prelude: In Defense of Eliot as Symboliste." In *T. S. Eliot: A Voice Descanting*, edited by Shyamal Bagchee, 1–27. New York: St. Martin's Press, 1990.

Anderson, Perry. "Marshall Berman: Modernity and Revolution." In *A Zone of Engagement*, 25–55. New York: Verso, 1991.

Apter, Emily. "Global *Translatio*: The 'Invention' of Comparative Literature, Istanbul, 1933." *Critical Inquiry* 29, no. 2 (2003): 253–81.

Arac, Jonathan. "Anglo-Globalism." *New Left Review*, no. 16 (2002): 35–45.

Arendt, Hannah. *The Origins of Totalitarianism*. New York: Harcourt Brace & Company, 1979.

Arnold, Matthew. "The Incompatibles." In *Complete Prose Works Vol. 9*, edited by R. H. Super, 238–85. Ann Arbor: University of Michigan Press, 1977.

———. "On the Study of Celtic Literatures." In *Complete Prose Works Vol. 3*, edited by R. H. Super, 291–386. Ann Arbor: University of Michigan Press, 1960.

Arrighi, Giovanni. *The Long Twentieth Century: Money, Power and the Origin of Our Times*. New York: Verso, 1994.

Barolini, Teodolinda. "Bertran De Born and Sordello: The Poetry of Politics in Dante's *Comedy*." *PMLA* 94, no. 3 (1979): 395–405.

Barthes, Roland. "The Reality Effect." In *French Literary Theory Today: A Reader*, edited by Tzvetan Todorov, 11–17. Cambridge: Cambridge University Press, 1982.

Bartolovich, Crystal. "Introduction: Marxism, Modernity and Postcolonial Studies." In *Marxism, Modernity and Postcolonial Studies*, edited by Crystal Bartolovich and Neil Lazarus, 1–17. Cambridge: Cambridge University Press, 2002.

Bartolovich, Crystal, and Neil Lazarus, eds. *Marxism, Modernity, and Postcolonial Studies*. Cambridge: Cambridge University Press, 2002.

Baucom, Ian. *Out of Place: Englishness, Empire, and the Locations of Identity*. Princeton, NJ: Princeton University Press, 1999.

Beck, Ulrich. "The Cosmopolitan Society and Its Enemies." *Theory, Culture & Society* 19, no. 1–2 (2002): 17–44.

Beer, Gillian. *Arguing with the Past: Essays in Narrative from Woolf to Sidney*. New York: Routledge, 1989.

Begam, Richard, and Michael Valdez Moses, eds. *Modernism and Colonialism: British and Irish Literature, 1899–1939*. Durham, NC: Duke University Press, 2007.

Benhabib, Seyla. "The Liberal Imagination and the Four Dogmas of Multiculturalism." *Yale Journal of Criticism* 12, no. 2 (1999): 401–13.

Benjamin, Walter. *Charles Baudelaire: A Lyric Poet in the Era of High Capitalism*. Translated by Harry Zohn. New York: Verso, 1997.

———. *Illuminations*. Translated by Harry Zohn. Edited by Hannah Arendt. New York: Schocken Books, 1968.

———. *The Arcades Project*. Translated by Howard Eiland and Kevin McLaughlin. Cambridge, MA: The Belknap Press of Harvard University Press, 1999.

Bhabha, Homi. "Signs Taken for Wonders: Question of Ambivalence and Authority under a Tree Outside Delhi, May 1817." In *The Location of Culture*, 102–22. New York: Routledge, 1994.

Booker, M. Keith. *Ulysses, Capitalism, and Colonialism: Reading Joyce after the Cold War*. Westport, CT: Greenwood Press, 2000.

Booth, Allyson. "Sir Ernest Shackleton, Easter Sunday & the Unquiet Dead in T. S. Eliot's *Waste Land*." *Yeats Eliot Review* 16, no. 2 (1999): 28–33.

Booth, Howard J., and Nigel Rigby, eds. *Modernism and Empire: Writing & British Coloniality, 1890–1940*. Manchester: Manchester University Press, 2000.

Brennan, Timothy. *At Home in the World: Cosmopolitanism Now*. Cambridge, MA: Harvard University Press, 1997.

———. "The National Longing for Form." In *Nation and Narration*, edited by Homi K. Bhabha, 44–70. New York: Routledge, 1990.

Brewer, Anthony. *Marxist Theories of Imperialism: A Critical Survey.* London: Routledge & Kegan Paul, 1980.

Brown, Bill. *A Sense of Things: The Object Matter of American Literature.* Chicago: University of Chicago Press, 2003.

———. *The Material Unconscious: American Amusement, Stephen Crane & the Economics of Play.* Cambridge, MA: Harvard University Press, 1996.

Brown, Nicholas. *Utopian Generations: The Political Horizon of Twentieth-Century Literature.* Princeton, NJ: Princeton University Press, 2005.

Brown, Wendy. *States of Injury: Power and Freedom in Late Modernity.* Princeton, NJ: Princeton University Press, 1995.

Bukharin, Nikolai. *Imperialism and World Economy.* (1917). New York: Monthly Review Press, 1973.

Bush, Christopher. *Ideographic Modernism: China, Writing, Media.* Oxford: Oxford University Press, 2010.

Bush, Ronald. "The Presence of the Past: Ethnographic Thinking/Literary Politics." In *Prehistories of the Future: The Primitivist Project and the Culture of Modernism,* edited by Elazar Barkan and Ronald Bush, 23–41. Stanford, CA: Stanford University Press, 1995.

Butler, Judith. "Universality in Culture." In *For Love of Country?* edited by Joshua Cohen, 45–51. Boston, MA: Beacon Press, 1996.

Cain, Peter J., and A. G. Hopkins. *British Imperialism, 1688–2000.* 2nd ed. New York: Longman, 2002.

Casanova, Pascale. *The World Republic of Letters.* Translated by M. B. DeBevoise. Cambridge, MA: Harvard University Press, 2004.

Casillo, Robert. *The Genealogy of Demons: Anti-Semitism, Fascism, and the Myths of Ezra Pound.* Evanston, IL: Northwestern University Press, 1988.

Castle, Gregory. *Modernism and the Celtic Revival.* Cambridge: Cambridge University Press, 2001.

Chakrabarty, Dipesh. "Universalism and Belonging in the Logic of Capital." *Public Culture* 12, no. 3 (2000): 653–78.

Cheng, Vincent J. *Joyce, Race, and Empire.* Cambridge: Cambridge University Press, 1995.

Chilcote, Ronald M., ed. *The Political Economy of Imperialism: Critical Appraisals.* Boston, MA: Kluwer Academic Publishers, 1999.

Childs, Donald J. *From Philosophy to Poetry: T. S. Eliot's Study of Knowledge and Experience.* London: The Athlone Press, 2001.

Chow, Rey. "The Interruption of Referentiality: Poststructuralism and the Conundrum of Critical Multiculturalism." *The South Atlantic Quarterly* 101, no. 1 (2002): 171–86.

Cleary, Joe. "Misplaced Ideas? Locating and Dislocating Ireland in Colonial and Postcolonial Studies." In *Marxism, Modernity and Postcolonial Studies,* edited by Crystal Bartolovich and Neil Lazarus, 101–24. Cambridge: Cambridge University Press, 2002.

Cleary, Joseph. "Toward a Materialist-Formalist History of Twentieth-Century Irish Literature." *Boundary* 2 31, no. 1 (2004): 207–41.

Clifford, James. *The Predicament of Culture: Twentieth-Century Ethnography, Literature, and Art.* Cambridge, MA: Harvard University Press, 1988.

Conrad, Joseph. *Heart of Darkness.* (1899). Edited by Robert Kimbrough. New York: W. W. Norton & Company, 1988.

Cook, Eleanor. "T. S. Eliot and the Carthaginian Peace." *ELH* 46, no. 2 (1979): 341–55.

Cribb, T. J. "Writing up the Log: The Legacy of Hakluyt." In *Travel Writing and Empire: Postcolonial Theory in Transit,* edited by Steve Clark, 100–112. New York: Zed Books, 1999.

Cuddy-Keane, Melba. "Modernism, Geopolitics, Globalization." *Modernism/Modernity* 10, no. 2 (2003): 539–58.

———. *Virginia Woolf, the Intellectual, and the Public Sphere.* Cambridge: Cambridge University Press, 2003.

Curtis, L. Perry. *Apes and Angels: the Irishman in Victorian Caricature.* Washington, D.C.: Smithsonian Institution Press, 1971.

Davis, Alex, and Lee Jenkins, eds. *The Locations of Literary Modernism.* Cambridge: Cambridge University Press, 2000.

Davis, Mike. *Late Victorian Holocausts: El Nino Famines and the Making of the Third World.* New York: Verso, 2001.

de Gay, Jane. *Virginia Woolf's Novels and the Literary Past.* Edinburgh: Edinburgh University Press, 2006.

de Grazia, Victoria. *Irresistible Empire: America's Advance through Twentieth-Century Europe.* Cambridge, MA: Harvard University Press, 2005.

Deane, Seamus. "Introduction." In *Nationalism, Colonialism, and Literature,* 3–22. Minneapolis: University of Minnesota Press, 1990.

———. "Joyce and Nationalism." In *James Joyce: New Perspectives,* edited by Colin MacCabe, 168–83. Bloomington: Indiana University Press, 1982.

———. "'Masked with Matthew Arnold's Face': Joyce and Liberalism." In *James Joyce: The Centennial Symposium,* edited by Morris Beja, 9–20. Chicago: University of Illinois Press, 1986.

Douglass, Paul. "Reading the Wreckage: De-Encrypting Eliot's Aesthetics of Empire." *Twentieth Century Literature* 43, no. 1 (1997): 1–26.

Doyle, Laura. "Toward a Philosophy of Transnationalism." *Journal of Transnational American Studies* 1, no. 1 (2009): 1–29.

Doyle, Laura, and Laura A. Winkiel. "Introduction: The Global Horizons of Modernism." In *Geomodernisms: Race, Modernism, Modernity,* edited by Laura Doyle and Laura A. Winkiel, 1–14. Bloomington: Indiana University Press, 2005.

Drain, Richard. "*The Waste Land*: The Prison and the Key." In The Waste Land *in Different Voices: The Revised Version of Lectures Given at the University of York in the Fiftieth Year of* The Waste Land, edited by A. D. Moody, 29–46. London: Edward Arnold, 1974.

Duffy, Enda. "Disappearing Dublin: *Ulysses*, Postcoloniality, and the Politics of Space." In *Semicolonial Joyce,* edited by Derek Attridge and Marjorie Howes, 37–57. Cambridge: Cambridge University Press, 2000.

————. *The Subaltern* Ulysses. Minneapolis: University of Minnesota Press, 1994.

Dumett, Raymond E., ed. *Gentlemanly Capitalism and British Imperialism: The New Debate on Empire*. New York: Longman, 1999.

Dussel, Enrique. "Beyond Eurocentrism: The World-System and the Limits of Modernity." In *The Cultures of Globalization*, edited by Fredric Jameson and Masao Miyoshi, 3–31. Durham, NC: Duke University Press, 1998.

Eliot, T. S. "A Letter." *Translatlantic Review* 1, no. 1 (1924): 95–6.

————. "Books of the Quarter." *The New Criterion*, October 1926, 751–7.

————. *Collected Poems, 1909–1962*. New York: Harcourt, Brace & World, Inc., 1963.

————. *Knowledge and Experience in the Philosophy of F. H. Bradley*. New York: Columbia University Press, 1964.

————. "Mr. Middleton Murry's Synthesis." *The Monthly Criterion*, October 1927, 340–7.

————. "Notes Towards the Definition of Culture." (1949). In *Christianity and Culture*. New York: Harvest/ Harcourt Brace Jovanovich, 1968.

————. *Selected Essays*. New York: Harcourt, Brace & World, Inc., 1964.

————. "The Beating of a Drum." *The Nation and the Athenaeum*, October 6 1923, 11–12.

————. *The Sacred Wood*. (1920). New York: University Paperbacks, 1964.

————. The Waste Land: *A Facsimile and Transcript of the Original Drafts Including the Annotations of Ezra Pound*. Edited by Valerie Eliot. New York: Harcourt Brace & Company, 1971.

————. "*Ulysses*, Order, and Myth." *The Dial* (1923): 480–3.

Ellmann, Maud. "The Imaginary Jew: T. S. Eliot and Ezra Pound." In *Between 'Race' and Culture: Representations of 'the Jew' in English and American Literature*, edited by Bryan Cheyette, 84–101. Stanford, CA: Stanford University Press, 1996.

Esty, Joshua. *A Shrinking Island: Modernism and National Culture in England*. Princeton, NJ: Princeton University Press, 2004.

Ferns, H. S. "Britain's Informal Empire in Argentina, 1806–1914." *Past and Present* 4, no. 1 (1953): 60–75.

Finn, Margot C. *After Chartism: Class and Nation in English Radical Politics, 1848–1874*. Cambridge: Cambridge University Press, 1993.

Fish, Stanley. "Boutique Multiculturalism, or Why Liberals Are Incapable of Thinking About Hate Speech." *Critical Inquiry* 23, no. 2 (1997): 378–95.

Flaubert, Gustave. *The Letters of Gustave Flaubert: 1830–1857*. Translated by Francis Steegmuller. Cambridge, MA: Belknap Press of Harvard, 1980.

————. *Three Tales*. (1877). Translated by Robert Baldick. New York: Penguin, 1986.

Fox, Alice. *Virginia Woolf and the Literature of the English Renaissance*. Oxford: Clarendon Press, 1990.

————. "Virginia Woolf at Work: The Elizabethan *Voyage Out*." *Bulletin of Research in the Humanities* 84 (1981): 65–84.

Friedman, Susan Stanford. "Definitional Excursions: The Meanings of *Modern/Modernity/Modernism*." *Modernism/Modernity* 8, no. 3 (2001): 493–513.

———. *Mappings: Feminism and the Cultural Geographies of Encounter*. Princeton, NJ: Princeton University Press, 1998.

———. "Modernism in a Transnational Landscape." *Paideuma* 32, no. 1–3 (2003): 39–74.

———. "Periodizing Modernism: Postcolonial Modernities and the Space/Time Borders of Modernist Studies." *Modernism/Modernity* 13, no. 3 (2006): 425–43.

Froula, Christine. "Out of the Chrysalis: Female Initiation and Female Authority in Virginia Woolf's *The Voyage Out*." *Tulsa Studies in Women's Literature* 5, no. 1 (1986): 63–90.

———. "The Beauties of Mistranslation: On Pound's English after *Cathay*." In *Ezra Pound & China*, edited by Zhaoming Qian, 49–71. Ann Arbor: University of Michigan Press, 2003.

———. *To Write Paradise: Style and Error in Pound's* Cantos. New Haven, CT: Yale University Press, 1984.

———. *Virginia Woolf and the Bloomsbury Avant-Garde: War, Civilization, Modernity*. New York: Columbia University Press, 2005.

Gallagher, John, and Ronald Robinson. "The Imperialism of Free Trade." *The Economic History Review New Series* 6, no. 1 (1953): 1–15.

Geist, Anthony L., and José B. Monleón, eds. *Modernism and Its Margins: Reinscribing Cultural Modernity from Spain and Latin America*. New York: Garland Publishing Inc., 1999.

Gikandi, Simon. *Maps of Englishness*. New York: Columbia University Press, 1996.

———. "Preface: Modernism in the World." *Modernism/Modernity* 13, no. 3 (2006): 419–24.

———. *Writing in Limbo: Modernism and Caribbean Literature*. Ithaca, NY: Cornell University Press, 1992.

Gluck, Mary. "The *Flâneur* and the Aesthetic Appropriation of Urban Culture in Mid-19th-Century Paris." *Theory, Culture & Society* 20, no. 5 (2003): 53–80.

Goodman, Kevis. *Georgic Modernity and British Romanticism: Poetry and the Mediation of History*. Cambridge: Cambridge University Press, 2004.

Gramsci, Antonio. *Selections from the Prison Notebooks*. Translated by Quintin Hoare and Geoffrey Nowell Smith. New York: International Publishers, 1971.

Guillory, John. *Cultural Capital: The Problem of Literary Canon Formation*. Chicago: University of Chicago Press, 1993.

Hawthorn, Jeremy. "'Ulysses,' Modernism and Marxist Criticism." In *James Joyce and Modern Literature*, edited by W. J. McCormack and Alistair Stead, 112–25. Boston, MA: Routledge and Kegan Paul, 1982.

Hayot, Eric. *Chinese Dreams: Pound, Brecht, Tel Quel*. Ann Arbor: University of Michigan Press, 2004.

―――. "Critical Dreams: Orientalism, Modernism, and the Meaning of Pound's China." *Twentieth Century Literature* 45, no. 4 (1999): 511–33.

Heine, Elizabeth. "The Earlier *Voyage Out*: Virginia Woolf's First Novel." *Bulletin of Research in the Humanities* 82, no. 3 (1981): 294–316.

Helgerson, Richard. *Forms of Nationhood: The Elizabethan Writing of England.* Chicago: University of Chicago Press, 1992.

Herr, Cheryl. *Joyce's Anatomy of Culture.* Chicago: University of Illinois Press, 1986.

Hilferding, Rudolf. *Finance Capital: A Study of the Latest Phase of Capitalist Development.* (1910). Translated by Morris Watnick and Sam Gordon. Edited by Tom Bottomore. Boston, MA: Routledge & Kegan Paul, 1981.

Hobsbawm, E. J. *The Age of Capital: 1848–1878.* New York: Charles Scribner's Sons, 1975.

―――. *The Age of Empire 1875–1914.* New York: Pantheon Books, 1987.

Hobson, J. A. *Imperialism: A Study.* London: George Allen & Unwin Ltd., 1905.

Horkheimer, Max, and Theodor W.Adorno. *Dialectic of Enlightenment: Philosophical Fragments.* (1969). Translated by Edmund Jephcott. Edited by Gunzelin Schmid Noerr. Stanford, CA: Stanford University Press, 2002.

Howes, Marjorie, and DerekAttridge. "Introduction." In *Semicolonial Joyce*, edited by Derek Attridge and Marjorie Howes, 1–20. Cambridge: Cambridge University Press, 2000.

Ingelbien, Raphael. "They Saw One They Knew: Baudelaire and the Ghosts of London Modernism." *English Studies* 88, no. 1 (2007): 43–58.

Innes, C. L. "Modernism, Ireland and Empire: Yeats, Joyce and Their Implied Audiences." In *Modernism and Empire: Writing & British Coloniality, 1890–1940*, edited by Howard J. Booth and Nigel Rigby, 137–55. New York: Manchester University Press, 2000.

Jameson, Fredric. *A Singular Modernity: An Essay on the Ontology of the Present.* New York: Verso, 2002.

―――. "Modernism and Imperialism." In *The Modernist Papers*, 152–69. New York: Verso, 2007.

―――. "The Realist Floor-Plan." In *On Signs*, edited by Marshall Blonsky, 373–83. Baltimore, MD: Johns Hopkins, 1985.

―――. "Third-World Literature in the Era of Multinational Capitalism." *Social Text* 15 (1986): 65–88.

―――. "*Ulysses* in History." In *James Joyce: A Collection of Critical Essays*, edited by Mary T. Reynolds, 145–58. Englewood Cliffs, NJ: Prentice Hall, 1993.

Jehlen, Myra. "History before the Fact: Or, Captain John Smith's Unfinished Symphony." *Critical Inquiry* 19, no. 4 (1993): 677–92.

Jennings, Michael. "On the Banks of a New Lethe: Commodification and Experience in Benjamin's Baudelaire Book." *boundary 2* 30, no. 1 (2003): 89–104.

Jessop, Bob. "The Political Scene and the Politics of Representation: Periodising Class Struggle and the State in the *Eighteenth Brumaire*." In *Marx's 'Eighteenth Brumaire': (Post)Modern Interpretations*, edited by Mark Cowling and James Martin. Sterling, 179–94. VA: The Pluto Press, 2002.

Joyce, James. *A Portrait of the Artist as a Young Man.* (1916). New York: Viking Press, 1964.
——. *Dubliners.* (1914). New York: Penguin, 1967.
——. *Stephen Hero.* New York: New Directions, 1963.
——. *The Critical Writings of James Joyce.* Edited by Ellsworth Mason and Richard Ellmann. Ithaca, NY: Cornell University Press, 1989.
——. *Ulysses.* (1922). New York: Random House, 1961.
Kadir, Djelal. "To World, to Globalize – Comparative Literature's Crossroads." *Comparative Literature Studies* 41, no. 1 (2004): 1–9.
Kearns, Cleo McNelly. *T. S. Eliot and Indic Traditions.* Cambridge: Cambridge University Press, 1987.
Kenner, Hugh. "Introduction." In *Ezra Pound: Translations*, 9–14. New York: New Directions, 1963.
——. *The Invisible Poet: T. S. Eliot.* New York: McDowell, Obolensky, 1959.
——. *The Pound Era.* Berkeley: University of California Press, 1973.
——. *Ulysses.* Baltimore, MD: Johns Hopkins University Press, 1987.
Kiberd, Declan. "James Joyce and Mythic Realism." In *Inventing Ireland*, 327–55. Cambridge, MA: Harvard University Press, 1996.
——. "Postcolonial Modernism." In *Modernism and Colonialism: British and Irish Literature, 1899–1939*, edited by Richard Begam and Michael Valdez Moses, 269–87. Durham, NC: Duke University Press, 2007.
Kim, Joon-Hwan. *Out of the "Western Box": Towards a Multicultural Poetics in the Poetry of Ezra Pound and Charles Olson.* New York: Peter Lang Publishing, 2003.
King, Mary C. "Hermeneutics of Suspicion: Nativism, Nationalism, and the Language Question in 'Oxen of the Sun'." *James Joyce Quarterly* 35, no. 2–3 (1998): 349–72.
Knapp, James F. *Literary Modernism and the Transformation of Work.* Evanston, IL: Northwestern University Press, 1988.
Kodama, Sanehide. *American Poetry and Japanese Culture.* Hamden, CT: Archon, 1984.
Kristal, Efrain. "Considering Coldly: A Reply to Franco Moretti." *New Left Review*, no. 15 (2002): 61–74.
Kyd, Thomas. *The Spanish Tragedy.* Edited by J. R. Mulryne. New York: W. W. Norton & Company, 1989.
Lacoue-Labarthe, Phillipe, and Jean-Luc Nancy. *The Literary Absolute: The Theory of Literature in German Romanticism.* Translated by Philip Barnard and Cheryl Lester. Albany: State University of New York Press, 1988.
Lan, Feng. *Ezra Pound and Confucianism: Remaking Humanism in the Face of Modernity.* Toronto: University of Toronto Press, 2005.
Larsen, Neil. *Determinations: Essays on Theory, Narrative and Nation in the Americas.* New York: Verso, 2001.
——. *Modernism and Hegemony: A Materialist Critique of Aesthetic Agencies.* Minneapolis: University of Minnesota Press, 1990.
Lazarus, Neil. "The Fetish of 'the West' in Postcolonial Theory." In *Marxism, Modernity and Postcolonial Studies*, edited by Crystal Bartolovich and Neil Lazarus, 43–64. Cambridge: Cambridge University Press, 2002.

Lenin, V. I. *Imperialism: The Highest Stage of Capitalism. A Popular Outline.* (1917). New York: International Publishers, 1939.

Leonard, Garry. *Advertising and Commodity Culture in Joyce.* Gainseville: University Press of Florida, 1998.

Levenson, Michael. "Does *The Waste Land* Have a Politics?" *Modernism/ Modernity* 6, no. 3 (1999): 1–13.

Lewis, Pericles. *Modernism, Nationalism and the Novel.* Cambridge: Cambridge University Press, 2000.

Lloyd, David. "Adulteration and the Nation." In *Anomalous States: Irish Writing and the Post-Colonial Moment,* 88–124. Durham, NC: Duke University Press, 1993.

———. *Anomalous States: Irish Writing and the Post-Colonial Moment.* Durham, NC: Duke University Press, 1993.

Lukács, Georg. "Franz Kafka or Thomas Mann?" In *The Meaning of Contemporary Realism,* 47–92. London: Merlin Press, 1963.

———. *History and Class Consciousness: Studies in Marxist Dialectic.* (1923). Translated by Rodney Livingstone. Cambridge, MA: The MIT Press, 1971.

———. *The Historical Novel.* (1937). Translated by Hannah Mitchell and Stanley Mitchell. Middlesex: Penguin Books, 1961.

———. "The Ideology of Modernism." In *The Meaning of Contemporary Realism,* 17–46. London: Merlin Press, 1963.

Luxemburg, Rosa. *The Accumulation of Capital.* (1913). Translated by Agnes Schwarzschild. New York: Routledge, 2003.

Mao, Douglas. *Solid Objects: Modernism and the Test of Production.* Princeton, NJ: Princeton University Press, 1998.

Mao, Douglas, and Rebecca L. Walkowitz. "Introduction: Modernisms Bad and New." In *Bad Modernisms,* edited by Douglas Mao and Rebecca L. Walkowitz, 1–17. Durham, NC: Duke University Press, 2006.

———. "The New Modernist Studies." *PMLA* 123, no. 3 (2008): 737–48.

Marx, Karl. *Capital, Volume 1.* Translated by Samuel Moore, Edward Aveling, and Ernest Untermann. Chicago: Charles H. Kerr & Company, 1912.

———. *Capital, Volume 1.* Translated by Ben Fowkes. New York: Penguin Books, 1990.

———. *Communist Manifesto.* (1848). Edited by Frederic L. Bender. New York: W. W. Norton & Company, 1988.

———. *Grundrisse.* Translated by Martin Nicolaus. New York: Penguin Books, 1973.

———. *The Class Struggles in France (1848–1850).* New York: International Publishers, 1964.

———. "The Eighteenth Brumaire of Louis Bonaparte." In *Marx's 'Eighteenth Brumaire': (Post)Modern Interpretations,* edited by Mark Cowling and James Martin, 19–109. Sterling, VA: The Pluto Press, 2002.

McClintock, Anne. *Imperial Leather: Race, Gender and Sexuality in the Colonial Contest.* New York: Routledge, 1995.

McClure, John A. *Late Imperial Romance.* New York: Verso, 1994.

McCormack, W. J. "James Joyce, Cliche and the Irish Language." In *James Joyce: The Augmented Ninth*, edited by Bernard Benstock, 323–36. Syracuse, NY: Syracuse University Press, 1988.

McGee, Patrick. *Joyce Beyond Marx: History and Desire in* Ulysses *and* Finnegans Wake. Gaineseville: University Press of Florida, 2001.

McLaughlin, Joseph. *Writing the Urban Jungle: Reading Empire in London from Doyle to Eliot*. Charlottesville: University Press of Virginia, 2000.

McVicker, Jeanette. "'Six Essays on London Life': A History of Dispersal, Part I." *Woolf Studies Annual* 9 (2003): 143–65.

———. "'Six Essays on London Life': A History of Dispersal, Part II." *Woolf Studies Annual* 10 (2004): 141–72.

Moretti, Franco. "Conjectures on World Literature." *New Left Review*, no. 1 (2000): 54–68.

———. "More Conjectures." *New Left Review*, no. 20 (2003): 73–81.

———. "The Long Goodbye: *Ulysses* and the End of Liberal Capitalism." In *Signs Taken for Wonders: Essays in the Sociology of Literary Forms*, 182–208. London: NLB, 1983.

———. *The Way of the World: The Bildungsroman in European Culture.* (1987). Translated by Albert Sbragia. New York: Verso, 2000.

Morrison, Paul. *The Poetics of Fascism: Ezra Pound, T. S. Eliot, Paul de Man.* New York: Oxford University Press, 1996.

Nicholls, Peter. *Ezra Pound: Politics, Economics and Writing.* London: Macmillan, 1984.

Nolan, Emer. *James Joyce and Nationalism.* London: Routledge, 1995.

North, Michael. *The Political Aesthetics of Yeats, Eliot, and Pound.* New York: Cambridge University Press, 1991.

Osborne, Peter. *The Politics of Time: Modernity and the Avant-Garde.* New York: Verso, 1995.

Palandri, Angela J. "The 'Seven Lakes Canto' Revisited." *Paideuma* 3 (1974): 51–4.

Palumbo-Liu, David. "Multiculturalism Now: Civilization, National Identity, and Difference before and after September 11th." *boundary 2* 29, no. 2 (2002): 109–27.

Park, JosephineNock-Hee. *Apparitions of Asia: Modernist Form and Asian American Poetics.* Oxford: Oxford University Press, 2008.

Parker, Andrew. "Ezra Pound and the 'Economy' of Anti-Semitism." In *Postmodernism and Politics*, edited by Jonathan Arac, 70–90. Minneapolis: University of Minnesota Press, 1986.

Peppis, Paul. *Literature, Politics, and the English Avant-Garde: Nation and Empire, 1901–1918.* Cambridge: Cambridge University Press, 2000.

Postone, Moishe. "Anti-Semitism and National Socialism." In *Germans and Jews since the Holocaust: The Changing Situation in West Germany*, edited by Anson Rabinbach and Jack Zipes, 302–14. New York: Holmes & Meier, 1986.

Pound, Ezra. *Collected Early Poems.* Edited by Michael King. New York: New Directions, 1976.

———. *Gaudier-Brzeska: A Memoir.* (1916). New York: New Directions, 1970.

———. *Guide to Kulchur.* (1953). New York: New Directions, 1970.

———. *Jefferson and/or Mussolini.* New York: Liveright Publishing, 1936.

———. *Literary Essays of Ezra Pound.* Edited by T. S. Eliot. New York: New Directions, 1968.

———. *Personae.* Edited by Lea Baechler and A. Walton Litz. New York: New Directions, 1990.

———. *Selected Prose: 1909–1965.* Edited by William Cookson. New York: New Directions, 1973.

———. *The Cantos of Ezra Pound.* New York: New Directions, 1986.

———. *The Spirit of Romance.* (1910). New York: New Directions, 1968.

———. "The State." (1927). In *Selected Prose 1909–1965*, edited by William Cookson, 214–15. New York: New Directions, 1973.

Prashad, Vijay. *Everybody Was Kung Fu Fighting: Afro-Asian Connections and the Myth of Cultural Purity.* Boston, MA: Beacon Press, 2001.

Qian, Zhaoming. *Orientalism and Modernism: The Legacy of China in Pound and Williams.* Durham, NC: Duke University Press, 1995.

———. "Painting into Poetry: Pound's Seven Lakes Cantos." In *Ezra Pound & China*, edited by Zhaoming Qian, 72–95. Ann Arbor: University of Michigan Press, 2003.

Rainey, Lawrence. *Revisiting* The Waste Land. New Haven, CT: Yale University Press, 2005.

Ramazani, Jahan. "A Transnational Poetics." *American Literary History* 18, no. 2 (2006): 332–59.

———. "Modernist Bricolage, Postcolonial Hybridity." *Modernism/Modernity* 13, no. 3 (2006): 445–63.

Redman, Tim. *Ezra Pound and Italian Fascism.* Cambridge: Cambridge University Press, 1991.

Richards, Thomas. *The Commodity Culture of Victorian England: Advertising and Spectacle, 1851–1913.* Stanford, CA: Stanford University Press, 1990.

San Juan, E., Jr. *Racism and Cultural Studies: Critiques of Multiculturalist Ideology and the Politics of Difference.* Durham, NC: Duke University Press, 2002.

Schlack, Beverly Ann. *Continuing Presences: Virginia Woolf's Use of Literary Allusion.* University Park: Pennsylvania State University Press, 1979.

Schwarz, Roberto. *A Master on the Periphery of Capitalism: Machado De Assis.* Translated by John Gledson. Durham, NC: Duke University Press, 2002.

Sena, Vinod, and Rajiva Verma, eds. *The Fire and the Rose: New Essays on T. S. Eliot.* Delhi: Oxford University Press, 1992.

Sherry, Vincent B. *The Great War and the Language of Modernism.* New York: Oxford University Press, 2003.

Shields, Rob. "Fancy Footwork: Walter Benjamin's Note on Flânerie." In *The Flâneur*, edited by Keith Tester, 61–80. New York: Routledge, 1994.

Shusterman, Richard. *T. S. Eliot and the Philosophy of Criticism.* London: Duckworth, 1988.

Sieburth, Richard. "In Pound We Trust: The Economy of Poetry/the Poetry of Economics." *Critical Inquiry* 14, no. 1 (1987): 142–72.

Simmel, Georg. "The Metropolis and Mental Life." (1903). In *The Sociology of Georg Simmel*, edited by Kurt H. Wolff, 409–24. London: The Free Press, 1950.

Snyder, Carey. "Woolf's Ethnographic Modernism: Self-Nativizing in *The Voyage Out* and Beyond." *Virginia Woolf Studies Annual* 10 (2004): 81–108.

Spivak, Gayatri Chakravorty. "Can the Subaltern Speak?" In *Marxism and the Interpretation of Culture*, edited by Cary Nelson and Lawrence Grossberg, 271–313. Chicago: University of Illinois Press, 1988.

Steinberg, Erwin R. "*Mrs. Dalloway* and T. S. Eliot's Personal Waste Land." *Journal of Modern Literature* 10, no. 1 (1983): 3–25.

Stone, Irving. "British Long-Term Investment in Latin America, 1865–1913." *The Business History Review* 42, no. 3 (1968): 311–39.

Surette, Leon. *Pound in Purgatory: From Economic Radicalism to Anti-Semitism.* Urbana: University of Illinois Press, 1999.

Taylor, Miles. "Rethinking the Chartists: Searching for Synthesis in the Historiography of Chartism." *The Historical Journal* 39, no. 2 (1996): 479–95.

———. "The 1848 Revolutions and the British Empire." *Past and Present* 166, no. 146–80 (2000).

Terrell, Carroll F. *A Companion to the Cantos of Ezra Pound.* Berkeley: University of California Press, 1993.

Torgovnick, Marianna. *Gone Primitive: Savage Intellects, Modern Lives.* Chicago: The University of Chicago Press, 1990.

Tratner, Michael. *Modernism and Mass Politics: Joyce, Woolf, Eliot, Yeats.* Stanford, CA: Stanford University Press, 1995.

Trotter, David. "Modernism and Empire: Reading *The Waste Land.*" *Critical Quarterly* 28, nos. 1 & 2 (1986): 143–53.

Wetherly, Paul. "Making Sense of the 'Relative Autonomy' of the State." In *Marx's 'Eighteenth Brumaire': (Post)Modern Interpretations*, edited by Mark Cowling and James Martin, 195–208. Sterling, VA: The Pluto Press, 2002.

Williams, Raymond. *Marxism and Literature.* New York: Oxford University Press, 1977.

———. *Politics and Letters: Interviews with the New Left Review.* London: Verso, 1981.

Williams, Rosalind H. *Dream Worlds: Mass Consumption in Late Nineteenth-Century France.* Berkeley: University of California Press, 1982.

Williams, Trevor L. "Dominant Ideologies: The Production of Stephen Dedalus." In *James Joyce: The Augmented Ninth*, edited by Bernard Benstock, 312–22. Syracuse, NY: Syracuse University Press, 1988.

Wolfe, Cary. "Ezra Pound and the Politics of Patronage." *American Literature* 63, no. 1 (1991): 26–42.

Wood, Ellen Meiksins. *Empire of Capital.* New York: Verso, 2003.

Woolf, Virginia. *Jacob's Room.* (1922). New York: Harcourt Brace Jovanovich, 1960.

———. *Mrs. Dalloway.* (1925). New York: Harcourt, Inc., 2005.

———. *Night and Day.* (1919). New York: Penguin, 1975.

———. *The Essays of Virginia Woolf: Volume One: 1904–1912*. Edited by Andrew McNeillie. 5 vols. Vol. 1. New York: Harcourt Brace Jovanovich, 1986.

———. *The Essays of Virginia Woolf: Volume Two: 1912–1918*. Edited by Andrew McNeillie. 5 vols. Vol. 2. New York: Harcourt Brace Jovanovich, 1987.

———. *The Essays of Virginia Woolf: Volume Three: 1919–1924*. Edited by Andrew McNeillie. 5 vols. Vol. 3. New York: Harcourt Brace Jovanovich, 1988.

———. *The Essays of Virginia Woolf: Volume Four: 1925–1928*. Edited by Andrew McNeillie. 5 vols. Vol. 4. New York: Harcourt Brace Jovanovich, 1994.

———. *The Essays of Virginia Woolf: Volume Five: 1929–1932*. Edited by Stuart N. Clarke. 5 vols. Vol. 5. New York: Harcourt Brace Jovanovich, 2009.

———. *The Pargiters*. Edited by Mitchell A. Leaska. New York: Harvest/Harcourt Brace Jovanovich, 1977.

———. *The Voyage Out*. (1915). New York: Penguin Books, 1992.

———. *To the Lighthouse*. (1927). New York: Harcourt, Inc., 1981.

Yip, Wai-Lim. *Ezra Pound's Cathay*. Princeton, NJ: Princeton University Press, 1969.

Žižek, Slavoj. "Multiculturalism, or, the Cultural Logic of Multinational Capitalism." *New Left Review* I, no. 225 (1997): 28–51.

Index

Milton Keynes UK
Ingram Content Group UK Ltd.
UKHW022205250823
427530UK00008B/50